PATHWAYS TO HIS PRESENCE

— A DAILY DEVOTIONAL —

CHARLES F. STANLEY

NELSON BOOKS
A Division of Thomas Nelson Publishers
Since 1798
www.thomasnelson.com

Published in Nashville, Tennessee, by Thomas Nelson, Inc.

Nelson Books titles may be purchased in bulk for educational, business, fund-raising, or sales promotional use. For information, please e-mail SpecialMarkets@ThomasNelson.com.

Visit CharlesStanleyInstitute.com for further study and personal training.

Library of Congress Cataloging-in-Publication Data [to come]

Stanley, Charles F.
    Pathways to his presence : a daily devotional / Charles F. Stanley.
      p. cm.
    ISBN 0-7852-2163-8 (hardcover)
    1. Devotional calendars. I. Title.
    BV4811.S8175 2006
    242'.2—dc22

2006019093

Printed in the United States of America

06 07 08 09 10 11 QW 9 8 7 6 5 4 3 2 1

CONTENTS

INTRODUCTION
PATHWAYS TO HIS PRESENCE

It is hard to resist the charm of a pathway:

- a winding trail leading deep into the forest
- a trail to a quiet retreat by the water
- a beautiful lane through a peaceful garden
- a rocky hillside path boasting spectacular views

But even more appealing are the spiritual pathways revealed in God's Word. These pathways are scriptural guidelines that, when followed, lead us into the presence of the almighty God. They are pathways to His presence.

This devotional guide focuses on twelve spiritual pathways that will guide you into the presence of God. Here are the pathways we will explore together during the coming year:

JANUARY:	PATHWAY TO GOD'S WILL
FEBRUARY:	PATHWAY TO FORGIVENESS
MARCH:	PATHWAY TO VICTORY
APRIL:	PATHWAY TO THE CROSS
MAY:	PATHWAY TO PRAYER
JUNE:	PATHWAY TO FAITH
JULY:	PATHWAY TO FREEDOM
AUGUST:	PATHWAY TO PEACE
SEPTEMBER:	PATHWAY TO ASSURANCE
OCTOBER:	PATHWAY TO SUCCESS

NOVEMBER:	PATHWAY TO SPIRITUAL MATURITY
DECEMBER:	PATHWAY TO THE FUTURE

As you walk these pathways, you will join a long list of biblical heroes who were called to move forward into impossible situations armed only with their trust in God. Of course, at times, these great men and women—Abraham, Sarah, Jacob, Moses, David, and many others—were filled with reservation and even fear. However, by choosing to place their lives in God's hands and to follow His call, each of them was able to accomplish great and mighty things in the name of the Lord.

It can be difficult to walk the dimly lit path of life with the lantern of God's guidance shining only a few steps ahead of us. We want to know more, we want to see what lies ahead, and we want to be guaranteed that we will succeed. Our worries and fears of the unknown, however, do not limit God. Instead, He desires that each of us step forward in faith. He has promised that when we do so, He will provide us with the guidance we long for:

> I will instruct you and teach you in the way you should go;
> I will guide you with My eye. (Psalm 32:8)

Our guide for our journey during this year is the Lord Jesus Christ, who declares:

> I am the way and the truth and the life. No one comes to the Father except through me. (John 14:6 NIV)

Our prayer is that of the psalmist David who requested:

> Cause me to know the way in which I should walk,
> for I lift up my soul to You. (Psalm 143:8)

Are you ready? The first pathway lies just ahead . . .

JANUARY
Pathway to God's Will

Your ears shall hear a word behind you, saying,
  "This is the way, walk in it,"
Whenever you turn to the right hand
  Or whenever you turn to the left.
                                    —Isaiah 30:21

WALKING WITH GOD

SCRIPTURE READING: GENESIS 6:9–7:1
KEY VERSE: GENESIS 7:1

Then the LORD said to Noah, "Come into the ark,
you and all your household, because I have seen that you
are righteous before Me in this generation."

A walk is a great way to get alone with someone special and discover more about that person. In today's Scripture passage, we see that Noah chose to spend his time walking with the most important being in his life: God. Because of this close relationship with the Lord, Scripture describes Noah in a most amazing way: "Noah walked with God" (Genesis 6:9).

The complete story of Noah and the great flood in Genesis 6–9 reveals what was involved for this one man to keep in step with his Lord. Noah's walk with God was notably marked by a steadfast faith and a willingness to trust God even when everyone else mocked him. His walk also set him apart from the wicked men and women of the world, none of whom cared to experience the power of a personal relationship with the Creator.

Most importantly, Noah's walk with God clearly represented the fellowship he enjoyed with the Lord. In a time when the world experienced its darkest day, the Lord looked to Noah and said, "I have seen that you are righteous before Me in this generation" (Genesis 7:1).

The wonderful news for you today is that God is just as excited about spending time with you as He was to fellowship with Noah. You are precious in His eyes, and He wants to develop a closer relationship with you. He wants to show you His amazing love in new ways. Will you walk with Him?

Lord, guide my feet so that they may not stray from the path that You
have created. I want to walk through my life with You at my side.

STANDING BEFORE AN OPEN DOOR

SCRIPTURE READING: 2 TIMOTHY 2:1–9
KEY VERSE: 1 CORINTHIANS 16:9

*For a great and effective door has opened to me,
and there are many adversaries.*

If we listen to the whispers of the world, it is possible for us to lose our focus in life. We can get caught up in life and forget about God's big picture of redemption. We could miss the open door of opportunity swinging wide in front of us.

As we enter into a relationship with God, we find out that as much as He cares about us, He cares just as deeply about everyone else in the world. And as we mature in our walk with God, what is important to Him should become important to us as well.

People are important to God. He cares about mankind—it's the motivation behind sending His only Son, Jesus Christ, to the earth to die for our sins. Paul wrote, "God our Savior . . . desires all men to be saved and to come to the knowledge of the truth" (1 Timothy 2:3–4).

So, here we stand at the beginning of a new year with opportunities circling all around us—opportunities that could impact the world in an eternal way. God doesn't open doors for us to simply peer through them; He opens them so we will pass through them with faith that He will empower us to do His kingdom work.

Standing before an open door never resulted in a single changed life. Walking through an open door has changed the lives of millions. Are you willing to walk through it?

Lord, give me the singularity of heart to seek the doors You open for me, and the courage to walk through them.

A Good Opportunity

SCRIPTURE READING: PSALM 78:1–8

KEY VERSE: PSALM 78:6

That the generation to come might know them,
The children who would be born,
That they may arise and declare them to their children.

A narrow mind can cripple our ability to reach people for Christ or to even think we can make a difference in this world. Being a Christian means much more than just avoiding hell at the end of life here on earth.

The door of opportunity before us as believers is great. In looking at the investments we make in other people's lives for Christ, the returns are eternal. Because God is forever—He always has been and He always will be—everything we do for Him also lasts forever:

> [God] established a testimony . . .
> That they should make them known to their children;
> That the generation to come might know them,
> The children who would be born,
> That they may arise and declare them to their children,
> That they may set their hope in God,
> And not forget the works of God,
> But keep His commandments. (Psalm 78:5–7)

Thinking about how we can reach the entire world might overwhelm us. But we can start simply where we are. What we do today has an impact both now and in the years to come. We all know people who don't know Jesus Christ personally, and by sharing our faith with them, both with our words and our deeds, we can begin to become a part of God's redemptive plan. By seizing the opportunities God presents to us, He will begin to use us to change our world.

Lord, I feel inadequate sometimes in sharing my faith with others.
Please give me wisdom and sensitivity as I seek to share the gift of
Your salvation.

GOD IS AT WORK

SCRIPTURE READING: EXODUS 1:7–14
KEY VERSE: EXODUS 3:7

*And the LORD said: "I have surely seen the oppression of My people
who are in Egypt, and have heard their cry because of their
taskmasters, for I know their sorrows."*

Pharaoh's reign over the Israelites had reached an unbearable point of oppression. As they increased in number, so did Pharaoh increase in hardness toward them. The Bible reports that the Egyptians "made their lives bitter with hard bondage" (Exodus 1:14).

As the weight of slavery crushed them, the Israelites called out to the God of their forefathers. Why? Because they knew He had been faithful to Abraham, Isaac, and Jacob. They knew how He had made Joseph into a mighty ruler and how His provision had saved them from the great famine. They knew He was faithful to answer their cries.

When life crushes the heart of a believer, the first response should be to cry out to God, being sure that, no matter the circumstance, His way is the best way.

Amy Carmichael writes, "Of one thing we are sure: prayer is heard; prayer is answered; forces are set in motion by prayer in the name of the Lord Jesus, which will not cease but will continue until that which has begun is perfected. Love will perfect that which it begins. It will not forsake the work of its own hands."

God heard the cries of Israel and delivered them out of Pharaoh's hands. He did not stop the work He started in them. Neither will He stop working to deliver you.

Lord, may Your name be on my lips in times of adversity and in times of prosperity. Help me to always remember that You are my deliverer.

EXPERIENCING GOD'S BEST

SCRIPTURE READING: JAMES 1:1–27
KEY VERSE: JAMES 1:17

Every good gift and every perfect gift is from above,
and comes down from the Father of lights, with whom there
is no variation or shadow of turning.

Here are some of the requirements to experiencing God's best during the coming year:

- An open and willing heart. Before you can experience the blessings of God, you must be open to His love and will for your life. He takes great joy in blessing those who love Him.
- "Ask and you shall receive" were the words Jesus spoke to His disciples. Being open to God's blessings does not mean just being open to receive something good from Him. It means being willing to receive whatever He sends your way. And in some cases, He may send something that you did not wish to receive. However, you can be sure that every gift is ultimately good and sent from a loving Father who has your best interests in mind.
- Obedience. This is a key to receiving and enjoying the goodness of God. Many times the obedience that we exercise is not noticeable to others, but God knows. When we take a step forward in obedience, the Lord always sends His blessings our way.
- The ability to dream. God wants us to look forward to His blessings. When we lose the ability to dream and think on the goodness of God, something inside of us dies. No matter how small your dream for the future appears, refuse to let go of it. Allow God to reshape it if necessary, but always believe in His loving ability to supply answers to your hopes and dreams.

Lord, please give me an open and willing heart. Make me obedient,
and give me the ability to dream.

THE RISK OF OBEYING GOD

SCRIPTURE READING: LUKE 5:1–11
KEY VERSE: LUKE 5:4

*When He had stopped speaking, He said to Simon, "Launch
out into the deep and let down your nets for a catch."*

Jesus was speaking to the crowds on the shore of the Sea of Galilee. As they listened, they pressed closer. When Jesus saw two boats lying on the edge of the water near where the fishermen were washing their nets, He got in Simon Peter's boat, continuing to teach.

When He was finished teaching, Jesus said to Peter, "Launch out into the deep and let down your nets for a catch" (Luke 5:4). Peter had a choice—either to obey or disobey God. He chose to obey. The result was so many fish that the nets began to break.

Through the simple act of obedience, Peter witnessed a miracle. He realized that Jesus had his best interest at heart, even when he did not understand what Jesus was telling him to do. Peter had toiled all night without catching any fish. But he was willing to obey.

What has God asked you to do that you are afraid to do? There are many reasons why we hesitate to obey God: fear of failure, the desire to control our own lives, or fear of what God may require of us.

What little thing has God been nudging you about? God wants you to trust and obey Him in the small things. Don't allow your unwillingness to obey God to cause you to miss the blessings He has for you. Every time God asks you to do something, He has something good in store for you.

*Father, help me trust You in the small things, knowing You have
something good in store for me.*

TRUSTING THE LORD

SCRIPTURE READING: PROVERBS 3:1–6
KEY VERSE: PROVERBS 3:6

*In all your ways acknowledge Him,
And He shall direct your paths.*

Seeing a sweet little dog wearing a large, white Elizabethan collar may make you chuckle. Though these large cone-shaped accessories look like the puppy had an unfortunate run-in with a bigger dog, they actually serve a very valuable purpose.

According to a popular pet Internet site, these collars "prevent pets from aggravating wounds that are healing and allow topical medications to work." The dogs do not understand why they have them on, but the collars impede them from hurting themselves.

Amazingly enough, many of the hindrances God has allowed in your life serve to protect you as well. When plans fall through or events don't turn out as you expect, your first instinct is often to blame God for the disappointment. However, Proverbs 3:5–6 has a different message. "Trust in the LORD with all your heart, and lean not on your own understanding; in all your ways acknowledge Him, and He shall direct your paths."

God knows far more about your future than you ever could. He allows roadblocks so that you will not be diverted from His best. Instead of giving in to self-pity, consider why God has prevented you from continuing. You will come to a deeper understanding of how He heals, protects, and directs you. And you will learn that He is truly trustworthy.

Lord, it is hard to trust before I understand. But You know all, and I bow to Your knowledge of what is best for my life, in good times and in bad.

An Extraordinary Life

SCRIPTURE READING: PROVERBS 3:7–12
KEY VERSE: PROVERBS 3:12

For whom the Lord loves He corrects,
Just as a father the son in whom he delights.

Early in his life, John Donne, one of England's great poets, was known for his controversial poetry and satirical criticism of religious denominations. However, Donne did not remain antagonistic toward God.

After joining the Church of England and marrying Anne More, Donne experienced immense suffering. He and Anne lost five of their twelve children and lived in despondent poverty. Donne continually struggled with depression and physical affliction. One would think that the suffering would have driven Donne further from God.

However, the exact opposite is true. During this time, Donne studied God's ways with fervor. Donne wrote:

> Batter my heart, three person'd God; for you
> As yet but knock, breathe, shine and seek to mend . . .
> Take me to you, imprison me, for I
> Except you enthrall me, never shall be free.

Donne understood that all his trials brought him closer to God. As Proverbs 3:12 says, "For whom the LORD loves He corrects, just as a father the son in whom he delights." If you are suffering greatly, do not think that God has abandoned you. Rather, like Donne, God is making your life into a sweet sonnet. Donne was not only one of England's great poets, but also one of its greatest preachers. God is making something extraordinary of your life too.

Father, I receive Your reproof. I know You have not abandoned me.
Make my life fruitful!

HOLY FEAR

SCRIPTURE READING: PSALM 25:1–22
KEY VERSE: PSALM 25:12

Who is the man that fears the Lord?
Him shall He teach in the way He chooses.

Life is one continuous decision-making process from childhood through the golden years. Often, the decisions you will be called upon to make will be very difficult and very serious. God is willing to give you clear guidance about every circumstance in your life. However, He desires to be rightly regarded and respected in your life. In fact, He asks you to fear Him.

John Owens explains, "That fear which keeps from sin and excites the soul to cleave more firmly to God, be the object of it what it will, is no servile fear, but a holy fear and due reverence unto God and His word."

Reverence to God means serving God instead of yourself. It means comprehending His sovereignty and having confidence in His character. Understanding that God is perfect in His knowledge, all-sufficient in His strength, and unconditionally loving toward you is key to trusting Him for your future. The person who does well is the one who reveres God, respects Him, yields to Him, seeks Him, and desires to know His mind. In fact, Psalm 25:12 promises, "Who is the man that fears the LORD? Him shall He teach in the way He chooses."

Are you in the midst of a difficult situation? Check your heart and analyze your attitude toward God. Reevaluate your situation in light of His trustworthy character.

Lord, I bend my knee and my spirit in reverence before Your greatness, which is beyond human understanding.

SATISFYING YOUR HEART

SCRIPTURE READING: COLOSSIANS 3:12–17
KEY VERSE: COLOSSIANS 3:15

*And let the peace of God rule in your hearts, to which also
you were called in one body; and be thankful.*

Wasn't life simpler when you could plunk down a quarter and get a steamy cup of java? Now, to buy coffee, you must make a hundred different decisions. Would you like a latte, cappuccino, expresso, macchiato, or frappucino? Flavored with mocha, caramel, vanilla, amaretto, or hazelnut? Would you like it caffeinated or decaf? Tall or grande? The options are endless and create a sense of satisfying whatever your heart desires. It is natural for situations to go from simplicity to chaos when the heart is involved.

However, Scripture has an indictment for the heart, as Jeremiah 17:9 instructs: "The heart is deceitful above all things, and desperately wicked; who can know it?"

Sometimes the reason circumstances become more complicated is because the simplest answers are challenging to the heart. Even though you really do know what to do, the decision would take a great deal of courage and commitment. As you wait to find a solution that caters to the whims of your heart, answers become increasingly difficult to find.

The only answer is for God to direct you. As Colossians 3:15 teaches, "Let the peace of God rule in your hearts." Is it Christ who rules your heart and directs your path? His is the greatest satisfaction your heart will ever know.

*Lord, my heart wanders as it wills. I give it to You, so that You may
guide it around the pitfalls of its own longings.*

MAKING IMPORTANT DECISIONS

SCRIPTURE READING: JOHN 16:7–15
KEY VERSE: JOHN 16:1

These things I have spoken to you,
that you should not be made to stumble.

God has definite plans for each of our lives and is very interested and involved in our every decision. In light of this fact, how should we go about making important decisions?

The Lord has our interests at heart every single second of our lives. There is no time at which He does not care about us or long for our very best. This is why He has promised in Psalm 16:11 to show us the path of life. Later, in Psalm 32:8, God promises to instruct us in the way we should go, and that He will guide us with His eye.

In his book *What God Wishes Christians Knew about Christianity*, author Bill Gillham reminds us that God has a "helicopter view" above the parade of our lives. While we can only see the parade as it marches by, God sees the beginning, middle, and end of our parade. Why, then, would we not beseech the Lord to give us guidance not only in major decisions but also in our daily choices?

Do you prayerfully submit to the Lord the choices you face? Do you rejoice in the fact that He has given you His Holy Spirit as a pilot in your search for guidance? Or do you navigate without first checking with your pilot, proceeding as if your personal philosophy holds that it is better to ask for forgiveness than permission?

Dear God, thank You for Your Holy Spirit who provides guidance
for my way and gives me wisdom for making important decisions.

SEEKING GOD'S GUIDANCE

SCRIPTURE READING: PSALM 32:1–8
KEY VERSE: PSALM 32:8

I will instruct you and teach you in the way you should go;
I will guide you with My eye.

In seeking the Lord's guidance, we must be careful to watch for pitfalls along our paths. Strong fleshly desires, wrong counsel, impatience, doubt, and pressures are all snares that will leave us with less than God's best if we cave in to their temptations. These reasons are why there are certain essentials to seeking God's guidance:

- Cleansing: Sin inhibits not your relationship with God, but your fellowship. If you are a believer, your relationship is secure. But constant sin will impede your fellowship with God, and He will not act until you walk away from the sin.
- Surrendering: God loves you and wants your best. So why not believe Him, let go of the worldly trappings you may hold so dear, and step out in faith?
- Asking: James said that we don't have because we don't ask or because our requests are made with wrong motives. Our heavenly Father is often just waiting for us to simply ask with a pure heart.
- Meditating: How often do you make decisions by intentionally seeking God's promises in His Word and meditating over them?
- Believing: To believe is to trust and obey. His Word says that whoever has His commands and obeys them is the one who loves Him.
- Waiting: This is difficult. But it's also when the Lord does His best work as sculptor of our souls.

Lord, I surrender to Your will. Cleanse me as I wait and meditate on You.

Knowing the Voice of God

Scripture Reading: 1 Kings 19:1–18
Key Verse: 1 Kings 19:12

*. . . and after the earthquake a fire, but the Lord was not in the fire;
and after the fire a still small voice.*

The most potent hearing aid known to man is the Holy Bible. It is the standard of truth against which you can test every message that comes your way.

Making a decision on an issue important to you can be extremely difficult. Sometimes it may seem as if you are hearing two or more voices, all of which make seemingly good points but also tug you in different directions. It is important that in these times you learn to discern the voice of God.

There are several principles you can apply to what you're hearing to gauge whether it is of God, but the most basic is whether the message conflicts with Scripture. God won't tell you to do something that counters what He already has recorded for all mankind. Therefore, the best way to know God's voice is to get to know Him. Spend time in His Word and soak in His truths. You must know God's Word before you can differentiate God's instructions from the messages Satan or your flesh is sending you.

Do you know how investigators are trained to recognize counterfeit money? They don't spend all of their time trying to keep up with the latest technological advances in creating false money. Instead, they first and foremost diligently study the original, the real thing.

Then, held against the standard, the counterfeit stuff stands out.

Help me to discern Your voice, dear Lord. I want to differentiate Your message from all others.

Is God Still Talking?

SCRIPTURE READING: PSALM 81:11–16
KEY VERSE: PSALM 81:13

Oh, that My people would listen to Me,
That Israel would walk in My ways!

If you've ever wondered whether God still talks to people, allow Him to use today's verse to give an answer: "Oh, that My people would listen to Me" (Psalm 81:13). God wants people to listen. Therefore, He must be talking. While God was speaking primarily to the nation of Israel in this psalm, you can be sure that His voice still guides, confirms, disciplines, and assures His children.

Generally, there are four reasons He speaks and four methods He uses to speak: God desires to have fellowship with us, His most precious creation, and loves us just as much as He loved the saints of the Bible; God knows that we need clear direction in a difficult world; God realizes we need comfort and assurance just as much as did Abraham, Moses, Peter, Paul, and others; and, most importantly, God wants us to get to know Him.

But how do we know when God is speaking to us? Today, He uses four primary ways to share His heart with ours: through His Word, the foremost tool He uses to impart His truth; through the Holy Spirit, who witnesses to our spirits; through other believers who are walking in His Spirit; and through circumstances He providentially arranges. It may be a still, small voice, but it resounds loudly because of whose voice it is.

Speak to me, Lord, through Your Word, Your Spirit, other believers,
and providential circumstances.

ARE YOU LISTENING?

SCRIPTURE READING: ACTS 9:1–9
KEY VERSE: JOSHUA 1:7

*Only be strong and very courageous, that you may observe to
do according to all the law which Moses My servant commanded
you; do not turn from it to the right hand or to the left,
that you may prosper wherever you go.*

It has been said that there are two ways in which God speaks to us today: with a whisper or a shout. Certainly none of us would choose the "shouting method," but often our insensitivity to His voice forces God to use methods that demand our undivided attention.

Incidents in the lives of Joshua and Saul demonstrated God's whisper/shout principle. Joshua heeded God's instructions, "Do not turn from [the Law] to the right hand or to the left, that you may prosper wherever you go" (Joshua 1:7). On the other hand, God secured Saul's attention on the Damascus road by knocking him to the ground and temporarily blinding him.

God communicated with the people of the Old and New Testaments through dreams, prophets, angels, and an audible voice. But what must He do to make us listen? God offers His Word to communicate His will and allows the Holy Spirit to speak to our hearts. God also sends others to bless and direct us. Even in our disappointments, God communicates that our failure today can make us a success tomorrow (Romans 8:28).

As a believer, you can know that in every situation God will speak to guide (Psalm 48:14), comfort (John 14:16), protect (Genesis 19:17–26), teach obedience (Joshua 6:18–19), or express His unfailing love to us (John 16:27). Do not allow the incessant noises of life to drown out His voice. When we fail to hear His gentle whisper, He has other effective ways of getting our attention.

Are you listening?

Lord, tune my ears to hear Your whispers, so that I may never need to hear You shout.

FINDING GOD

SCRIPTURE READING: PSALM 16:7–11
KEY VERSE: PSALM 16:11

You will show me the path of life;
In Your presence is fullness of joy;
At Your right hand are pleasures forevermore.

Men often have a bad reputation for refusing to request directions while driving. At the root of the issue is the fact that we do not like to admit that we do not know something. Even if it means going in circles for hours, many of us would rather stumble upon the right answer ourselves than to ask for help. This method works for us as long as we know the general area. However, if we must get to a specific destination in a strange town, we need to know how to get there!

The same can be said of our lives. We may believe that God has something specific set aside for us, and yet we may not seek His guidance for leading us safely into His plan. How can we arrive at God's destination if we do not consult the only One who can see where we are going?

The Lord has promised to give us direction. Psalm 16:11 says, "You will show me the path of life; in Your presence is fullness of joy; at Your right hand are pleasures forevermore." God's will is not something that we find "out there" through trial and error. Rather, it is something that we find "in Him," through prayer and Bible study as we strive to know His heart more clearly.

If you have been on a quest to "find God," stop your searching and simply talk to Him. He knows where you are, and He knows exactly where you need to go. No roadmap could promise more.

May I not waste precious time wandering, Lord, when I can come directly to You and seek direction for my life.

GOD'S PLAN FOR YOUR FUTURE

SCRIPTURE READING: JEREMIAH 29:11–14
KEY VERSE: JEREMIAH 29:11

For I know the thoughts that I think toward you, says the LORD,
thoughts of peace and not of evil, to give you a future and a hope.

Are you aware that God knows exactly where you are and what you are doing right now? What about tomorrow, or the next day, or the next? God is just as aware of what you will be doing at 10:42 A.M. on any random morning five years from now, as He is mindful of what you are doing now.

Contrary to secular thought, we are not bouncing around haphazardly through time and space. The same God who created the universe and everything in it also has a specific plan for every single person on earth. Because He is the God of yesterday, today, and tomorrow, He alone knows the ultimate outcome of each decision we make. Therefore, only God can be trusted to guide our daily steps as we seek to follow Him.

The Lord revealed through Jeremiah, "For I know the thoughts that I think toward you . . . thoughts of peace and not of evil, to give you a future and a hope" (Jeremiah 29:11). These two things—hope and the expectation of a bright future—are in short supply these days. However, we have the assurance of the almighty God that He already has a plan to provide us with both.

In Christ, the hope for our eternal future is secure. However, God is still intimately interested in your day-to-day living as well. Invite Him into your decisions; only He knows how to get you where He wants to take you.

Father, I am so thankful that You are interested in my day-to-day living. I invite You to guide me in every decision and get me where You want to take me.

THE REVELATION OF GOD

SCRIPTURE READING: HEBREWS 1:1–4
KEY VERSE: HEBREWS 1:2

[God] has in these last days spoken to us by His Son, whom He has appointed heir of all things, through whom also He made the worlds.

As evidenced in the Scriptures, God spoke to His people in the Old and New Testaments in many creative and powerful ways. But in these opening paragraphs of Hebrews chapter one, a new way of speaking is defined.

"[God] has in these last days spoken to us by His Son" (verse 2), it says. Why this change? you may be wondering. Verses 2–4 provide insight. Carefully and beautifully, the author of Hebrews explains that God speaks to us through His Son for these reasons:

- Jesus has been appointed heir of all things. Through Jesus, God made the world. Jesus is the radiance of God's glory. Jesus is the exact representation of God's nature, and He upholds all things by the word of His power.
- Jesus provided purification of sin and sits at the right hand of God. Jesus is higher than the angels and has inherited a most excellent name.
- Jesus Christ is the final expression of the heart of God. He is the final word about salvation and the final word of revelation. A revelation is defined as truth that God gives that could not be received in any other way. Therefore, Jesus came to speak to us and to die for us since God's message of love could not have been delivered in a more perfect way.

As you reflect on today's Scripture reading, consider the sacrifice that was made for you through Jesus Christ. What is God saying to your heart?

Father, I am humbled by Your great gift to me of Your Son, and through Him the gifts of being a fellow heir, purified from sin and a receptacle for Your truth.

BLIND TO THE TRUTH

SCRIPTURE READING: 2 CORINTHIANS 4:1–4
KEY VERSE: 2 CORINTHIANS 4:4

*. . . whose minds the god of this age has blinded, who do not believe,
lest the light of the gospel of the glory of Christ, who is the
image of God, should shine on them.*

Why is it that so many people in our world today remain ignorant of the gospel even when it is presented in so many ways? Modern-day missionaries are now able to deliver the message of salvation across the globe via radio, television, the Internet, books, and traditional word-of-mouth presentations. And still, there are those who will not receive Christ.

Though distressing, this situation is not new. When Paul addressed the church at Corinth in 2 Corinthians 4:4, he identified this same problem and offered a reason for its existence—Satan blinded the minds of the unbelieving.

We need only to turn on the news or pick up a newspaper to find supporting evidence for this problem. How many times do we hear confessions from criminals who claim to have acted in God's name? "A voice in my mind told me to commit this crime," they say in defense.

The sad truth is that the voices these people are hearing are not of the living God but of "the god of this world," the god of evil. Just as Paul said, these poor souls have been blinded to God's truth.

In your time of prayer today, thank God for drawing you to Himself with His truth. After doing this, intercede for someone in your family or community who has not yet accepted Jesus Christ. Pray for this person's salvation, asking God to lift the "scales" of spiritual blindness from his or her eyes.

I am so grateful, dear Lord, that You have lifted the scales from my eyes. I pray for the hardened hearts of those around me, that they may be softened to receive You.

GOD'S GOAL IN SPEAKING

SCRIPTURE READING: GALATIANS 1:11–17
KEY VERSES: GALATIANS 1:15–16

*But when it pleased God, who separated me from my mother's
womb and called me through His grace, to reveal His Son in me,
that I might preach Him among the Gentiles, I did not
immediately confer with flesh and blood.*

When God speaks to us, He always has something very specific to say. Never speaking in generalities, He has a goal in mind to reach the human heart. Using today's passage from Galatians as our guide, we can identify three clear objectives of God's speaking. God speaks because He wants us to:

- comprehend and understand His truth;
- be conformed to and shaped by this truth; and
- be equipped to communicate truth to others.

In Galatians chapter 1, the apostle Paul used the example of his own life, preconversion and postconversion, as evidence of God's objectives. Beginning in verse 12, he explained how God first revealed truth to him through the revelation of Jesus Christ. This was the beginning of Paul's understanding of the truth.

Next, Paul wrote that, despite his advancement in the teachings of Judaism, the Lord called him through His grace (verse 15). This was the beginning of a process that involved Paul being conformed, or shaped, to the truth.

Finally, we are given Paul's grace-filled account of the Lord's plan for his life. "God . . . called me through His grace, to reveal His Son in me, that I might preach Him among the Gentiles" (verses 15–16). Clearly, Paul received and embraced his call to communicate God's truth to others.

What better proof do we have of God's objectives being perfectly revealed and carried out in one believer's life?

*Thank You for Your truth in my heart. Please use it to shape me to
Your will, so that I may share Your truth with others.*

Conformed to the Truth

Scripture Reading: Romans 12:1–5
Key Verses: Romans 12:1–2

I beseech you therefore, brethren, by the mercies of God, that you present your bodies a living sacrifice, holy, acceptable to God, which is your reasonable service. And do not be conformed to this world, but be transformed by the renewing of your mind, that you may prove what is that good and acceptable and perfect will of God.

Yesterday we were reminded that God speaks to us so that we may be conformed to His truth and communicate His message to others. But what does it mean to be conformed to the truth?

We are provided with an answer in Romans 12:1–2. The passage may be divided into three interrelated goals for the believer to pursue:

- Present your body as a living sacrifice.
- Do not be conformed to the world.
- Be transformed by the renewing of your mind.

Being a living sacrifice, we are told, is our spiritual service of worship to God (verse 1). No longer must we give burnt offerings. Instead, we are to live in a way that glorifies God.

Not conforming to the world means that we should not live according to, or be negatively influenced by, the standards of our secular environment.

Transformation is a continual process that happens from the inside out. Our minds should be constantly renewed or refreshed by a new way of thinking—replacing our selfish wants with desires to serve and obey God.

A final thought is given in verse 2. We must change so that we "may prove what is that good and acceptable and perfect will of God."

God has clearly communicated these goals to you. Where are you in this important process: presentation, conformity, or transformation?

Lord, my mind is Yours. Take it and reconstruct it so that my whole person can be reshaped into the person whom You intended me to be.

FOLLOWING GOD'S COUNSEL

SCRIPTURE READING: GENESIS 3:1–7
KEY VERSE: GENESIS 3:6

So when the woman saw that the tree was good for food, that it was pleasant to the eyes, and a tree desirable to make one wise, she took of its fruit and ate. She also gave to her husband with her, and he ate.

We serve a loving God who desires to lead His children into sound, wise decisions. However, even though we call on God for guidance and direction, we do not always follow His counsel. What can we expect when we fail to listen to Him?

Take a moment to read Genesis 3:1–7. In these verses, we find Eve faced with a conflict between what the Lord has told her and what she wants for herself. Sadly, she ultimately decides to base her decision on the words of the tempter, and as a result, sin enters the world.

This mistake demonstrates a pitfall that we often make in our day-to-day decisions: we listen to the wrong voices. In today's passage, Eve knows very well what the Lord requires of her, yet she gives in to the allure of Satan's offer. She weighs each option against the desires of her own heart and unfortunately chooses the one that appeals most.

When we follow similar patterns in our lives, we are in effect saying, "Thanks for Your advice, God, but I'm going to do things my way instead." Even though we may not say these words outright, it doesn't mean that our actions are not conveying this message. We must be careful how we respond to God's call.

God has made Himself approachable and available. He wants us to seek His mind for our decisions. When we receive His guidance, we must then decide to heed His advice. To remain obedient to God, pray for the strength to follow His wise counsel.

Dear Lord, I thank You that You are approachable and available. Give me the strength to follow Your wise counsel.

THE BLAME GAME

SCRIPTURE READING: GENESIS 3:8–13

KEY VERSE: JAMES 1:4

*But let patience have its perfect work, that you may
be perfect and complete, lacking nothing.*

Adam and Eve's fall into sin was the result of listening to the voice of the tempter, and their actions resulted in shame, guilt, and fear. Their shame is immediately evident in the awareness of their nakedness. Moreover, when faced with the presence of God, they choose to hide. They are simply afraid to face Him because, for the first time, Adam and Eve are aware of good and evil, and they realize the evil in their actions.

When questioned by God, Adam demonstrates yet another common response to sin: redirected blame. In Genesis 3:12, he tries to blame Eve for what he has done. How often do we still employ this tactic today?

"It's not my fault! The devil made me do it!" Maybe you have your own common catchphrases to shift blame elsewhere. At the root of this, however, is our own guilt over our wrongdoings. In desperation, we reach out and attempt to pin the blame on whoever may be readily accessible.

We must realize that we cannot be made to sin. James 1:14 makes this point clear: "But each one is tempted when he is drawn away by his own desires and enticed." When it comes to straying from God's desires for us, the blame game falls short. We must instead confess our sins to God, who stands ready to forgive everything that leads us to shame, guilt, and fear.

*Lord, help me not to blame others, but to take personal responsibility
for my own sin.*

RECOGNIZING THE VOICE OF GOD

SCRIPTURE READING: MATTHEW 16:24–27
KEY VERSE: MATTHEW 16:24

Then Jesus said to His disciples, "If anyone desires to come after Me,
let him deny himself, and take up his cross, and follow Me."

The world is filled with countless voices, all vying for our attention. Television personalities tell us to buy this or that, and government officials tell us what to believe. We pore over magazines and newspapers, surf Web pages for hours, and strap radio headsets to our ears. How, in the midst of this chaos, can we hope to recognize the voice of God?

One way to make sure you have heard a word from the Lord is to confirm that message with Scripture. God will never speak in contradiction to His holy, perfect Word. If you believe God has spoken and yet what you have heard goes against the Bible, you must dismiss the contrary message.

Rather than relying upon Scripture to verify God's messages to us today, many people use their own desires and morality as the litmus test. This is a tragic mistake, because our fleshly desires are simply not trustworthy. Our personal sense of right and wrong may ebb and flow, but the Word of God is forever unchanging and therefore continually reliable.

Another mistake in interpreting God's voice is to assume that His message to us will fit right into our normal lives. The truth is, His call is often life changing. Therefore, we should not assume that He might only want to "tweak" details of your life; He may want to change it completely.

God has a special word for each of us, and we must strive to hear Him clearly so we may act upon that message with boldness, confidence, and conviction.

Lord, thank You for giving us Scripture so that we can test the voices
we hear against Your enduring wisdom.

The Voice of the Shepherd

SCRIPTURE READING: JOHN 10:1–5
KEY VERSE: JOHN 10:4

*And when he brings out his own sheep, he goes before them;
and the sheep follow him, for they know his voice.*

Have you ever seen a child who cannot find his mother in a crowd? Although she may be out of sight, the little tyke may still hear her voice. It is almost as though his inner radar scans the sounds around him, looking for that one familiar tone. Did you know that Jesus encouraged His hearers to have that same familiarity with the voice of God?

In today's passage from the Gospel of John, Jesus likens His followers to sheep under the direction of the Great Shepherd. In this parallel, we see that only the shepherd can approach the flock without causing alarm. If an unknown intruder were to come near, the sheep would immediately sense danger, and the doorkeeper would not open the stable door. Also, we see that the sheep follow the shepherd wherever he leads because they know his voice. Just like a child listening for his mother, sheep instantly recognize the shepherd by his voice.

Why is this analogy important to us today? It is because we are the sheep and Jesus is the Shepherd. He has entered our "flock" by stepping into human history, and He calls us to Himself by word and deed.

Can you hear the word of the Lord? He desires to make Himself known in your life. If you have trouble hearing His voice, stop and pray for help in quieting the noises of the world so that you can focus intently on the voice of your Great Shepherd.

Lord, when I can't discern Your voice, help me not to ask You to speak louder but, rather, to spend more time listening for it.

CHOOSING THE PERFECT PATH

SCRIPTURE READING: 2 CORINTHIANS 4:8–12
KEY VERSE: HEBREWS 13:15

*Therefore by Him let us continually offer the sacrifice of praise to God,
that is, the fruit of our lips, giving thanks to His name.*

When you are faced with a very crucial decision and you really want to do God's best, what do you do? When you are rejected and criticized by someone you love very dearly, how do you respond? When you are tempted to indulge your carnal desire, where do you turn?

If you depend on your own calculations to negotiate an important decision in life, there is absolutely no guarantee that your action will yield God's best. While you may make a smart choice, your inability to see what lies ahead in life limits your capacity for decision making. But God, who sees all things, has plans to prosper you and to give you hope for your future. If you allow Him, He will make certain that you choose the perfect path for your life.

Rejection and criticism can be literally debilitating, particularly when they come from loved ones. But there is no one who loves you more than your Father in heaven. When Jeremiah's heart was faint, he turned to God to be his comforter (Jeremiah 8:18–19). You can too.

The apostle Paul instructed believers to pray for deliverance from temptation. When you are in the throes of ungodly provocation, invoke the name of God. Direct your prayers to Him, and your heart will follow.

A wise person looks to God to be his stronghold through trials. Realizing that you are no match for the snares of the enemy, it is always prudent to put your trust in God, who will never leave or forsake you.

*Lord, on my own I am nothing. Thank You that You are always there
to give me love and guidance when I am feeling battered.*

GETTING GOD'S VIEWPOINT

SCRIPTURE READING: 2 CORINTHIANS 4:16–18
KEY VERSE: 2 CORINTHIANS 4:17

*For our light affliction, which is but for a moment, is working
for us a far more exceeding and eternal weight of glory.*

If you have traveled on an airplane, you have experienced the thrill of liftoff. As the plane surges up and up, the objects on the ground become smaller until the plane finally breaks through the clouds. Then, with the pillowy mist below, you are transported to a tranquil wonderland with a new perspective.

When hardships and problems invade our lives, we often fix our focus on them, looking down as we would from an airplane. The result is that we sometimes forget that God has a completely different vantage point. From His view, every event has a purpose that fits perfectly into His plan.

Today's Scripture passage provides additional encouragement, saying that our momentary afflictions are producing eternal glory (verse 17). It also reminds us that, while we are on earth, it is not the visible things but the unseen things that are eternal (verse 18).

What "light affliction" in your life is causing you to look away from God? Has someone hurt you? Are you disappointed? Are discouraging circumstances hindering your joy? God, your heavenly Father, longs to relieve you of these burdens. He wants to show you His perspective.

When you have God's viewpoint, you will be able to face your circumstances with the confidence that He will see you through your difficulty. And as a result, the Lord will allow you to soar past your hardships into a new horizon of spiritual growth.

Heavenly Father, give me Your viewpoint. Help me face my circumstances with confidence that You will be with me through every difficulty.

LETTING GOD SPEAK

SCRIPTURE READING: 2 SAMUEL 7:8–22
KEY VERSE: 2 SAMUEL 7:18

*Then King David went in and sat before the Lord; and he said:
"Who am I, O Lord GOD? And what is my house,
that You have brought me this far?"*

Of all the heroes of the Bible, few are spoken of as respectfully as King David. What was so special about David? That was a question he asked himself. The best answer is simply this: David was a man who listened to God.

It is impossible to live a godly life if we do not listen to God. When we listen, we gain guidance, direction, discipline, and encouragement from our heavenly Father. This was certainly true in David's life (Psalm 63:1–8). In the Psalms, we get a beautiful picture of David's prayer life. Note four things he did when meditating on God:

- First, he reviewed the past. Though David had made some serious mistakes, those hard times produced a necessary humility. Looking back helped him remember God's faithfulness.
- Second, David reflected upon God Himself. When we focus on God's character, we grow in our understanding of who He is. This results in a more personal, interactive relationship.
- Third, David remembered God's promises. God had directed David's steps throughout his life, and always with great success.
- Finally, David made requests of his heavenly Father. God never intended us to go through life alone. He is always ready to act on our behalf.

If your prayer life is dominated by your own talking, you probably need to make some adjustments. Just as He spoke to David, God has many things to say to you, if you will simply let Him speak.

Lord, I know You have important things to say to me. Help me to listen, knowing You will speak.

LISTENING FOR GOD'S VOICE

SCRIPTURE READING: MATTHEW 6:5–13
KEY VERSE: MATTHEW 6:6

*But you, when you pray, go into your room, and when you have
shut your door, pray to your Father who is in the secret place;
and your Father who sees in secret will reward you openly.*

Imagine yourself standing in the middle of a full auditorium, with thousands of people surrounding you. If every person there was speaking at the same time, would it be possible to hear any individual in the great crowd? More than likely, you would never be able to distinguish one voice from another.

This same principle holds true for our prayer lives. In our normal, everyday lives, we are surrounded by countless voices in need of our attention. Our children cry for it, our employers demand it, and our loved ones yearn for it. With all of these calls, is it any wonder that God's voice sometimes seems so muffled or distant?

Effective meditation demands seclusion. If we do not make an effort to find a moment or two to escape the demands of our daily lives, then our ability to hear God's voice will be weakened.

Jesus was well aware of this need for isolation. In teaching the disciples how to pray, Jesus told them to go into their rooms and close the door behind them. He knew that it was vital to take a break from the demands of life in order to truly commune with the Father.

The modern world works against this need, however. Mobile phones, e-mail, and other technological advances have brought us the blessing— and the curse—of constant communication.

At some point today, turn off the television, cell phone, and computer, and simply listen for His voice. Your schedule will not surrender time easily, so make a decision to claim a block of time for the Lord.

*Lord, I am surrounded by countless voices in need of my attention.
Help me to stop, listen, and hear Your voice today.*

SIMPLY BE STILL

SCRIPTURE READING: PSALM 46:1–11
KEY VERSE: PSALM 46:10

Be still, and know that I am God;
I will be exalted among the nations,
I will be exalted in the earth!

Don't just stand there! Do something!" This is a familiar call to action in our modern world. However, there is something inherently dangerous when we try to force this way of thinking into our spiritual lives.

Too often, whether we voice the belief or not, we act as though God needs our help. We wrestle with God for some degree of control over the events in our lives. In effect, we make a proud stand and proclaim, "Okay, God. I think this is what You want to happen, so I'm going to work and work and work and make it come about."

Somewhere in the back of our minds, we hear the time-honored counsel, "God helps those who help themselves." In fact, the vast majority of Christians believe that this word of advice is in the Bible. It is not.

Actually, this statement is 100 percent contrary to the Word of God, which instead tells us to be still. The Father knows that we cannot help ourselves. That is the very reason He sent His Son to die—because we were utterly helpless to improve our sinful condition (Romans 5:8).

While we seek to do God's will, we must not forget His fundamental call to stillness before Him. When we are still and quiet in His presence, we put ourselves in the most teachable position possible.

Are you too busy trying to keep up with God? Lay down your efforts and simply be still. What you discover in the stillness may revolutionize your call to Christian service.

Lord, I cease from my own efforts. I wait in stillness before You.

THE BLESSINGS OF INTIMATE RELATIONSHIP

SCRIPTURE READING: EPHESIANS 1:16–19
KEY VERSE: JOHN 16:33

These things I have spoken to you, that in Me you may have peace.
In the world you will have tribulation; but be of good cheer,
I have overcome the world.

Our time spent with God has a dramatic impact on our daily lives. When we spend time focusing upon and listening to Him, several changes—both subtle and dramatic—begin to occur in our lives:

- We begin to gain a godly perspective. The apostle Paul was certainly mindful of this. In Ephesians 1:16–19, we see that Paul actively prayed for himself and others to receive God's outlook. When we begin to see through enlightened eyes, the whole world becomes much clearer, as does our understanding of how to deal with these issues.
- Spending time with God causes the pressures of life to dissipate. Jesus warned His disciples that they would (just as all of us will) face trouble in this world, but He assured them that they had no real reason to be afraid. Why fear a foe that Christ has already conquered (John 16:33)?
- Meditation brings peace. In our thoroughly troubled world, we frequently find ourselves in need of peace. Jesus promised us that true peace can be found in Him alone (John 14:27). Not only can the world not offer this genuine peace, but Paul even said that the world cannot understand God's peace (Philippians 4:7).

The search for personal satisfaction should not be our only reason for spending time with the Lord, but we cannot deny the blessings that accompany an intimate relationship with Him.

Thank You, dear Lord, that I can have an intimate relationship with You, enabling me to hear Your voice and walk in Your ways.

FEBRUARY
Pathway to Forgiveness

"For if you forgive men their trespasses, your heavenly Father will also forgive you. But if you do not forgive men their trespasses, neither will your Father forgive your trespasses."
—Matthew 6:14–15

A Path to His Presence

SCRIPTURE READING: JOHN 1:1–9
KEY VERSE: PSALM 32:5

I acknowledged my sin to You,
And my iniquity I have not hidden.
I said, "I will confess my transgressions to the Lord,"
And You forgave the iniquity of my sin. Selah

Do you know people who attend church every Sunday and profess the love of Christ, yet do not express His love to others? Could one of those people be you? It is easy to embrace the intellectual theology of Christ's love, but quite another thing to let that love flow in and through your heart to a needy world.

One of the primary reasons people fail to experience God's love flowing through them is that a barrier of bitterness and resentment obstructs it. When you are bitter, you build a wall around your heart to protect yourself from pain. If you build it high enough, you may become entirely isolated from the world. Safe, but isolated. Your protective mechanism eventually leads to loneliness and ineffectiveness.

The root of this condition sometimes can be traced to an unforgiving spirit. When you enclose yourself in a cell of unforgiveness, you work, fellowship, and even worship behind bars. But this need not be the case. We know from Scripture that Jesus came to set the captives free. He did so through a divine act of love and forgiveness.

The power of Christ's strength to forgive even the most degenerate is available to you, if you are willing to accept it. If you are captive to your own anger and hostility, allow the Lord to exchange those attitudes for the love you need in order to forgive. In doing so, you yourself will experience the love of your heavenly Father and will, at the same time, become a vessel for sharing it with others—even those who hurt you.

Forgiveness is a pathway into the presence of God.

Dear Lord, give me the strength to forgive. I refuse to be held captive to anger and hostility. Give me the love I need in order to forgive others.

HEALING OUR HURTS

SCRIPTURE READING: EPHESIANS 4:26–32
KEY VERSE: EPHESIANS 4:32

*And be kind to one another, tenderhearted, forgiving one another,
even as God in Christ forgave you.*

Whether it is the driver who cut you off in traffic, a relative who gets under your skin, or a coworker who irritates you, there will always be someone in your life who needs forgiveness.

Sometimes the pardon is easily doled out, and anger is soon forgotten. Yet sometimes, deep roots of hurt prevail and the bitterness tightens its grip on your spirit and makes reconciliation very difficult.

Christian author Dag Hammarskjöld writes, "Forgiveness breaks the chain of causality because he who forgives you—out of love—takes upon himself the consequences of what you have done. Forgiveness, therefore, always entails a sacrifice."

Ephesians 4:32 proclaims, "And be kind to one another, tenderhearted, forgiving one another, even as God in Christ forgave you."

Pardon is most easily given when remembering the immense debt of which Christ has relieved you. Each person knows the wrongs they have done, yet Christ freely forgives because of His unmatchable love for His children. He heals your hurts first by forgiving you and then by teaching you how to forgive others. Out of thankfulness to Him, reflect the grace that you have been shown.

Forgiveness is God's grace lived out in a practical way. You will never resemble Christ more than when you do what He did for you: forgive.

Lord, grant me the strength to give up my anger and resentment toward others so that I may be a mirror of Your grace.

COMING OUT OF HIDING

SCRIPTURE READING: GENESIS 3:8–13
KEY VERSE: GENESIS 3:10

So he said, "I heard Your voice in the garden, and I was afraid because I was naked; and I hid myself."

Adam and Eve did their best not to give away their hiding places. Soon enough, the familiar voice was calling to them, as it consistently did in the cool of the day. Adam and Eve knew that eventually they would have to face the Lord God. In Genesis 3:10, Adam explained his hiding because he was ashamed of his nakedness.

Perhaps you are not hiding in the bushes or covered with fig leaves, but most people understand what it is to conceal their most private, intimate thoughts, faults, and failures. Afraid that the deepest hurts will be exposed— naked for all to see—a person hides behind defensive responses. You may think, *This is the way I am. I've had a hard life, and I can't change.*

However, the Bible exhorts that each person has a responsibility to live a godly life. In other words, each person has the ability to respond in a God-honoring manner. James Rhinehart admonishes, "I've learned that our background and circumstances may have influenced who we are, but we are responsible for who we become."

God is calling to you, and He wants you to come out of hiding. Will you open yourself up to really knowing the Father?

Lord, I offer You the feeble fig leaves that I use to cover my weaknesses so that I may wear Your garment of righteousness.

IN NEED OF GRACE

SCRIPTURE READING: 1 JOHN 4:17–21
KEY VERSE: 1 JOHN 4:20

If someone says, "I love God," and hates his brother, he is a liar;
for he who does not love his brother whom he has seen,
how can he love God whom he has not seen?

In your life there will always be someone you know who will irritate you in the most frustrating manner. He will know how to effectively push the buttons that lead to aggravation, fear, and anger.

You will be tempted to hate him and, perhaps, even seek revenge. However, the Bible has a strong warning for you in 1 John 4:20: If you say you love God, but hate your brother, do you really love God?

This person in your life is not a foe, for you have no human adversaries. Rather, this person has been placed in your life so that God can grow godliness within you and exercise your faith.

Wayne W. Dyer explains, "The only thing blame does is to keep the focus off you when you are looking for external reasons to explain your unhappiness or frustration. You may succeed in making another feel guilty of something by blaming him, but you won't succeed in changing whatever it is about you that is making you unhappy."

Whoever is tempting you to anger is a person in need of grace. It will take all of your trust in God to deal with that person in a godly manner, but you are called to no less. Trust God to give you the power to forgive.

Oh Father, I am unable on my own to love those who irritate me.
You alone can give me the strength to love them as I ought.

THE RIGHT WAY TO LIVE

SCRIPTURE READING: LUKE 6:27–31
KEY VERSE: LUKE 6:27

But I say to you who hear: Love your enemies,
do good to those who hate you.

It has been said that every person you will ever meet is fighting a difficult battle. However, some people are obviously trying to make the battle you are fighting that much harder. Though God desires that everyone should be saved, some people are so contrary and opposed to God that their very fruit is evil. How do you respond to such people?

In Luke 6:27, Jesus commanded His followers to love their enemies. He understood coming in direct contact with people who want to take your life. You cannot change them, but you can control your reaction to them.

On the cross, Jesus asked the Father to forgive His persecutors. Here on earth, you are instructed to act as Christ would. "Beloved, do not avenge yourselves, but rather give place to wrath; for it is written, 'Vengeance is Mine, I will repay,' says the Lord. Therefore 'If your enemy is hungry, feed him; if he is thirsty, give him a drink; for in so doing you will heap coals of fire on his head.' Do not be overcome by evil, but overcome evil with good" (Romans 12:19–21).

As Christ's representative, you are responsible for how you respond. Therefore, do not give others a reason to criticize you. Rather, do good, and by so doing, show the right way by which to live.

Lord, if I hate those who hate me, how will I change the world? Take my heart and shape it to love in Your extraordinary fashion.

YOUR MOST LOYAL ALLY

SCRIPTURE READING: 2 TIMOTHY 2:24–26
KEY VERSE: LUKE 6:35

But love your enemies, do good, and lend, hoping for nothing in return; and your reward will be great, and you will be sons of the Most High. For He is kind to the unthankful and evil.

In Luke 6:35, Jesus taught His disciples to love their enemies, giving up anything they might receive in return.

Jesus was the model for treating persecutors with kindness so that the door would be open for all men to come to repentance. He instructed the disciples to show grace to their adversaries in hopes that enemies someday would become friends.

Though often conflicts with people seem insurmountable, the power and grace of God can do things beyond a person's imagination. The disciples learned the truth of this soon enough when Christian-persecuting Saul was transformed into Christ-centered Paul.

Having received this great grace, Paul wrote, "And a servant of the Lord must not quarrel but be gentle to all, able to teach, patient, in humility correcting those who are in opposition, if God perhaps will grant them repentance, so that they may know the truth, and that they may come to their senses and escape the snare of the devil, having been taken captive by him to do his will" (2 Timothy 2:24–26).

It is the Lord's will that you treat others with forgiveness and love so that they might be saved. So be kind and gentle to all. You may just find that your greatest adversary has become your most loyal ally.

Lord, bend my unforgiving spirit into a loving one so that Your Holy Spirit's workings in me will lead my enemies to You.

THE GIFT OF FORGIVENESS

SCRIPTURE READING: PSALM 130:1–8
KEY VERSES: PSALM 130:3–4

If You, LORD, should mark iniquities,
O Lord, who could stand?
But there is forgiveness with You,
That You may be feared.

Sometimes well-meaning believers proclaim that their anger toward something or someone is "righteous indignation." They may even note that Jesus Himself turned over the tables of the money changers in the temple and often rebuked religious leaders.

Jesus was perfect, however, and we are not. The problem with our indignation and anger is that we often let it ferment until it spoils our hearts. When someone sins against us or wrongs us, it can be tempting to raise an eyebrow, tug our symbolic robes, and esteem ourselves better than our oppressor.

Too often, we worsen the situation by letting it simmer for long periods. One pastor compared this to buying beautifully ripe fruit, only to leave it in a bowl on the counter for a month. What once was vibrant and perfectly conditioned becomes bitter and rotten if left to ferment.

Forgiveness is God's gift to us through the shed blood of His Son, Jesus Christ. He expects us, in turn, to share forgiveness with those who sin against us. We cannot allow pride to dictate our reaction. It requires humility to give a gift as precious as forgiveness.

It is difficult to function in the present or look to the future when we are constantly looking back and weighing how we have been treated. God tells us not to let the sun go down on our anger, because He wants us to deal with it immediately.

Bitterness, wrath, and anger are by-products of failing to promptly deal with a problem. However, the timing of a tender heart is impeccable.

Lord, cleanse me from bitterness, wrath, and anger. Help me to forgive others as You have forgiven me.

THE RESULTS OF FORGIVENESS

SCRIPTURE READING: ROMANS 6:1–6
KEY VERSE: ROMANS 6:6

. . . knowing this, that our old man was crucified with Him,
that the body of sin might be done away with, that we
should no longer be slaves of sin.

Perhaps you have been hurt by someone you love. If you don't deal with the problem early enough, there is a likelihood that some form of bitterness will sink roots deep within your spirit.

The consequences of an unforgiving spirit are severe. First, if you allow your heart to harden toward others, you can expect to suffer emotional bondage, especially as it relates to the source of your pain. Your joy and freedom in Christ will be limited because you have chosen to harbor resentment and derision. This can have a paralyzing effect throughout your life.

One of the worst effects of unforgiveness is that it erodes our fellowship with God. He provided the ultimate sacrifice for our sins and expects us to remember Christ's death on the cross and graciously extend forgiveness to others, even when they don't ask for it. There is no true rationalization for holding a grudge while also claiming to live in the shadow of the cross.

Unforgiveness also leads to broken relationships. The words "I'm sorry; please forgive me" are very difficult to utter. The words "I accept your apology, and I forgive you" also require humility and a heart and mind led by the Lord's Spirit. When both parties approach a hardship in this manner, God can restore a relationship to even fuller love. Jesus took upon Himself the sin of the world, and we should demonstrate love and liberty as a result.

Dear heavenly Father, help me forgive and accept forgiveness. I want
to demonstrate Your love to a needy world.

FORGIVING YOURSELF

SCRIPTURE READING: PSALM 51:1–19
KEY VERSE: PSALM 51:1

Have mercy upon me, O God,
According to Your lovingkindness;
According to the multitude of Your tender mercies,
Blot out my transgressions.

Guilt settled in like a thick fog. David had sinned horribly against God by taking another man's wife, committing murder, and making sure that his actions had remained undiscovered. Then, when it appeared that the coast was clear, he breathed a sigh of relief. That is when God sent the prophet Nathan to awaken King David's conscience.

Crushed and broken in spirit, David threw himself to his knees. Fear crept into his mind as he thought, *How can I approach God now? Have I completely destroyed my relationship with the Lord?*

Armed only with a broken and contrite heart, the fallen David approached the Lord. He prayed, "Have mercy upon me, O God, according to Your lovingkindness; according to the multitude of Your tender mercies, blot out my transgressions" (Psalm 51:1).

After asking for a clean heart (verse 10), David boldly stated his belief that God can and will restore him. Not only did God forgive, but He continued to actively use David. Despite his guilt and shame, David's failures did not exclude him from serving his Lord. Because God forgave him, he was able to forgive himself.

If guilt is preventing you from fully experiencing the joyful forgiveness God offers, pray today for His help in laying down your chains and escaping the bondage of unholy guilt.

Lord Jesus, I offer to You the sins I have committed and the guilt that makes me feel worthless. I thank You that I am blameless because of Your sacrifice for me.

UNCHANGING LOVE

SCRIPTURE READING: ROMANS 6:7–12
KEY VERSE: ROMANS 8:1

There is therefore now no condemnation to those who are in
Christ Jesus, who do not walk according to the flesh,
but according to the Spirit.

After God exposed David's sin with Bathsheba, David's heart was filled with remorse. His spirit was crushed by what he had done, and evidence of his sin and steps of repentance is found in 2 Samuel 11–12.

At one point, David's shame became so great he cried out: "I have sinned against the Lord"(2 Samuel 12:13). Notice David did not deny his sin or excuse it. No. He owned up to what he had done and sought God's forgiveness.

When we confess our sin to the Lord, we are in essence agreeing with Him that what we have done is wrong and not in keeping with His moral standards. It is at this point that we acknowledge our sin and decisively turn from it. This is what David did.

Sin has its consequences. Bathsheba became pregnant with David's baby who later died. Not only did David have to endure the sorrow connected with his sin, but he also had to face the death of his son. Yet we never hear David wallowing in guilt and shame. He sought God's forgiveness in humility and then set his heart on continuing to be the king God had called him to be.

When you sin, pray as David did. Know God's mercy keeps you. Confession and repentance are your hope. The moment you seek His forgiveness, He restores you. And it is there that you will find His love is unchanged by your failure.

Lord, I ask Your forgiveness for the times I have wallowed in my
guilt. I want to walk forward with You, not looking back.

YOU ARE FORGIVEN

SCRIPTURE READING: COLOSSIANS 3:5–9

KEY VERSE: ROMANS 5:8

But God demonstrates His own love toward us,
in that while we were still sinners, Christ died for us.

Many people quake in fear after reading the list of sins in 1 Corinthians 6:9–10. Others read the list and breathe a sigh of relief, because their sins are not on the list. Unfortunately, the apostle Paul continued his list of vices in Galatians 5:19–21, Ephesians 5:3–5, and Colossians 3:5–9.

When these passages are seen together, it becomes very clear that every believer has some aspect of sin in his or her life. Clearly, Paul took a very hard view of sin. In many of these passages, he refers to the sinners listed as those who will not enter the kingdom of God. This is the ultimate punishment, and this is what we each deserve.

However, the hope offered to the Corinthians is still our hope today. We are washed in Jesus' blood. It has removed the stain of our sin; we are sanctified because our union with Christ has drawn us into the people of God; and we are justified by Christ's work on the cross that has drawn us into a restored, personal relationship with the Creator God.

There is joy in knowing that we have been forgiven. We must remember that our sin does not surprise God; on the contrary, "while we were still sinners, Christ died for us" (Romans 5:8). Knowing who and what we are, our loving Father sent His Son to save us. Ask God to help you forgive yourself, just as He has already forgiven you in Christ.

Lord Jesus, through Your death and resurrection You have washed
my soul and removed the stains of sin. Thank You.

THE GRACE TO FORGIVE

SCRIPTURE READING: ROMANS 6:13–17
KEY VERSE: ROMANS 6:16

*Do you not know that to whom you present yourselves slaves to obey,
you are that one's slaves whom you obey, whether of sin leading to
death, or of obedience leading to righteousness?*

All of our lives, we have heard the old adage, "Time heals all wounds." While this rings true occasionally, it is certainly not an all-encompassing rule. There are times when we can actually subvert the effectiveness of time to heal our wounds. Moreover, we can actually work against the power of God to heal our hurts.

What would cause us to do this? It is a matter of forgiveness. When we allow unforgiven hurts to dominate our lives, we are in effect saying, "I do not want to be free from this pain. I want to keep it, nurse it, feed it, and help it to grow. Then, when the time is right, I will thrust this pain upon someone else, hoping to bring misery upon him as well." Most likely, we never actually voice these intentions, but the effect is the same: we refuse to forgive, and therefore we suffer the pain anew every day.

As Christians, we celebrate that God has chosen not only to forgive our sins but to absolutely forget them as well. According to Psalm 103:12, "As far as the east is from the west, so far has He removed our transgressions from us." You see, when God forgives us, our sins and failures are totally removed. They are gone—never to be seen, thought of, or heard from again. Ask God today to search your heart and reveal any unforgiven sins that have caused you pain, and ask for the grace to forgive and forget.

Lord, do not let me use the chains of unforgiveness to rebind that which You have set free—my soul and that of my neighbor.

SHARING THE WEALTH

SCRIPTURE READING: ROMANS 6:18–23
KEY VERSE: ROMANS 6:23

*For the wages of sin is death, but the gift of God is
eternal life in Christ Jesus our Lord.*

Who has hurt you this week? Was the offender sorry, or did it seem to be intentional? How are we supposed to respond to those who attack us on all fronts?

Most likely, we will rise up and proclaim, "It is not fair! I am innocent, and yet you hurt me deeply!" We may foolishly expect to be treated well by another, just because we have treated him well. We are like a character in C. S. Lewis's *The Great Divorce*, who proclaims, "I only want my rights. I'm not asking for anybody's charity."

How crazy it is to seek out what we deserve! How easily we forget how hurtful, malicious, and rebellious we ourselves have been. Remember Romans 3:23: "For all have sinned and fall short of the glory of God." We have all hurt the Lord far worse than any individual has ever hurt us personally. What do we deserve? Romans 6:23: "For the wages of sin is death." Far more serious than any interpersonal dispute, our rebellion against the Lord deserves only death. But we serve a merciful God: "The gift of God is eternal life in Christ Jesus our Lord."

Ephesians 4:32 ends with the command to forgive others "even as God in Christ forgave you." You have been forgiven already. Now, go out and share the wealth, spreading that forgiveness to others.

Lord, I have no right to claim forgiveness or fairness as my right. Help me to be mindful that it is a gift to be given to others, not demanded for myself.

The Fine Is Paid

SCRIPTURE READING: 1 CORINTHIANS 6:9–11
KEY VERSE: 1 CORINTHIANS 6:20

*For you were bought at a price; therefore glorify God in
your body and in your spirit, which are God's.*

There you are, driving down the interstate toward home. The speed limit
is 60 mph, and you are cruising along at 73. Then the unthinkable happens: you zoom past a police car. Immediately, your eyes dart to the rearview
mirror. Did he see you? Has his car pulled onto the road? Without a doubt,
this scene has happened to most of us; these moments are sometimes the
clearest instances of self-realization that we ever have.

The truth is, the police car represents a greater truth: drivers are not
supposed to speed. Even though you may know this simple little rule, seeing
a police officer probably makes you look at your speedometer, in order to
make sure you are within the legal limits. Whether you are speeding or not,
you always hope the squad car stays where it is, and you always feel better
when it is safely behind you.

Does this sound at all like your spiritual life? How often do you go about
your day, without a care in the world, and then suddenly find yourself caught
in a moment of extreme spiritual awareness? If the Lord appeared right now,
would He catch you "speeding"?

Ask Jesus to help you understand that He is always beside you, seeing all
that you do. Here is the bonus, though: even if Jesus gives you a spiritual
"ticket," take joy in the fact that you are already forgiven. He has already paid
your fine.

*Lord, help me to live my life as if You are a police officer traveling
in my car as I drive life's highway.*

WHEN YOU ARE ABUSED

SCRIPTURE READING: JOHN 13:31–35
KEY VERSE: JOHN 13:34

A new commandment I give to you, that you love one another;
as I have loved you, that you also love one another.

Have you ever been harshly judged by a fellow Christian? If so, you know that having a peer's self-righteous condemnation poured out on you can be irritating, if not painful. Far too many nonbelievers are turned away from the Cross as a result of the actions of abusive Christians.

Muhatma Ghandi once said that he liked Jesus, but could not come to accept the Christians he had met. It is important for Christians to uphold high moral standards, but there is a difference between discipline and abuse.

Discipline is always directed toward a specific behavior and is rooted in love. For example, talking to a friend about his or her problem with dishonesty in a way that demonstrates genuine concern can be helpful.

Abuse, on the other hand, is directed toward a person and is rooted in the abuser's own anger and hatred. Telling another person that they are ungodly because they wear clothing that is different from yours or have different musical tastes could result in building resentment, rather than helping that individual know and embrace the love of Jesus.

When we allow our carnal feelings to fuel a moral rebuke of another person, our behavior is anything but Christian. Three times on the eve of His crucifixion Christ said, "Love one another" (John 13:34). Throughout the New Testament are instructions to believers on how to treat people. There is never an excuse for a Christian to damage or harm another person.

Lord, guard my heart so that I may not use You as an excuse for hurting others.

FORGIVING ABUSES

SCRIPTURE READING: PROVERBS 3:1–4
KEY VERSE: PHILIPPIANS 4:8

*Finally, brethren, whatever things are true, whatever things are noble,
whatever things are just, whatever things are pure, whatever things are
lovely, whatever things are of good report, if there is any virtue and
if there is anything praiseworthy—meditate on these things.*

When we are abused, the time and energy we spend focusing on the wrong done to us frequently exceed the actual affliction we've endured. Have you ever brooded for hours, days, even weeks over a minor infraction leveled against you? If so, you are not alone.

But God commands us, for our own sakes, to forgive our abusers. Because Christ forgave us, there is no biblical justification for an unforgiving spirit. An unforgiving spirit is worse than cancer. Dwelling on harm done to us only magnifies our misery and intensifies our pain.

Unforgiveness is simply the determination to keep punishing our abusers. Yet God tells us that vengeance belongs to Him. Instead of focusing on bringing justice to others, we should pray for our abusers; we should pray for God to reveal the motivations behind their actions, that we might better understand our situation.

God never instructs us to retaliate. Instead, He shows us a way to move forward. The past cannot hold us back from doing what God desires of us, unless we allow it to. By seeking God's guidance in dealing with abuse, we open ourselves to godly healing.

The next time you are the object of someone else's venom, look for God to make something good of that experience. When you are tempted to dwell on negative thoughts, fill your mind with helpful things instead (Philippians 4:8).

I know that when I brood on the injustices committed against me, I am passing up an opportunity for grace. Tell me, Lord, when I am doing this, and open my ears to hear.

THE STRUGGLE OF UNFORGIVENESS

SCRIPTURE READING: COLOSSIANS 2:11–14
KEY VERSE: COLOSSIANS 2:13

*And you, being dead in your trespasses and the uncircumcision of
your flesh, He has made alive together with Him,
having forgiven you all trespasses.*

From God's perspective, forgiveness is immediate. However, we must
desire His forgiveness. Often this means listening for His still, small voice
to direct us in our confession.

In her devotional book, *Streams in the Desert*, Mrs. Charles Cowman writes:

Christmas Evans tells us in his diary that one Sunday afternoon he was
traveling a very lonely road to attend an appointment, and he was convicted
of a cold heart. He says, "I tethered my horse and went to a sequestered
spot, where I walked to and fro in agony as I reviewed my life.

"I waited three hours before God, broken with sorrow, until there broke
over me a sweet sense of His forgiving love. . . . As the sun was westering, I
went back to the road, found my horse, mounted it and went to my
appointment. On the following day I preached with such new power to a
vast concourse of people gathered on the hillside, that a revival broke out
that day and spread through all Wales."

When we do sin, a humble heart quickly ushers us into the throne room
of God. Seek to be sensitive to the moving of God's Spirit in your life. If He
is pressing you to be still and listen for His guidance, then take the opportunity to do so. From time to time, God may draw you aside to be with Him
in prayer in order to cleanse and refresh you. A marvelous blessing comes
whenever you obey His Spirit's call.

*Father, I sometimes struggle with unforgiveness. Help me to hear Your
still, small voice to direct my confession and obey the Spirit's call.*

GIVING LOVE

SCRIPTURE READING: 1 THESSALONIANS 3:11–13
KEY VERSE: 1 THESSALONIANS 3:12

*And may the Lord make you increase and abound in love to
one another and to all, just as we do to you.*

How freely do you love others? Do you give love without needing or expecting love in return? While each of us desires love, it is far more rewarding to give rather than receive.

In a note to a friend, Amy Carmichael wrote:

A few minutes ago I read words that sum up my desires for you: 1 Thessalonians 3:12 [KJV], "The Lord make you to increase and abound in love one toward another." This poor world is a cold place to many. I pray that no one who comes to us may ever feel chilled here, but rather that all chilliness may melt, melted by the blessed glow of heavenly love. Don't let us ever be afraid of being too loving. We can never love enough.

So I pray, "Lord, keep us free to love. Never let the slightest shade of suspicion to shadow any heart. Help each to think the best of every other. Through all the chances and changes of life, hold all together in tender love. Let nothing quench love. Let nothing cool it. Keep every thread of the gold cord unbroken, unweakened, even unto the end. O my Lord, Thou Loving One, keep my beloveds close together in Thy love forever."

How you love others reflects the love you have for Jesus. Be patient in love, willing to receive little or no thanks for something you have done in love for another, and quick to forgive. Remember, no act of love, including forgiveness, is ever wasted.

Lord, help me remember that no act of love is wasted. Help me increase and abound in love.

RELEASE FROM BONDAGE

SCRIPTURE READING: MATTHEW 18:21–35
KEY VERSES: MATTHEW 18:21–22

*Then Peter came to Him and said, "Lord, how often shall my brother
sin against me, and I forgive him? Up to seven times?" Jesus said to him,
"I do not say to you, up to seven times, but up to seventy times seven."*

Can you think of a person in your life, the very sight of whom would
cause you to cringe? Perhaps you were once in a relationship that ended
in disappointment, or perhaps you worked for a boss who unfairly fired you
from a job.

When other people wound us, it is easy to allow bitterness to creep into
our hearts. Feelings of rejection and hurt run deep within us and frequently
linger for years. The Bible tells us to forgive those who hurt us, but far too
often we ignore this wisdom and seek out other avenues for advice.

When we are weakened by pain, our minds are fertile soil for Satan. He
puts his own spin on the situation and fills our heads with thoughts that can
yield only bondage. Here is what happens: Someone hurts us, and we develop
an angry spirit toward that person. Satan excuses our anger by saying, "You've
been hurt; it's all right to be angry. After all, the person who wounded you has
never apologized. You're a little bit disillusioned right now."

Never once does Satan suggest that we might have an unforgiving spirit
toward that person. Never once does he encourage us to forgive. He knows all
too well that as long as we allow ourselves to be dejected and angry, we will continue to sink in the mire of self-pity. If you are holding someone captive to your
own unforgiveness, purpose to loose the chains of anger that bind them. You
may find, in the end, that it is you who have been the prisoner all along.

*Lord, I have waved the flag of self-pity. I surrender it to Your greater
plan for my life.*

When Others Fail Us

SCRIPTURE READING: 2 TIMOTHY 4:9–18
KEY VERSE: 2 TIMOTHY 4:17

*But the Lord stood with me and strengthened me, so that the message
might be preached fully through me, and that all the Gentiles might
hear. Also I was delivered out of the mouth of the lion.*

In times of trouble, why are we sometimes forsaken by those we trust? Why
do the friends we believed we could count on suddenly disappear during
our worst days? These questions are painful to consider, but sometimes they
represent harsh reality. Truly, there are many reasons that others fail us. And
although examining the cause may not erase our pain, it can help us to process
and understand why we are often disappointed by our friends.

Perhaps you have witnessed some of these situations or emotions in the
lives of friends who have walked out on you:

- Feeling inadequate to help
- Disassociation from trouble
- Jealousy, insensitivity, or a critical spirit
- Fear of facing a similar problem
- Self-centeredness

The apostle Paul was certainly familiar with this list. As he penned his letter
to Timothy, he stood abandoned by his friends and was left to face his final court
trial alone. "No one stood with me, but all forsook me," he said in verse 16.

Yet look at what he said in the very next line: "But the Lord stood with me
and strengthened me" (verse 17). Paul's faith in the Lord he loved and trusted
shone through, despite his discouraging situation.

The good news is that God offers His strength and presence to us in the
same way today. Even if all others leave, the Lord will remain faithful.

*Father, when others fail me, help me remember that You remain
faithful. I rejoice in Your strength and presence. I am not alone.*

RELEASING OFFENSES

SCRIPTURE READING: LUKE 23:33–43
KEY VERSE: LUKE 23:34

Then Jesus said, "Father, forgive them, for they do not know what they do." And they divided His garments and cast lots.

You can barely believe it! You just witnessed a fellow brother or sister in Christ commit an act of sheer disobedience against the Lord. Even when the initial shock wears off, you cannot erase the incident from your mind. You are disappointed, discouraged, and disillusioned. What should you do?

- First, we must never allow the acts of another person to pull us away from our relationship with God. Instead, we should cling to the promise that He is the One who will never fail us, even when others do. God stands firm when others fall, and He provides strength, support, and refuge. Regardless of what is happening around us, He will never disappoint us.
- Second, we should forgive those who offend us. Harboring resentment or bitterness is never the Christlike thing to do. Luke 23:34 supports this notion by pointing out that Christ forgave the Roman soldiers even as they led Him to His crucifixion.
- Third, we can draw comfort from the Great Comforter, the Holy Spirit. When we are grieved by things that displease God, we must remember that our greatest source of comfort is the Holy Spirit who resides within us for this very purpose.

The next time you are failed by another person, remember: draw near to God, forgive your offender, and allow the Holy Spirit to bring comfort.

Is there an offense that needs to be erased from your mind? Release it to God right now, and pray for the person who disappointed you.

Lord, Sometimes I just can't get past the offenses other Christians have committed. Help me turn my eyes to You, so that I can forgive them.

THE PROCESS OF FORGIVENESS

SCRIPTURE READING: PSALM 103:1–12
KEY VERSE: PSALM 103:12

As far as the east is from the west,
So far has He removed our transgressions from us.

An unforgiving spirit is like an insidious cancer that eats away at a person until it has a devastating impact. But while physical cancer often can't be seen or felt until it is a real danger, the cancer of unforgiveness often steals a person's joy for years. Yet there is a sure healing process for this cancer:

- Repentance: You must assume responsibility for your unforgiving spirit toward someone and then have a change of mind. You must ask forgiveness for your unforgiveness, and then you must forgive the person in mind.
- Release: No longer should you hold over someone the debt you feel they owe you. This release is an act of the will. Feelings have nothing to do with it, though some people sense a "release" of their own at this point.
- Recognition: You acknowledge that the person's wrongdoing toward you exposed a weakness in your life. Your resentment, hostility, bitterness, and desire to seek vengeance are areas God wishes to whittle away.
- Remembrance: You should remember continuously how often God forgives you. How many times have you asked His forgiveness? How many times has He said no?

You cannot truly experience the joy of God's forgiveness until you follow His model and forgive those who have wronged you. Life is so much sweeter when the heart is tender and not tainted.

Lord, I release my resentment and the damage that it has done to me and my relationships. Your forgiveness of me has set me free.

REJECTING ACCUSATION

SCRIPTURE READING: 1 JOHN 3:16–21
KEY VERSE: 1 JOHN 3:20

*For if our heart condemns us, God is greater than our heart,
and knows all things.*

How often have you heard someone say, "I know God has forgiven me, but I will never be able to forgive myself"?

Such self-condemnation can spring from several sources, but it is, in any case, an enemy God has already defeated. Romans 8:1 tells us, "There is therefore now no condemnation to those who are in Christ Jesus." This encouraging statement covers all condemnation, including self-recrimination. How, then, should we deal with those condemning voices?

First of all, we need to distinguish between remorse and guilt. It is appropriate to feel sorrow and remorse for past deeds, but to carry guilt for them is not necessary. The Bible assures us that if we confess our sins, God is faithful to forgive us (1 John 1:9). Any lingering feelings of guilt after this are enemies trying to rob us of our freedom in Christ.

Sometimes these feelings of guilt stem from the mistaken notion that we still must pay for our sins, so we unconsciously embrace perpetual remorse as a way to make restitution for past wrongs. Such a practice suggests the faulty notion that Jesus did not really pay for all sin by the shedding of His precious blood. When we realize that He has stamped "paid in full" on our account, then we must never dare to side with those who would have us believe otherwise.

Since God has given us His Word, we can reject all accusing voices and rest on His promise: "For if our heart condemns us, God is greater than our heart, and knows all things" (1 John 3:20).

Lord, I reject all accusing voices and rest on Your promises. You are greater than condemnation and accusation.

EXAMINING YOUR HEART

SCRIPTURE READING: LUKE 17:1–4
KEY VERSE: LUKE 17:4

*And if he sins against you seven times in a day, and seven times in a
day returns to you, saying, "I repent," you shall forgive him.*

Some say that the failure to offer or receive forgiveness lies at the heart of
most of the serious emotional and spiritual disorders that we experience.
While this may be an unprovable assertion, it is clear that unforgiveness provides fertile soil for a remarkably diverse crop of weeds. It is the source of
much that can go sour in personal relationships, and it can hide behind many
different masks.

People sometimes say in an angry tone that they have forgiven past
offenses, but their obvious bitterness betrays them. Unforgiveness can lodge
in your heart and hide from you. The following questions will help you
examine your heart to see if you need to forgive someone:

1. Do you still secretly hope that someone will get what he/she
   deserves?
2. Are you still talking negatively about this person to others?
3. Do you indulge in fantasies of revenge—even mild ones?
4. Do you spend time mulling over what he/she did to you?
5. How do you feel when something good happens to him/her?
6. Have you quit blaming this person for how your life has turned
   out?
7. Do you find it difficult to be open and trusting with people?
8. Are you frequently angry, depressed, or bitter?
9. Do you find it difficult or impossible to thank God for your
   offender?

Let God examine your heart. Does He find any unforgiveness there?

*Dear Lord, examine my heart. I do not want to harbor unforgiveness.
Expose it so I can deal with it in Your strength.*

THE DEPTH OF GOD'S FORGIVENESS

SCRIPTURE READING: HEBREWS 10:29–31
KEY VERSE: HEBREWS 10:30

*For we know Him who said, "Vengeance is Mine, I will repay,"
says the Lord. And again, "The LORD will judge His people."*

There are many hindrances blocking our attempts to truly forgive our offenders. Chief among them is a failure to fully understand and appreciate the depth of God's forgiveness for us.

How can you lift the debt from your debtors if you don't comprehend or are still struggling with your own indebtedness? The feeling that you somehow have to even accounts with God or pay Him off can be so oppressive that you have no freedom to release someone else. How can you offer something that you yourself have never received? How can you give when you are totally consumed with acquiring?

Not until you are fully conscious that God has paid the sin-debt on your account will you cease your efforts to collect from others. Once this glorious freedom has been achieved by taking God at His word, you can then begin the process of offering your offenders full forgiveness. You must now make a deliberate choice (no matter how devoid of feeling) to leave all punishment or retaliation up to God. It is essential that you surrender your so-called "rights," whether it is your right to get even or to get justice.

At this point, it might be helpful to write out a list itemizing all the offenses against you that you can think of. Then bring them one by one before God and leave them at the cross. By doing this and by asking for God's help, you can let your offender off the hook and release him to the One who claimed vengeance as His own (Hebrews 10:30).

Lord, my lack of self-worth hinders my ability to accept Your forgiveness and, in turn, to forgive others. Help me to see myself through Your eyes.

WHY WE STRUGGLE

SCRIPTURE READING: HEBREWS 10:16–18
KEY VERSE: HEBREWS 10:17

*Then He adds, "Their sins and their lawless deeds
I will remember no more."*

All of us have been hurt at one time or another, and the offender may well have been someone we love. We often attempt to get past the pain of such situations with comments like "That's okay" or "Don't worry about it," and yet we just can't seem to shake that penetrating sting. Why aren't we able to let it go?

One reason we struggle with unforgiveness is a simple matter of pride. Why don't we forgive? "Because that person hurt ME," we cry. As a result of our offended pride, the injustice grows much greater than we should allow. It becomes an issue of personal insult rather than an honest mistake or flash of insensitivity.

Another factor in our unforgiveness is bitterness. We become resentful when we refuse to deal honestly with hurt feelings, and then allow the matter to fester in our heart. A growing sense of irritation spreads through our spirit like an infection.

It has been rightly said that bitterness is like a poison that you prepare for someone else and then drink yourself. While it silently destroys our life, the person who hurt us may remain completely unaware of our dark feelings.

Finally, we struggle with unforgiveness because we often have a poor idea of what it is all about. Or we might be sitting around waiting for an apology that may never come.

If you have been hurt recently, pray for the strength and honesty to approach the offender and say, "You did this and it hurt me. But I love you and refuse to allow this to destroy our relationship."

Lord, cleanse me from bitterness. Help me understand the true spirit and power of Your forgiveness manifested to and through me.

A CALL TO REPENTANCE

SCRIPTURE READING: ISAIAH 50:7–10
KEY VERSE: ISAIAH 50:7

For the Lord God will help Me;
Therefore I will not be disgraced;
Therefore I have set My face like a flint,
And I know that I will not be ashamed.

Genuine repentance of sin includes: agreeing with the Lord that our behavior or thought pattern is ungodly; establishing in our thinking that this sinful habit is displeasing to God; identifying—with the Spirit's help—what would please Him; and taking steps under the Spirit's power to turn from sin and walk in godliness. Whether we are nonbelievers starting to come to faith in Jesus or believers wrestling with sin, we all need to practice biblical repentance.

Three key words describe the process of repentance: recognition, agreement, and commitment. Unless we recognize that our behavior or thoughts are sin, we will not see any need to confess them to God. Recognition comes as we study God's Word and learn what He identifies as sin. We must then agree that God's pattern for life is correct and ours is wrong.

The epistles to the Ephesians and Galatians are both helpful in revealing what pleases and displeases God. Without agreement, our confession would be more of an "I am sorry about the consequences" statement. Commitment is also necessary. Isaiah proclaims, "For the Lord GOD will help Me; therefore I will not be disgraced; therefore I have set My face like a flint, and I know that I will not be ashamed" (Isaiah 50:7). We must commit ourselves to turning away from sin and choosing God's way.

We who belong to Jesus can change permanently. Remember: Christ promises that those He sets free will be free indeed (John 8:36).

Lord, thank You for the freedom that comes through repentance. I recognize my sin, agree with what Your Word says about it, and commit my life to You. Forgive me.

GENUINE FORGIVENESS

SCRIPTURE READING: JOHN 15:12–17
KEY VERSE: JOHN 15:9

As the Father loved Me, I also have loved you; abide in My love.

If you constantly struggle to forgive people who have wronged you, you may consider yourself incapable of that kind of forgiveness. Many people are convinced that forgiveness is simply a feeling that can be experienced in the face of conflict. What a faulty understanding!

Genuine forgiveness is not a feeling but an action. If you find it hard to forgive others, the following four guidelines can help:

1. Acknowledge and confess an unforgiving spirit. No, it is not always easy to forgive. We are sometimes the target of tremendously hurtful offenses. However, we are not accountable for other people's behavior; we are responsible only for our own. God commanded us to be loving, forgiving people. If we are unforgiving, that is our problem and no one else's. We must repent of this sin and ask God to help our unforgiveness.
2. Release the other person. Make a conscious decision to release the offender in your mind. If you find yourself reliving details of the upsetting behavior, force yourself to stop.
3. Forgive the offender forgetfully. By keeping details fresh in your mind, you trap yourself in a cycle of pain. Choose instead to separate the individual from the painful memory.
4. Forgive with finality. True forgiveness is complete. This means that you cannot "forgive" someone and then continually bring the subject up. Forgive them and move on.

If you've been nursing a grudge, pray for the strength to forgive. Then do it!

Lord, I confess my unforgiving spirit. I release those who have offended me and forgive them once and for all!

TRULY FORGIVEN

SCRIPTURE READING: 2 TIMOTHY 2:19–22
KEY VERSE: 2 TIMOTHY 2:19

*Nevertheless the solid foundation of God stands, having this seal:
"The Lord knows those who are His," and, "Let everyone who
names the name of Christ depart from iniquity."*

Sin is a big problem. It worms its way into our lives, distorts our viewpoints, and influences every decision. God knew that none of us could have defeated the power of sin, so He acted on our behalf by sending His Son into the world to conquer sin. For those of us who have received Jesus as Lord and Savior, that victory has removed the penalty of sin from our lives.

Unfortunately, though, our acceptance of Christ does not stop us from sinning. Although we love the Lord and rejoice in His saving hand, we find ourselves continually struggling with sin in our lives.

This is a great surprise to many new Christians, who come to Christ thinking that their old passions will simply disappear. This is rarely, if ever, the case. Instead, we must take responsibility for our sinful actions and cravings. This does not mean that we should attempt to "clean ourselves up"; rather, we must be honest with God about our sin and invite His cleansing power into our darkest parts.

Second Corinthians 7:1 calls us to "cleanse ourselves from all filthiness of the flesh and spirit, perfecting holiness in the fear of God." We "cleanse ourselves" by becoming aware of the sin in our lives, laying it down, and walking away from it. That is what repentance means—to turn from old behaviors.

Thank You, Lord, that I am truly forgiven. Because I am forgiven, I can forgive others. I rejoice in Your forgiveness!

MARCH
Pathway to Victory

But thanks be to God, who gives us the victory
through our Lord Jesus Christ.
—1 Corinthians 15:57

The First Step to Victory

SCRIPTURE READING: ROMANS 8:26–28
KEY VERSE: ROMANS 8:28

*And we know that all things work together for good to those who love
God, to those who are the called according to His purpose.*

Our pride deceives us into thinking that failure is for the weak, not for us. We assume that God is working through our victories. But what does God's Word say?

Paul wrote, "And we know that all things work together for good to those who love God, to those who are the called according to His purpose" (Romans 8:28). In relation to failure, this verse explains that God works through our failures for His glory. Failure is actually the first step to victory.

God's ultimate goal is to transform us into His image so that we more vividly reflect His glory, and He will do whatever is necessary to achieve that within our hearts. And sometimes, failure in our lives is essential for God to bring about a greater purpose.

We may wonder why failure is happening in our lives. We ask ourselves, "What am I doing wrong? Doesn't God love me? Doesn't He want me to be victorious?"

Above achieving victory, God wants to transform us into His likeness. And when we fail, self-reflection occurs. We look upon our hearts and wonder what we could have done differently.

If we are willing to ask God what He is trying to teach us through our failures, He gladly will reveal lessons. We begin to recognize that failure leads to victory—the triumphant transformation of our hearts to totally trust God with control of our lives.

*Lord, take my victories and my failures and shape them into paths
that lead to You.*

VICTORY THROUGH LIFE'S UPS AND DOWNS

SCRIPTURE READING: 2 CORINTHIANS 12:1–9
KEY VERSE: 2 CORINTHIANS 12:9

And He said to me, "My grace is sufficient for you, for My strength is made perfect in weakness." Therefore most gladly I will rather boast in my infirmities, that the power of Christ may rest upon me.

Life sometimes feels like an endless roller coaster, full of surprising twists and turns—some that excite us and others that severely disappoint us. And during the ride of life, our weaknesses are revealed. As believers, we need to know how to handle the ups and downs so that our relationship with Christ remains consistent in its nature and we can have a victorious walk.

When our weaknesses are revealed, we discover our inability to accomplish something to its full potential. The world leads us to believe that weakness is a liability; however, in our relationship with Christ, it can oftentimes be our greatest asset.

Paul realized his weaknesses. Agonizing over them and bemoaning his situation never accomplished what was necessary. Yet Paul's accepting attitude of his weaknesses resulted in the avenue God needed to intervene.

In his letter to the church in Corinth, Paul wrote, "I take pleasure in infirmities, in reproaches, in needs, in persecutions, in distresses, for Christ's sake. For when I am weak, then I am strong" (2 Corinthians 12:10).

Paul discovered that strength was found in weaknesses. Instead of trying to lug his cross up a hill, Paul decided it was best turned over to the Lord. When Paul's strength was insufficient, he turned to God. As a result, Paul humbly walked through life's ups and downs with a perspective that kept his eyes forever focused on Jesus.

Lord, I realize that my weakness is an opportunity for Your strength to be revealed. Through You, I can have victory over the ups and downs of life.

GOD'S CHOICE TOOL

SCRIPTURE READING: 2 CORINTHIANS 12:7–10
KEY VERSE: 2 CORINTHIANS 12:10

Therefore I take pleasure in infirmities, in reproaches, in needs,
in persecutions, in distresses, for Christ's sake.
For when I am weak, then I am strong.

Like pressure turns coal into a beautiful diamond, adversity can become a starting point for God to do something beautiful in our lives. He can transform our hearts, change our attitudes, teach us what it means to trust Him and walk in true victory.

However, instead of growing embittered and distrustful of God, we must look beyond the present struggle and recognize what God is doing. Adversity is God's choice tool for building character and equipping us for future ministry. Not only does adversity put an edge on our relationship with Christ, it also enables us to minister to those we will meet in the future with whom we share a similar experience.

Adversity hits us in our weakest areas—the very areas in which God desires to strengthen us. Paul wrote that he was actually strong when he was weak (2 Corinthians 12:10). He recognized that his strongest areas were his weakest.

God has a design and purpose behind every adversity in our lives. Even when the enemy attempts to destroy us or our faith through an attack, God can take the situation and bring a tremendous victory from it.

Instead of hardening our hearts toward adverse situations, we must seek to discover what God desires to do in our hearts and give Him full authority to do so.

Lord, I am too human to seek adversity in order to grow stronger, yet
I recognize, and thank You, that when I am at my weakest, in You
I am also strongest.

Applying Truth for Victory

SCRIPTURE READING: PHILIPPIANS 4:10–13
KEY VERSE: PHILIPPIANS 4:13

I can do all things through Christ who strengthens me.

In grasping a clear picture of how we can weather the dangers that come with both victory and defeat, we must not forget to apply what we know. Understanding that God is our strength in weakness is one thing, but applying that truth in an effective way is another.

The apostle Paul said he had learned the secret of contentment in any situation—Christ, the source of strength (Philippians 4:12–13). We must do more than just acknowledge God's awesome power—we need to get it into our lives. We must submit our will to His will. Asking God to give us strength to accomplish our will results in burnout. God never promises us strength for our own plans, only for His. That's why submitting to His will is the first step to seeing His power begin to permeate our lives.

We must also trust Him to control our circumstances for His purposes. Once we realize that God's plans and purposes are greater than we could imagine, we also have to realize that the path He is leading us down will result in His glory.

The result of relying on God's strength is that we cease to struggle against that which we cannot control. And victory is found in trusting in the Lord's strength.

Heavenly Father, I trust Your strength as I face the challenges of life today. I praise You because I will walk in victory!

FACING LIFE'S CHALLENGES

SCRIPTURE READING: 2 CHRONICLES 20:1–30
KEY VERSE: 2 CHRONICLES 20:12

*O our God, will You not judge them? For we have no power against
this great multitude that is coming against us; nor do we
know what to do, but our eyes are upon You.*

Jehoshaphat had a choice. In 2 Chronicles 20, we read how a tremendous army had come against the nation of Israel with one intention: destroying the people of God. Most armies in Israel's position would have been plotting their survival. Wisely, Jehoshaphat chose to lead the people in a prayer that confessed their total dependence on the Lord: "O our God, will You not judge them? For we have no power against this great multitude" (verse 12).

You may think that you do not have an option when facing a difficult challenge, but you do. You can choose to turn to God and bow down before Him, or you can turn and run away in fear.

If Israel caved into fear, the people would be running for the rest of their existence. Jehoshaphat was wise enough to know that his nation wouldn't survive without God's intervention.

The enemy has one goal for your life, and that is discouragement—to influence people to give up and become ineffective for God. You are called to follow Christ for a purpose. When challenges come, go to God in prayer. Confess your inability and your need for Him. Humility is a sign of great strength, not weakness.

Then trust God to do the impossible in your situation and give you the victory.

Heavenly Father, You have a solution for the challenges I am facing today. I trust You to do the impossible and bring the victory.

TRUE VICTORY

SCRIPTURE READING: ROMANS 12:9–11
KEY VERSE: ROMANS 12:9

Let love be without hypocrisy. Abhor what is evil.
Cling to what is good.

When life sends us sprawling, our response is an excellent measuring stick for how mature we are in our relationship with Christ. A response that demonstrates total and complete trust in the Lord is what He desires to see. That is the measure of true victory.

If we are careless, the tragic events that unfold in our lives can leave us jaded. Quickly forgetting who our God is, and the role He plays in our lives, will lead to the wrong responses. When we drift away from a passionate pursuit of God in the midst of adversity, we react in a way that goes against God's Word. We might blame others or God for our current situation. We might search for an escape through drugs and alcohol. We might pity ourselves or just give up.

Turning to the Lord in difficult situations reinforces where our strength and hope reside. Paul, who experienced more than his share of adversity following his conversion, gave us great direction as to how we should respond in adversity, beginning with this: "Cling to what is good" (Romans 12:9).

As we enter the storms in our lives, clinging to the Lord reveals where our hearts are. Clinging is an action of determined grip, unwilling to let go no matter what the cost. And we know that, with Him, we will be able to endure anything that comes our way in life, and emerge victorious.

Lord, when all else fails, I know that I can count on You. I cling to Your promise that Your goodness will prevail.

ENGINEERED BY GOD

SCRIPTURE READING: PSALM 4:1–8

KEY VERSE: PSALM 4:5

Offer the sacrifices of righteousness,
And put your trust in the LORD.

The thought of failing can stir up feelings of anxiety and fear. We wonder to ourselves, *If I fail, what will others think of me? If I am defeated instead of constantly victorious, how will that reflect upon my life?*

Failure is sometimes engineered by God to bring about a stark revelation about ourselves: we need to trust God in every aspect of our lives. Whether our failure relates to a particular sin that seems impossible to conquer or a venture within ministry or a business or a relationship, it helps us to understand that we need to depend totally upon God. There are times in our lives where we strike out on our own, possibly even attempting to do something for God. But when we try these things in our own strength, failure is imminent.

David understood both failure and victory, experiencing both in many different areas of his life. And it was through his defeats that he recognized how desperately he needed God to permeate every place in his heart.

As we place our dependence upon God, an incredible freedom and peace will begin to rest in our hearts. And reaching that point in our lives makes every failure worth it.

Lord, permeate my being so that in failure I can see victory, and in victory I can see You.

A New Beginning

SCRIPTURE READING: JOHN 4:1–26
KEY VERSE: ROMANS 8:1

There is therefore now no condemnation to those who are in Christ Jesus,
who do not walk according to the flesh, but according to the Spirit.

There is nothing more hope-filled than being given a new beginning, especially after we have suffered a defeat. This is what God gives to those who seek His forgiveness.

He provides a chance to begin again. While it is true that there are consequences to sin, God will never condemn us for our bad choices (Romans 8:1). Nor will He leave us in the mess that our sin or doubt has created.

The key to living above your circumstances is realizing that God has a plan for your life even when you make a mistake. He never stops loving you, and He will never give up on you. He may not change the results of a poor decision, but He certainly knows how to take a bad circumstance and bring good out of it.

Jesus made a point of meeting with the woman at the well. From a human perspective, her life was filled with failures. Jesus, however, only saw potential. Even though the woman had been married several times, Jesus did not hesitate to express His love for her.

While God's love for us is unconditional, it is not without responsibility. Love like this demands our complete devotion. Jesus came so that this woman—and each of us—might know and experience the eternal love of God. We are transformed when we draw near to God's amazing love.

Oh Father, Your love is so deep that I cannot comprehend it, yet I know that it is that love that is transforming me. Thank You.

RESTORATION FOR YOUR SOUL

SCRIPTURE READING: ROMANS 7:15–25
KEY VERSE: ROMANS 7:22

For I delight in the law of God according to the inward man.

How can we possibly restore our lives to victory when we have just experienced a particularly difficult time? The best way to restoration is through focusing on God's truth. This means refusing to listen to the nagging voice of the enemy.

Satan tempts us to doubt God's goodness by telling us that we are not worthy of God's love. The enemy interjects thoughts of doubt, worry, and anxiety into our minds so that we will become paralyzed and melt with fear. The enemy also assaults our minds with lies, but God's truth brings hope and restoration to our souls.

Are you facing a time of intense pressure? If so, you may wonder how you will get through it. Christ has the answer. When the storms of life hit, you can retain a strong sense of peace and calm by meditating on the fact that God is in control, and He has nothing but good in mind for your life. He wants you to be victorious spiritually.

When the burden you are carrying becomes too heavy, give it to God. He is your source of strength. In *Telling Yourself the Truth*, author William Backus writes that there are three steps to becoming a person of contentment and peace:

1. Locate your misbeliefs, those things that the enemy uses to discourage you.
2. Ask God to help you remove them.
3. Replace misbeliefs with God's truth.

Lord, I give all doubt and fear to You. For me, they are insurmountable roadblocks, but in Your hands, they are nothing.

The Value of Defeat

SCRIPTURE READING: PSALM 98:1–9

KEY VERSE: PSALM 98:1

Oh, sing to the LORD a new song!
For He has done marvelous things;
His right hand and His holy arm have gained Him the victory.

Paul tried to do the right thing, but, like us, sometimes he failed. In his letter to the Romans, Paul seemed to agonize over his inability to triumph over sin at every confrontation in his life. Don't we all feel like Paul at times? We want to do what's right, but our actions don't always represent our true desires.

However, Paul learned that failure shouldn't be condemning—in fact, it taught him an invaluable lesson about victory: Christ's strength could shine through any situation, no matter how weak that situation may have made Paul (2 Corinthians 12:10).

Here are some things to remember about defeat:

1. Defeat is often engineered by God. God isn't after self-improvement. He is after death—death to our flesh, which leads to life in Him.
2. Defeat is often essential for God to fulfill His purposes in our lives. When we are broken to the point that the only place we can look is up, and see Him, then we begin to see the purposes and plans He has for our lives.
3. Defeat exposes our weaknesses and inadequacies. Our best efforts never match what God can—and wants to—do in us and through us.

Defeat in our lives doesn't mean we are defeated. It is merely God's way of pointing us to ultimate victory.

Lord, let me realize that defeats are simply signposts along the road to point me to ultimate victory.

NEVER ALONE

SCRIPTURE READING: 2 TIMOTHY 4:16–18
KEY VERSE: 2 TIMOTHY 4:16

At my first defense no one stood with me, but all forsook me.
May it not be charged against them.

Most of us can identify with Paul's words in 2 Timothy. In fact, as we read them, we probably can sense the heaviness and thoughtfulness with which they were written: "At my first defense no one stood with me, but all forsook me" (4:16).

Have you ever been in a position where you had to take a stand for something that you knew was not right, and no one was willing to stand with you? Maybe you had to say no to a project that was in the process of being developed. You knew that if things continued, the company you worked for would suffer.

Or perhaps your son or daughter came to you and asked permission to do something you felt was not best. All the other moms and dads had said yes, but for some reason, you sensed that you should say no, and this is what you did. Suddenly, you were very unpopular. Those who had once supported you now felt you were acting prudish and legalistic.

The Spirit of God leads us in the way that we should go. Godly decisions require godly courage. From a human perspective, Paul was alone. No one was with him. But he was not alone. Jesus was beside him and with him.

You are never alone. Life's trials provide a wonderful opportunity for God to display His power and wisdom in your life. Be courageous and do not fear (Joshua 1:9). The Lord your God is with you, and He will give you strength, wisdom, and victory.

Lord, I need Your courage in order to stand strong when I feel forsaken or alone. Let me not forget that my strength comes from You.

A Messenger of Victory

SCRIPTURE READING: ACTS 18:9–11
KEY VERSE: ACTS 18:9

Now the Lord spoke to Paul in the night by a vision,
"Do not be afraid, but speak, and do not keep silent."

Corinth was a difficult place to live, especially for a believer. It was a port city, one that embraced visitors and businessmen from all over the known world. Along with an atmosphere of open commerce, was a very liberal view of religion. Paganism and cult worship were common practices.

Warren Wiersbe writes, "Corinthians' reputation for wickedness was known all over the Roman Empire. . . . Money and vice, along with strange philosophies and new religions, came to Corinth and found a home there."

God is not afraid to send His messengers to places where evil abounds. These are the very places the gospel message is needed. Therefore, God sent Paul to Corinth, but the ministry was under tremendous attack. The conversion of Crispus, a well-known Jewish leader, was the evidence that Paul needed to continue preaching God's message of truth. We must never abandon the post God has given us.

In Acts 18, the Lord spoke to Paul through a dream, encouraging him not to let fear hold him back from speaking (verses 9–10). This was just the encouragement that Paul needed, and it is the same encouragement He has for you.

God is aware of your situation. Take courage and be full of hope. His truth will be taught or spoken. You are His messenger to those who need it most, and you will be victorious in your labors.

Lord, let me be a light in darkness, bringing the message of the gospel to those who need it most.

His Power Will Triumph

SCRIPTURE READING: JUDGES 7:1–11
KEY VERSE: JUDGES 7:2

And the LORD said to Gideon, "The people who are with you are too many for Me to give the Midianites into their hands, lest Israel claim glory for itself against Me, saying, 'My own hand has saved me.'"

Gideon understood fear and hopelessness. Imagine his circumstances: Gideon, with a very small army, was called by God to defeat a large army of Midianites. It seemed as though the odds were against him. But he trusted God and obeyed the Lord's commands.

Then the Lord gave Gideon the news: "The people who are with you are too many for Me to give the Midianites into their hands, lest Israel claim glory for itself against Me, saying, 'My own hand has saved me'" (Judges 7:2). Gideon's small, insignificant army was to be reduced even further. Why? To bring God more glory when the tiny army found victory over the legions of Midianites.

Have you ever encountered such a challenge, where your meager resources are cut even smaller, and your only recourse is to trust God? Perhaps you find yourself in that situation right now and feel intimidated by the task.

A. B. Simpson offers a word of encouragement: "When God wants to bring more power into your life, He brings more pressure." The more impossible your circumstance seems, the more glory God will receive when your situation is rectified.

As your circumstances become more impossible and the odds seem against you, do not be discouraged. God faithfully brought the victory to Gideon, and He will give you victory too. Trust Him, and watch His power triumph.

Lord, when the tools I have seem inadequate for the job, help me to recognize that the miraculous is where You dwell.

WHEN THE ODDS ARE AGAINST YOU

SCRIPTURE READING: JUDGES 7:12–15
KEY VERSE: JUDGES 7:12

*Now the Midianites and Amalekites, all the people of the East,
were lying in the valley as numerous as locusts; and their camels were
without number, as the sand by the seashore in multitude.*

Do you need special encouragement today? Does it feel like all your sources of security have crumbled around you? Gideon understood feeling like all the odds were against him. He faced the challenge of his life: fighting the mighty battalions of Midian with an army of only three hundred men.

Judges 7:12 reported that the Midianites and the Amalekites appeared as numerous as locusts. Their camels appeared as numerous as the sand on the seashore. Can you imagine how Gideon's heart must have sunk upon seeing the awesome view? However, God did not allow Gideon to remain discouraged. When he returned to the camp, he heard two men discussing a dream that, being interpreted, was of God giving Midian over to the Israelites. Upon hearing this, Gideon worshiped God.

Gideon's boldness was renewed. Yours can be too. Such courage is available to you, though all the odds appear stacked against you. This is because you can know for sure that God will not leave you to face your foes alone. No matter what you face today, God is greater. Trust Him, and He will use you in a mighty, wonderful way to effect victory.

Thank You, Lord, that You will use me today to effect victory in Your name. I move forward with confidence and trust.

FACING LIFE'S MOUNTAINS

SCRIPTURE READING: ZECHARIAH 4:6–10
KEY VERSE: ZECHARIAH 4:6

*So he answered and said to me: "This is the word of the Lord
to Zerubbabel: 'Not by might nor by power, but by My Spirit,'
says the Lord of hosts."*

The Bible uses the word *mountain* to mean different things: a geographical location such as Mount Zion (Psalm 2:6); an example of stability (Psalm 30:7); and a barrier, hindrance, or obstacle (Zechariah 4:7).

As a disciple of Christ, you are not guaranteed an easy life. You may face many mountains—trials, difficulties, and hardships—throughout your life. How do you respond when facing what appears to be an overwhelming obstacle or problem? Do you panic? Do you feel discouraged? Do you feel like giving up?

When God calls you to a task, He assumes the responsibility of removing the hindrances that would keep you from succeeding. "Not by might nor by power, but by My Spirit" (Zechariah 4:6).

What do you feel is looming before you like an impossible mountain? Work, relationships, finances, health, the future?

Isaiah 41:10 provides words of comfort for us to hold close to our hearts: "Fear not, for I am with you; be not dismayed, for I am your God. I will strengthen you, yes, I will help you, I will uphold you with My righteous right hand."

No matter what you are facing or how easy or difficult the task may be, always look toward God for victory. He is your eternal, unfailing hope (Psalm 123:2).

*Lord, help me to see that the mountain I consider impossible to climb
is the one that You see as an opportunity for a better view.*

Overcoming Obstacles to Victory

SCRIPTURE READING: JOSHUA 6:1–20
KEY VERSE: JOSHUA 6:5

*It shall come to pass, when they make a long blast with the ram's horn,
and when you hear the sound of the trumpet, that all the people shall
shout with a great shout; then the wall of the city will fall down flat.
And the people shall go up every man straight before him.*

It was huge, and it stood in their way. As Joshua looked at the fortifications of Jericho, he realized that taking the city was no small task, especially with the seemingly impenetrable wall that stood before him.

However, God promised Joshua that Israel would triumph, and Joshua believed Him. Joshua 6:5 records God's command: "It shall come to pass, when they make a long blast with the ram's horn, and when you hear the sound of the trumpet, that all the people shall shout with a great shout; then the wall of the city will fall down flat. And the people shall go up every man straight before him."

For generations to come, the children of Israel would ask about the onslaught at Jericho, to which their parents would respond that it was by shouts and trumpet blasts that the walls were destroyed, because the power of God was with them. No battering ram technology, no modern warfare strategy was necessary—only obedience. The lesson for you remains that God has a way for you to overcome every obstacle by His power. It may not be what you expect, but it is exactly what is needed.

As Theodore Parker prayed, "Give me, Lord, eyes to behold the truth; a seeing sense that knows the eternal right; a heart with pity filled, and gentlest truth; a manly faith that makes all darkness light."

*Lord, You are the Creator, the innovator in the face of the impossible.
I give You all my obstacles, for I know that You alone can overcome
them.*

VICTORY IN A PIG PEN

SCRIPTURE READING: LUKE 6:1–20
KEY VERSE: LUKE 15:18

I will arise and go to my father, and will say to him, "Father,
I have sinned against heaven and before you."

Imagine the prodigal son looking at the pigs he was feeding. As he dropped pods into their sty, his stomach growled, and he realized that the swine were eating better than he was. He was at such a low point that he was actually envying the hogs! The only alternative he could imagine was to return to his father in humility (Luke 15:18).

When the prodigal son considered his options, he chose the last place he had experienced grace. Even though he was determined to offer himself to his father as a hired hand, he must have known in his heart that his father's arms would be open to him. No matter how far you are from God, His arms are open to you. God's grace is always available to you to lift you from sin and defeat back to victorious living.

Catherine of Genoa writes, "I clearly recognize that all good is in God alone, and that in me, without Divine Grace, there is nothing but deficiency. . . . The one sole thing in myself in which I glory, is that I see in myself nothing in which I can glory."

You have not slipped too far away from Him, because the only good in you was from Him in the first place. Do not envy the pigs, but run back to the Father. He desires to restore you by His grace and fill you with all of His goodness.

Lord, show me the areas where I have been prodigal and call me
back to the safety of Your love.

Walking in Victory

Scripture Reading: 2 Corinthians 1:1–7
Key Verses: 2 Corinthians 1:3–4

Blessed be the God and Father of our Lord Jesus Christ, the Father of mercies and God of all comfort, who comforts us in all our tribulation, that we may be able to comfort those who are in any trouble, with the comfort with which we ourselves are comforted by God.

When you are suffering—whether it be a personal tragedy or one of public magnitude—what do you do? Do you tell others about it? Do you hide it in hopes of denying it? Do you pray that the Lord removes it?

How we respond to tragedy provides us a unique opportunity for the type of spiritual growth that results in victorious Christian living. Once we trust Jesus Christ as our Savior, the rest of our days are devoted to growing. While we would often choose otherwise, the pain we suffer or tragedy we experience is useful.

Second Corinthians 1:4 tells us that we suffer so that God can comfort us. The first usefulness of hardship is for us to grow in our knowledge of God. We will soon know His comfort when we reach out in times of hurting. How could we know this aspect of our Father's love if He didn't allow our hearts to break?

The second point of practicality for our suffering is so that we can comfort others. Anyone who has ever experienced real heartache understands how unfulfilled it feels to be thrown shallow phrases in the midst of turmoil.

Yet how would we as humans be able to offer anything more than fluffy words to each other were it not for the deep, penetrating comfort we ourselves have received from the Lord? Know that your pain is real. It is important to the Lord. Your suffering, in fact, is precious to Him. By it, He reveals Himself to you and all those who come in contact with you.

Lord, I seek Your embrace in my pain. Help me not to seek comfort longer than I need but, rather, to share that comfort with others.

Tragedy and Victorious Living

SCRIPTURE READING: 2 CORINTHIANS 1:8–11
KEY VERSE: 2 CORINTHIANS 1:9

*Yes, we had the sentence of death in ourselves, that we should not
trust in ourselves but in God who raises the dead.*

Paul knew what real pain and devastation felt like. He called his burden "excessive, beyond his strength," even causing him to despair of life (2 Corinthians 1:8). He knew what it felt like not to want to live anymore.

Maybe you're going through a time right now when you feel so barraged by hardship that your life hardly seems worth its pain. Walking in victory seems like an illusion. While you endure suffering, looking to the Lord for comfort, remember one thing: God initiated a relationship with you. Therefore, He initiates His comfort for you too.

Paul understood this when he wrote, "We should not trust in ourselves but in God who raises the dead" (2 Corinthians 1:9). The Lord understands our pain even before we cry out to Him. However, it's at the point of us crying out to God that we understand what Paul understood: we cannot trust in ourselves for relief; we must trust in our sovereign God.

Admit to the Lord exactly how you feel. Ask Him to heal your hurting heart, restore your joy, and help you to walk in victory.

When I go through the deepest mire of life, Lord, help me to lift my eyes and see, not just the cross, but the risen Christ.

Our Greatest Victories

SCRIPTURE READING: ISAIAH 55:1–9
KEY VERSES: ISAIAH 55:8–9

"For My thoughts are not your thoughts,
Nor are your ways My ways," says the Lord.
"For as the heavens are higher than the earth,
So are My ways higher than your ways,
And My thoughts than your thoughts."

How do you normally respond when the world seems to turn against you? The wrong way to respond, sadly, is what we most often experience. This is marked by bitterness, doubt, depression, and hopelessness. These feelings mount up, causing the pressure of adversity to increase. This pressure is usually released in one of several common ways: we look for someone to blame, develop a deep desire to escape, deny the problem, or fall into depression. These are certainly not the results God wants to see in our lives!

In contrast to these wrong responses, there are a few things we can do to make the best of hardships in our lives:

- First, we must strive to view everything from God's perspective. His ways are not our ways (Isaiah 55:8), and He wants us to examine the issue from beyond our normal human point of view.
- Second, we must pray, "Father, what is Your goal for my life in this adversity?" God can turn any time into a teaching moment.
- Third, we must surrender to the will of God and then rest in His faithfulness to see us through the ordeal.

Sometimes, our lives require a major disruption in order to realign our thoughts with the Lord's. Though sometimes painful, these times can become our most life-altering moments and lead to our greatest victories, depending on how we respond.

Lord, in difficult times, help me to turn from bitterness, blame , and depression and seek to discover and surrender to Your perspective.

A Dose of Pain

SCRIPTURE READING: 1 PETER 1:3–9
KEY VERSES: 1 PETER 1:6–7

In this you greatly rejoice, though now for a little while,
if need be, you have been grieved by various trials, that the
genuineness of your faith, being much more precious than gold that
perishes, though it is tested by fire, may be found to praise, honor,
and glory at the revelation of Jesus Christ.

Twentieth-century scholar, writer, and theologian C. S. Lewis was no stranger to pain. He lost his mother at a young age and was subsequently raised in various boarding schools throughout Europe. His father, though a decent man, was at a loss in parenting without his late wife's help.

After many years, Lewis met and fell in love with his wife, Joy, whom he also lost to illness. An alcoholic brother, a close friend killed in battle, and many other challenges marked the life of one of the century's most profound Christian thinkers.

In his book *The Problem of Pain*, Lewis writes, "One dynamic benefit of pain is that it shatters the illusion that what we have, whether good or bad in itself, is our own and enough for us. Without pain, humans revert to an innate sense of self-sufficiency. We find God an interruption," he continues, "or as a friend of mine said, 'We regard God as an airman regards his parachute; it's there for emergencies but he hopes he'll never have to use it.'"

God is not a parachute. People do not have a ripcord with which they can pop God out of a neatly packed backpack to help with a temporary crisis, only to be refolded and stuffed away. Without a personal, active, growing relationship with God, no one's life is complete. Sometimes, even though it hurts, it takes a dose of pain to help us remember that.

Please, Lord, let me never treat You as a parachute, handy for
emergencies. Rather, You are the only One who is always there, in
prosperity and in want.

A Full Harvest of Victory

SCRIPTURE READING: MATTHEW 13:3–9
KEY VERSES: GALATIANS 5:22–23

But the fruit of the Spirit is love, joy, peace, longsuffering,
kindness, goodness, faithfulness, gentleness, self-control.
Against such there is no law.

There is something special about biting into a piece of fresh fruit. While Christians should make a habit of offering thanks for every meal, a juicy green apple almost seems to deserve an extra word of appreciation.

Most food requires preparation from many people before it is ready to be consumed. Breads are mixed, kneaded, and baked. Meats are carefully selected, sliced, and preserved. Fruit, however, seems to go straight from the tree to the market. It does not require any preparation; it is perfect the way God made it.

Just as God cultivates apples and oranges, He works to produce a ripe crop of spiritual fruit within His people. In Galatians 5:22, Paul listed the nine specific fruits of the Spirit as love, joy, peace, patience, kindness, goodness, faithfulness, gentleness, and self-control. As with food, the quality of these things can surpass any personal characteristics that you may develop on your own.

If God is the planter and the Spirit is the seed, what is missing? The soil! Fruit—even spiritual fruit—cannot grow without something in which to sink its roots. For Christians, that soil is often adversity.

The believer's response to pain provides a fertile field from which God can raise a cornucopia of fresh fruit. Trust Him with your adversity. There will be a full harvest of victory on the horizon!

Help me, Lord, to remember that when life is most difficult, Your truth is rooting itself deeper in my life in order to produce richer fruit.

When Things Go Wrong

SCRIPTURE READING: JAMES 1:1–4
KEY VERSE: MATTHEW 6:34

*Therefore do not worry about tomorrow, for tomorrow will worry
about its own things. Sufficient for the day is its own trouble.*

Have you ever heard the expression "hitting the wall"? It sounds painful, doesn't it? "The wall" is sometimes used among individuals who have recently begun a new athletic endeavor, most often jogging. Symptoms include a racing heart rate, perspiration pouring down, and lungs gasping for breath in loud, painful inhalations. For new runners, this is the point at which one simply cannot go another step.

After experiencing this sensation, many people give up running. After all, exercise is supposed to make you feel good, right? The problem for these new runners is that they have not yet reached the point of physical endurance. This is what enables runners to continually grow stronger and better able to jog farther each day. Endurance is the result of determination, discipline, and the willingness to suffer in order to achieve results. This is true in your spiritual life as well as on the racetrack.

James 1:2–4 shows the progression of spiritual stamina. In the passage, joy in the face of extreme trials produces endurance, the end result of which is maturity, or "perfection." Pray for God's help in meeting your everyday trials with the joy that comes from Christ, so that you may develop spiritual endurance and, ultimately, victorious maturity in Christ.

*Lord, help me to respond properly as I face my trials today. Enable
me to rejoice, knowing that You are developing spiritual endurance
which will result in victory.*

AFTER THE DARKNESS

SCRIPTURE READING: COLOSSIANS 1:13–16
KEY VERSES: COLOSSIANS 1:13–14

He has delivered us from the power of darkness and conveyed us into the kingdom of the Son of His love, in whom we have redemption through His blood, the forgiveness of sins.

Think about a time in your life when you were sitting comfortably in a brightly lit room during a thunderstorm. Perhaps you had an overhead light, a lamp, and the television illuminating everything in view. Then, without warning, you heard a loud crash of thunder and everything in the house went completely dark. Suddenly, your own corner of the world disappeared, and you sat shaken in a blanket of darkness.

The dark can be rather intimidating, can't it? In one fell swoop, our masterfully created eyes are rendered useless. In a room through which we normally run without thinking, we are required to go slowly, one step at a time, judging each stride carefully against a mental image of the room's layout.

While most people do not like this feeling of helplessness, there are some benefits. For example, the slow pace causes us to stop and make decisions: Do I take one more step? Is this as far as I should go? Also, the dark times make us better appreciate the moments in life when things are crystal clear.

Sometimes, our spiritual lives seem to darken a bit, and we find ourselves inching along with our hand stretched out before us as we desperately seek the Lord. Don't fear these times. Instead, treasure them as moments when God wants you to tread carefully and make wise decisions. When the darkness is over, you will be amazed at how brightly His glory can shine.

Lord, when life is at its darkest and I am inching my way along, rather than give in to fear, help me to trust You to guide my steps.

The Benefits of Darkness

SCRIPTURE READING: JOHN 15:1–5
KEY VERSE: JOHN 15:5

I am the vine, you are the branches. He who abides in Me, and I in him, bears much fruit; for without Me you can do nothing.

Have you ever experienced a time in your life when it seemed like your whole world was shattered? Maybe a loved one passed away, a spouse left home, or you or someone close to you was diagnosed with a serious illness. No one—not even committed Christians—are exempt from these dark times of life.

It has been said that the greatest growth in the Christian's spiritual life occurs during periods of darkness. How can this be so? How can any good come out of the most hideous horrors imaginable? Consider these ways:

- Hard times prevent us from thinking of ourselves as invulnerable. A hard fact of life is that we cannot do everything by ourselves. In fact, according to Scripture, we can do nothing apart from Christ (John 15:5).
- Life-shattering hardships cause us to fall at the foot of the cross with open, empty hands. God is not impressed with how much we can handle "on our own"; rather, He desires us to come to Him utterly broken, realizing that He alone can restore our lives (Psalm 51:17).
- The darkest life is the one that is affected most by the light of Christ. Just as a single candle has tremendous impact on a dark room, so does the blazing light of Jesus illuminate our hearts.

Pray for a clearer understanding of the dark times in your life, so that you may be better prepared to understand and accept the grace that God desires to pour out.

Lord, help me to understand that the darkness makes Your light shine brighter and makes me realize my need for it.

STANDING IN THE STORM

SCRIPTURE READING: PSALM 62:1–12
KEY VERSE: PSALM 62:1

Truly my soul silently waits for God;
From Him comes my salvation.

Truly my soul silently waits for God; from Him comes my salvation. He only is my rock and my salvation; He is my defense; I shall not be greatly moved" (Psalm 62:1–2).

This moving passage can bring to mind many images, but a favorite may be a photograph of a tiny bird wedged into a small crevasse within a rocky cliff. Just outside his hiding place, a brutal storm rages. Strong winds and rain beat down, upturning leaves and breaking tree branches. Yet the bird is safe and still and his life is spared, thanks to the solid rock around him.

Can you recall a time in your life when it seemed as if you would be blown away by a physical or emotional storm? Think back to what you did in response to this trial. Did you venture out into its midst or retreat into the shelter of God's protective arms?

When the next storm blows into your life, remember the words of Psalm 62. Give special attention to the phrase, "my soul silently waits for God." In the photograph mentioned above, the bird was not chirping and fretting. Instead he was resting quietly until the storm passed. His confidence was in the source of his protection, and he did not need to panic.

Though God always hears our cries of distress, we can be assured that once we call for Him, He will be with us. We can release our anxieties and rest in Him until the storms die down and we emerge once again victorious from our hiding place.

Lord, as the birds calmly seek shelter to wait out the storm, let me
also be quick to seek shelter in You when life buffets me about.

DOING THE BEST HE CAN

SCRIPTURE READING: COLOSSIANS 2:3–6
KEY VERSE: GALATIANS 5:16

*I say then: Walk in the Spirit, and you
shall not fulfill the lust of the flesh.*

Many people think that life will be easy after they get saved. Instead, they frequently find they seem to have even more struggles than before. We should not be dismayed, however; this is the normal Christian life. Before we met the Savior, we were walking aimlessly; but upon our salvation, we commenced a journey that would take us through rough terrain and high mountains.

In the epistle to the Galatians, the apostle Paul warned us not to use our newfound freedom in Christ as an excuse to revert—instead of drifting back into our aimless ways, we must take the yoke of Jesus and learn to walk in the Spirit. Paul specifically said "walk" (Galatians 5:16) because the Christian life has direction. We are climbing new heights toward a specific goal, and climbing means struggling.

Every day, we grapple with jealousy, lust, and pride because we live in a world filled with such things. At the same time, we can learn to walk by the Spirit and rise above our temptations and enemies. Yes, it is tough to be in a perpetual fight, and many people have no stomach for such constant exertion. When they see the high standard of Jesus' example, they sometimes drop out of the contest and settle for doing the best they can in their own strength.

But doing the best we can is exactly what Paul said will not work—it simply isn't good enough. That's why the Holy Spirit came. By fully submitting to Him, we can learn to let the Spirit of God do the best He can. Then we will walk in victory.

Lord, I want to walk in victory, not just do the best I can. Do the best You can through me.

WELL EQUIPPED FOR VICTORY

SCRIPTURE READING: EPHESIANS 6:10–18
KEY VERSES: EPHESIANS 6:10–11

Finally, my brethren, be strong in the Lord and in the power
of His might. Put on the whole armor of God, that you may
be able to stand against the wiles of the devil.

In the lifelong struggle with temptation and natural desire, believers are told to "put on" the Lord Jesus Christ. This becomes a daily activity by which you decide who is going to live your life for you today. Are you going to live in the flesh, or is Jesus going to have the privilege of living His life through you?

People have different terms for the "flesh," but simply put, it is the natural part of each person that desires to operate in opposition to God. It usually manifests itself by challenging the restrictions that the Lord set for mankind's good.

Once we are saved, we fluctuate between two mind-sets—that of the Spirit leading toward God and that of the flesh leading away from Him. While we will always retain old fleshly patterns of thinking, we do not have to succumb to living by them, because we have the Holy Spirit dwelling within us.

But since our two ways of thinking are in opposition to each other, conflict and warfare naturally result. We are in a real battle, which requires real weapons. The Lord has given us the helmet of salvation so that we will not surrender our minds to ungodly thinking. The breastplate of righteousness protects our emotions from giving way to natural desires. We also put on the belt of truth, which enables us to walk in keeping with godly principles rather than according to the flesh. And the Lord has provided a true shield of faith for us because there are actual darts of doubt.

In other words, we are at war, but we are well equipped for it. God always leads us in triumph.

Thank You, Lord, that You always lead me in triumph. Thank You for the weapons of spiritual warfare that assure my victory.

THE TROUBLEMAKER WITHIN

SCRIPTURE READING: 1 PETER 4:1–5
KEY VERSE: 1 PETER 3:18

For Christ also suffered once for sins, the just for the unjust,
that He might bring us to God, being put to death in the flesh
but made alive by the Spirit.

I used to wonder if the Christian life really worked. Even after I had been a pastor for a while, I still wondered. I'd look at the Scriptures and then at my life, and they did not always match.

Even though most people have the idea that the Christian life does not work out the way the Bible says it does, I could not be content with doubting what the Word of God says. So I fasted and prayed, confessing to the Lord everything I could think to acknowledge. Still, I believed I was missing something.

I soon discovered the actual reason my Christian life was not working according to Scripture. I had been overlooking one very important truth—a truth that would ultimately transform my life of faith from a burden to a buoyancy. The problem was coming from within me. That is, our greatest troublemaker is our flesh. The main cause of defeat for the believer is the propensity to sin.

We receive a new nature the moment we are saved. However, Scripture reveals that because of the way our thinking has been "programmed," we retain certain longings that do not fit a child of God. These attitudes and desires may come and go for the rest of our life, but they no longer define who we are. We are new creatures in Christ because He broke the power of the flesh. Therefore, it is clear that we cannot live the Christian life without God.

There is a battle waged between our flesh and the Holy Spirit, and the only way to win is by allowing Jesus Christ to live His life through us.

Dear heavenly Father, please reprogram my attitudes and desires.
Give me a new way of thinking that is in accord with Your Word.
Help me win the battle over the troublemaker within.

Obstacles to Righteousness

Scripture Reading: Proverbs 23:20–21
Key Verse: 1 Corinthians 2:14

*But the natural man does not receive the things of the Spirit of God,
for they are foolishness to him; nor can he know them,
because they are spiritually discerned.*

When we set our minds on things of the flesh—sinful attitudes, ideas, and habits in our life—we are decreeing death to the things of God. What makes such desires hard to resist is that they are natural and involve common worldly aspirations like money, sex, prominence, and power.

But 1 Corinthians 2:14 says the natural man does not receive the things of God. Just because something is natural or "only human" does not mean it is right. Notice that there is nothing wrong with eating, but the Scriptures consider gluttony sinful (Proverbs 23:20–21). Nor is there anything immoral about sex when it is practiced within God-given parameters.

As long as our desires and appetites are subdued and brought under subjection to the Holy Spirit, our fellowship with God can continue harmoniously. But when yearnings are unrestrained, our closeness and communication with the Lord are hindered, and we cease to walk in spiritual victory.

To give control of our lives over to the Holy Spirit, we must be persuaded that we cannot live righteously in our own strength. Most of us already realize the attempt to live in a God-pleasing manner is a struggle; to correct the situation, we must surrender our entire being to Him: mind, will, emotion, and conscience. Ask God to reveal areas of weakness, and then give Him each frailty as it comes to light. This needs to be done not once, but every day.

Dear heavenly Father, today I'm totally Yours. I can't live the Christian life, but You can live through me. Eliminate the obstacles to righteousness from my life.

THE POWER WITHIN

SCRIPTURE READING: 2 CORINTHIANS 13:4–9
KEY VERSE: 2 CORINTHIANS 13:4

*For though He was crucified in weakness, yet He lives by the power
of God. For we also are weak in Him, but we shall live with
Him by the power of God toward you.*

Spiritual power is the divine energy God is willing to express in and through us and the divine authority needed to carry out the work God has called us to do victoriously.

We cannot "harness" the power of the Holy Spirit. This power is not just for preachers, evangelists, or people who work in special ministry; rather, it is available to every believer who willingly surrenders moment by moment in submission and obedience to the Holy Spirit.

We cannot garner the power of the Spirit in order to use God. Conversely, we experience His power when we surrender to be used by Him. God releases His power through us as we walk in obedience to Him.

He releases His power to us in several ways:

- Through the fruit of the Spirit: God's power, and only God's power, enables us to exhibit love, joy, peace, patience, goodness, kindness, faithfulness, gentleness, and self-control, which reveal the character of Christ in us.
- Through witnessing: Scripture always refers to the power of the Holy Spirit in relationship to witnessing and glorifying God. It is His power through us that emboldens us and carries out the work.
- Through the work we are called to do: God will not place you into a position or ask you to accomplish a task for which He will not fully equip you for total victory.

Father, thank You for releasing Your power through me by the fruit of the Spirit manifested in my life, in my witnessing, and in the work I am called to do. I am surely equipped for total victory!

APRIL
Pathway to the Cross

From that time Jesus began to show to His disciples that He must
go to Jerusalem, and suffer many things from the elders and chief
priests and scribes, and be killed, and be raised the third day.
                                                    —Matthew 16:21

The Supreme Moment in History

SCRIPTURE READING: COLOSSIANS 2:11–15
KEY VERSES: COLOSSIANS 2:12–13

*. . . buried with Him in baptism, in which you also were
raised with Him through faith in the working of God, who raised
Him from the dead. And you, being dead in your trespasses and the
uncircumcision of your flesh, He has made alive together with
Him, having forgiven you all trespasses.*

In our lives, there are defining moments determining what path we will take. There are events that forever change us. The moment we see the truth brought to light, we run for it, realizing that all we have ever known pales in comparison.

For the world, that moment was when Jesus died on the cross. His death at Calvary closed the chapter on mankind's separation from God, making a way for all to know Him—and know Him intimately. As the perfect sacrifice for the entire world, Jesus served as the atoning death necessary for us to come into relationship with our heavenly Father.

Jesus' death on the cross changed the way we live and interact with Him today. God judged sin. With the world's sin on Jesus' shoulders, God showed us how much He abhors sin, letting His Son die. God defeated Satan. Our heavenly Father triumphed over the enemy, stripped him of his powers, and exposed him as a liar and a destroyer.

Paul wrote that God made us alive, forgiving us, and paying the price for our sin (Colossians 2:13–14). Through Christ's death, the barrier between God and us has been removed.

*Lord, there is no place for me to take my burden, other than the cross.
Thank You for triumphing over sin and setting me free.*

A Call to Repentance

SCRIPTURE READING: LUKE 24:44–49
KEY VERSES: LUKE 24:46–47

Then He said to them, "Thus it is written, and thus it was necessary for the Christ to suffer and to rise from the dead the third day, and that repentance and remission of sins should be preached in His name to all nations, beginning at Jerusalem."

The truth is that all have sinned. Everyone has done things that are wrong and made bad decisions. All people have hurts and concerns. There is not a person who has absolutely no regrets, and there is not one living soul who can be saved without Jesus.

In Luke 24:46–47, Jesus said forgiveness of sins would be proclaimed in His name. The good news is that every person can escape the consequences of sin through the blood of Christ.

Christians often attempt to construct great arguments about why accepting Christ as Savior is profitable and good. Yet the beauty of the gospel is its simplicity. Everyone has sinned. Everyone needs forgiveness from sin. Jesus provides that forgiveness. Repent and accept Him as your Savior.

All people have sins and hurts with which they need help. The call to repentance is the pathway to Christ. Lead them to Jesus, and you will have fulfilled the goal of the Cross.

Lord, let me never forget that where religion is complicated, faith is simple: Jesus died for my sins and through repentance I am reconciled to God.

At the Foot of the Cross

SCRIPTURE READING: 2 CORINTHIANS 7:8–12
KEY VERSE: 2 CORINTHIANS 7:10

For godly sorrow produces repentance leading to salvation, not to be regretted; but the sorrow of the world produces death.

Paul wanted the best for the people in Corinth. He loved the church and worked for the good of its members. During a trip to Macedonia, Paul realized that the ethical and doctrinal problems in Corinth were so great that, without correction, they would result in the ruination of the church. So Paul wrote a stinging disciplinary letter to the church. Preferring the people of Corinth to be wounded in correction and healed rather than continue on the pathway of sin and death, he rebuked them.

It is the concept that one finds in cancer treatments. The manner by which cancer is treated is by radiation or chemotherapy, which destroys harmful cells. Though the remedy is often harsh and draining, it stops the cancer's consumption of the body. In 2 Corinthians 7:10, Paul wrote that our sorrow produces repentance that leads to salvation.

God does not desire to see you face pain and suffering, but at times there are such destructive things at work in your life that He must root them out. His desire is that you would repent. He kills the cancerous cells of sin so that you might be able to enjoy the abundant life He has for you.

God invites you to come to the foot of the cross and confess your sins to Him. Acknowledge the sins that plague you so He can help you live the full life you were intended to experience.

Lord, the sting of correction is less painful than the cancer of sin. Search my heart and reveal to me the areas where my sin is hidden.

A SECOND CHANCE

SCRIPTURE READING: JOHN 8:1–11
KEY VERSE: JOHN 8:11

She said, "No one, Lord." And Jesus said to her,
"Neither do I condemn you; go and sin no more."

The love Jesus demonstrated at the Cross is unconditional. True love reaches out to the unlovely.

The woman caught in adultery sought affection, but reaped a scandal. As the scribes and Pharisees brought her before Jesus, they demanded that her punishment be stoning. Jesus reacted in love. Stooping down, He began writing something in the sand.

Then He related the basic truth that only the sinless have a right to cast stones. Knowing that sinlessness was not something they could claim, the crowd of religious men dispersed. Only Jesus was left, and He refused to condemn her.

Jesus' ministry always allowed for second chances. His interest was not to hold on to records of wrong, but to give people the chance to accept Him and do right. We do well to reflect His love by giving others second chances. Our greatest acts of love may be offering forgiveness to someone who has wronged us or to reach out to someone others have judged as unlovely.

Always remember the love and forgiveness God has shown you as you deal with other people. You will be less likely to cast stones and more likely to give second chances.

Father, thank You for the offer of a second chance. I accept. Thank
You for Your love and forgiveness.

LESSONS IN GETHSEMANE

SCRIPTURE READING: 2 CORINTHIANS 5:1–9
KEY VERSES: 2 CORINTHIANS 5:7–8

For we walk by faith, not by sight. We are confident, yes, well pleased rather to be absent from the body and to be present with the Lord.

One of the most painful experiences in Jesus' life on earth was the night He spent with His disciples in the Garden of Gethsemane before He went to the cross. The thought of being separated from God—if even for a few days—was excruciating to Him. Despite the pain that Jesus endured, His obedience to God's plan allowed Him to triumph over death and for mankind to find salvation.

Whenever we find ourselves in our own Garden of Gethsemane experiences, we can reflect upon Jesus' night there with hope. What God did was more perfect and more amazing than any man could ever imagine. In the midst of our pain and suffering, we find God is at work. God will spare no experience, effort, or pain to prepare us for His good plans and purposes.

Paul wrote that it was God that prepared us for his purposes (2 Corinthians 5:5, 7–8). The way God prepares us is not always easy, but it is perfecting us to accomplish something in the future that we cannot foresee. Our nights in the Garden of Gethsemane result in bright days ahead.

Through our obedience to God during these times, His perfect plan for our lives begins to unfold and we see His perfect purpose.

Lord, I fear separation from You. Yet those times when I walk through dark valleys, I know You are working out Your purposes. Thank You that I can entrust my life to You.

The Refining Process

SCRIPTURE READING: MATTHEW 26:36–46
KEY VERSE: MATTHEW 26:41

*Watch and pray, lest you enter into temptation. The spirit
indeed is willing, but the flesh is weak.*

One of the most reassuring traits of Jesus is the fact that He can relate to us. Regardless of how discouraged we might be or how weak and weary we feel, Jesus knows how we feel because He, too, felt likewise. But our weakness is not a sin. It is actually our pathway to strength.

While Jesus never sinned, He struggled like everyone, including in His prayer life. In the Garden of Gethsemane, Jesus wanted to know if there was another way for God to accomplish His great plan without this impending painful separation.

Jesus was weak and weary, yet His trust in His heavenly Father remained firm. He knew this day was coming and this was God's purpose for His life on earth, but it did not make the situation any easier. Jesus did not take up the cross lightly.

Jesus knew that His suffering was necessary to bring the world back into personal relationship with God. But it was still hard. It was still agonizing. Despite Jesus' knowledge of how His death and resurrection would impact mankind forever, He struggled to pray. However, Jesus was without sin. The struggles in His prayer life, much like ours from time to time, show how struggling is a natural by-product of entering a battle for God's kingdom.

But the struggles produce a refining process in us that glorifies our Lord and sharpens us more into His image.

*Lord Jesus, You struggled with human weakness, with weariness,
with temptation, and yet You didn't sin. Give me the strength to rise
above temptation too.*

GOD'S PLAN FOR THE RESURRECTION

SCRIPTURE READING: 1 CORINTHIANS 15:12–28
KEY VERSE: 1 CORINTHIANS 15:20

*But now Christ is risen from the dead, and has become the
firstfruits of those who have fallen asleep.*

The foundation of Christianity is the resurrection of Jesus Christ. The apostle Paul told the Corinthian church that without belief in this primary tenet of our faith, then our faith is in vain.

Since we believe in Jesus' bodily resurrection from the grave after His crucifixion, then we also believe in the promise of *our* bodily resurrection into eternity. The alternative is to believe in nothing that is real, nothing that is hopeful or redeeming.

We cannot separate these truths. Jesus is the firstfruits of those raised from the dead. When Paul said this in 1 Corinthians 15:20, he used a verb tense in the Greek that means Jesus not only was raised but is still alive. He lives forevermore.

George Sweeting writes:

In Glendale, California, at Forest Lawn Cemetery, hundreds of people each year stand before two huge paintings. One pictures the crucifixion of Christ. The other depicts His resurrection. In the second painting the artist has pictured an empty tomb with an angel near the entrance. In the foreground stands the figure of the risen Christ. But the striking feature of that huge canvas is a vast throng of people, back in the misty background, stretching into the distance and out of sight, suggesting the multitude who will be raised from the dead because Jesus first died and rose for them.

Lord, thank You for Your death on the cross and Your resurrection. I rejoice in this hope. I praise You!

Our Ultimate Assurance

SCRIPTURE READING: JOHN 20:19–29
KEY VERSE: JOHN 20:29

Jesus said to him, "Thomas, because you have seen Me, you have believed. Blessed are those who have not seen and yet have believed."

The Resurrection sometimes loses its powerful meaning with us. We forget that Jesus rising from the dead was more than a mere miracle from God. Jesus' resurrection was the beginning of the fulfillment of all God's promises to us.

This was not simply an event to change the minds of a few doubting men and women in that day. It was an event God used to change the hearts of men and women forever. Because of Jesus' resurrection, we realize that God's promises are real, not manipulative double-talk to keep us hoping that one day our lives will change. God's Word is true. Everything He has said about Himself is undeniably the truth.

Following Jesus' resurrection, the early church began to see how all of God's promises had been—and still were being—fulfilled. They began to understand that Jesus was indeed the Savior, regardless of what they expected the Messiah to be. They saw that a personal relationship with God the Father was possible. And they began a life empowered by the Holy Spirit. Jesus promised His disciples that the Holy Spirit would be the help they needed after He left earth.

Through Jesus' resurrection, we discover that God's promises are the basis by which we can live our lives. Faith in His promises guarantees a changed life forever.

Jesus, with Your resurrection, we caught our first glimpse of what Messiah means. Thank You that You are still showing us. Please help my heart to understand.

THE RICHES OF GOD'S GRACE

SCRIPTURE READING: EPHESIANS 1:3–6
KEY VERSES: EPHESIANS 1:5–6

. . . having predestined us to adoption as sons by Jesus Christ to Himself, according to the good pleasure of His will, to the praise of the glory of His grace, by which He made us accepted in the Beloved.

Have you ever questioned your acceptability? Have you ever wondered if you are truly loveable? When God holds out His salvation to you, He is not extending a membership to an obscure club. He is inviting you to a profound, wonderful relationship that was made possible through His death on the cross.

Ephesians 1:5–6 teaches us that God's will was to adopt you as His own through the work of Christ. It was His will that your bond to Him be the strongest it could be, so He did it through the most precious relationship He has ever created: He is accepting you as His child. William E. Brown of Baker's *Evangelical Dictionary* writes, "God is a father who graciously adopts believers in Christ into his spiritual family and grants them all the privileges of heirship. Salvation is much more than forgiveness of sins and deliverance from condemnation; it is also a position of great blessing. Believers are children of God."

The riches of God's grace provide a wonderful family for you. God does not want a detached relationship. His desire is for deep communion, because He loves you with an overwhelming love. You are accepted by God and special to Him. Enjoy your position as His child.

Lord, thank You for the riches of Your grace. Thank You that I have been adopted into Your family and that I am loved and accepted by You.

THE MESSAGE OF ETERNAL LIFE

SCRIPTURE READING: 1 CORINTHIANS 15:50–58

KEY VERSE: 1 CORINTHIANS 15:54

So when this corruptible has put on incorruption, and this mortal has put on immortality, then shall be brought to pass the saying that is written: "Death is swallowed up in victory."

If you knew for certain that this life was all there was, it would affect your thinking substantially. It would change the way you make decisions, big and small.

The truth is that many people in this world live by the cliché, "Eat, drink, and be merry, for tomorrow we will die." Earthly death, however, is not the end. Rather, on the other side of our physical death is eternity. Our Lord declared the message of eternal life several times throughout His ministry. Why is this such a vital promise to the believer?

- Jesus wanted His followers to know for certain that they are secure in Him forever. This means that death is nothing to be feared. Instead, our departure from earth is the moment of our entrance into His eternal presence.
- The Lord wanted to give His children hope in the face of death. The most common question in the minds of funeral attendees is, "Will I see him again?" Jesus did not want to leave His people unaware; He gave them the assurance necessary to endure the loss of a loved one.
- Jesus wanted to inspire every believer to be faithful until death. Because we know we will have to give an account to the Lord for our lives, we can live with the end in mind. Temptations to sin are then measured by the question, "Will God approve of this?"

Jesus conquered death so that we can enter into God's eternal presence. Because we do not have to fear tomorrow, we can more fully rejoice in Him today.

I rejoice, Lord, that because You conquered death, I, too, shall live.

The Sign of the Cross

SCRIPTURE READING: MARK 10:35–45
KEY VERSE: MARK 10:45

*For even the Son of Man did not come to be served, but to serve,
and to give His life a ransom for many.*

Crosses. We see them dangling from people's necklaces, on car bumpers, and printed on T-shirts and coffee cups. Crosses are everywhere. The Christian cross is such a familiar symbol that we can easily trivialize its significance. But it's what took place there—the death of Jesus—that lays the foundation for the Christian faith.

At the center of our faith is the cross. It is symbolic of the place where Jesus forever changed history, the place where our sin was forgiven. The cross and the death that occurred there bring life, joy, and hope. In Mark 10:45, Jesus said that He came to serve, not to be served. Jesus' death on the cross was the place in history where the debt for sin was paid in full. God demanded retribution for the sins of the world, and Jesus paid for them in one act with His own life.

For all the signs and wonders that Jesus did while He walked on earth, it was what He did hanging from the cross that brought about the beautiful gift of salvation, which isn't limited to just a few, but is available to all.

When we think upon the Cross, we should do so with great awe and reverence. It is the heartbeat of our faith, the place where our sins were paid in full by the most sacrificial act ever done by one man.

Lord, when I start to treat a cross as a decoration, help me to see Your hands, Your feet, and my hope hanging on the cross of Calvary.

WHAT THE CROSS REPRESENTS

SCRIPTURE READING: LUKE 2:25–35
KEY VERSES: LUKE 2:34–35

Then Simeon blessed them, and said to Mary His mother, "Behold,
this Child is destined for the fall and rising of many in Israel,
and for a sign which will be spoken against (yes, a sword will
pierce through your own soul also), that the thoughts of
many hearts may be revealed."

We loosely toss around the phrase "the cross" like everyone understands the validity and weight of the object to which we are referring. But many people do not understand at all what the cross represents—even some Christians.

The cross is the place where Jesus died a sinner's death for us, the place where all shame, guilt, and sin are laid bare, the place where life begins. Despite the wrong choices we have made in life, the heaviness of our sins, or the inconsistency of our faith, we can all find common ground at the foot of the cross—the place where we can cast aside the troubles of our mind and receive the benefits of salvation. It is there that God redeems our lives into something truly valuable and beautiful, just as He has always planned for us.

Upon seeing Jesus as a baby, Simeon exclaimed, "Behold, this Child is destined for the fall and rising of many in Israel, and for a sign which will be spoken against (yes, a sword will pierce through your own soul also), that the thoughts of many hearts may be revealed" (Luke 2:34–35).

The cross, though thick and dull, is the place where hearts are seared before God and true freedom begins. Despite what we may perceive about God, He desires the best for our lives and wants us to receive the freedom He has so readily made available to those who are willing to accept it.

Lord, my life, my eternal life, began at Your cross. Thank You for setting me free by yielding to death by crucifixion.

Oh, the Wonderful Cross!

Scripture Reading: Romans 5:1–8
Key Verse: Romans 5:6

For when we were still without strength,
in due time Christ died for the ungodly.

The Cross is where love became a five-letter word. Eternal, incomprehensible, unconditional love is spelled C-R-O-S-S.

Romans 5:1–5 explains this great love and how God expressed it by sending His Son, Jesus Christ, to die on the cross for our sins. The Cross is the hinge point of history where a holy God made a way for fallen, sinful man to have a relationship and fellowship with Him.

In one awesome, indescribable moment, justice and mercy met at the Cross. There was enough justice at the Cross to punish every sin of all humanity. There was enough mercy at the Cross to envelop all of humanity in God's wonderful, loving forgiveness. God not only poured out His wrath on sin—which is justice—but He even exhibited mercy by lovingly providing Jesus so we would not have to face the death penalty of sin.

God also demonstrated His wisdom at the Cross. His goal was the redemption of mankind, the forgiveness of mankind's sins. God's plan and purpose are always the very best, and He chose the best route to accomplish His plan when He sent Jesus to die on the cross.

Was there any other way in which a holy God could breech the divide between Himself and sinful man and still remain just? Think about it. No other plan could so perfectly accomplish His will and yet direct all of the honor and glory to God and not one shred of glory to man.

Lord, thank You for demonstrating Your love at the Cross. Thank You, Lord, that Your mercy was great enough to envelop all of humanity—including me!

The Blood of Christ

SCRIPTURE READING: JOHN 1:19–29
KEY VERSE: JOHN 1:29

Behold! The Lamb of God who takes away the sin of the world!

Christian doctrine features several terms that are essential in comprehending the importance of the blood of Christ shed on the cross of Calvary:

- Redemption: Believers have been redeemed and forgiven. Our salvation has been purchased through the shed blood of Jesus Christ, the sinless Son of God who died for our sins and took upon Himself our guilt and penalty for those sins (Ephesians 1:7).
- Justification: God has justified us, or declared us not guilty, because by the gift of faith we have accepted Christ as Savior. He also has declared us righteous in His sight, applying the righteousness of Christ to our accounts (Romans 5:9, 17).
- Reconciliation: Jesus' blood makes it possible for God to bring us back into a right relationship with Him. The Bible says we were enemies of God until we accepted Christ. Christ's blood is the bridge, the peace offering, that reconciles us to God (Colossians 1:19–22).
- Sanctification: Sanctification is God's cleansing and setting us apart unto Himself for His purposes and His will. He sanctified us when we were saved, and He continues to sanctify us to make us clean vessels properly prepared for His good works (Hebrews 12:14).
- Access: Finally, we would not have access to God's throne of grace without the shedding of Christ's blood. The reason we can cry out and be heard by God is Christ's sacrificial death.

Praise the Lord for the glory of the blood (Hebrews 10:19).

Heavenly Father, thank You that I am redeemed, justified, reconciled, sanctified, and that through the blood, I have access to You.

THE LAMB OF GOD

SCRIPTURE READING: ROMANS 3:21–26
KEY VERSE: ROMANS 3:23

For all have sinned and fall short of the glory of God.

In her book *The Vision of His Glory,* Anne Graham Lotz explains the importance of the blood of Christ. She writes that under the Law of Moses, when someone sinned, the person was required to bring a lamb without blemish to the priest at the temple. The sinner was required to grasp the lamb with both hands and confess his sin. Lotz continues:

> It was as though the guilt of the sinner was conveyed through his arms, down to his hands, and transferred to the lamb. Then the sinner took the knife and killed the lamb, so the lamb died as a direct result of the sinner's action. The priest then took the blood of the lamb and sprinkled it on the altar to make atonement for the person's sin. . . . When John the Baptist observed Jesus of Nazareth walking beside the Jordan River, he exclaimed, "Look, the Lamb of God, who takes away the sin of the world." . . .
>
> Today, when we grasp the Lamb of God with our "hands" of faith and confess our sin, the guilt of our sin is transferred to the Lamb. Although the Romans physically crucified Jesus, it was your sin and mine that was responsible for putting Him to death. He died as my personal sacrifice— and yours. His blood was sprinkled on the altar of the cross for your sin, and God accepted the sacrifice, granting you atonement, redemption, forgiveness, and a way back into His Presence through the substitutionary death of Jesus Christ.

Lord, thank You for the substitutionary death of Your Son, Jesus, whose blood was shed for my sin.

GOD'S AMAZING LOVE

SCRIPTURE READING: PSALM 139:1–18
KEY VERSE: PSALM 139:13

For You formed my inward parts;
You covered me in my mother's womb.

In *The Gift for All People*, Max Lucado describes the event of the Cross in this way:

> Christ came to earth for one reason: to give His life as a ransom for you, me, for all of us. He sacrificed Himself to give us a second chance. He would have gone to any lengths to do so. And He did. He went to the cross, where man's utter despair collided with God's unbending grace. And in that moment when God's great gift was complete, the compassionate Christ showed the world the cost of His gift.

As you strengthen your relationship with Jesus, you will begin to understand the amazing truth that He died specifically for you. Though His sacrifice freed the world from the penalty of sin, Jesus was intimately familiar with you as an individual as He accepted and fulfilled His sentence of death upon the cross.

The Bible tells us that God knew you before you were formed in your mother's womb (Psalm 139:13). That means that when He sent His Son to die on the cross over two thousand years ago, God knew you and included the sins you would commit in the future among those to be forgiven.

What a beautiful gift! What a reason to rejoice! Yet so many people take Christ's sacrificial death for granted. In the holy Easter season, take time to thank Him for His amazing love that is demonstrated to us all each day.

Father, I am speechless at the thought that You knew who I was when You sent Your Son to die for me. Thank You for loving me that much.

THIS GRACE IS YOURS

SCRIPTURE READING: JOHN 1:19–29
KEY VERSE: JOHN 1:29

The next day John saw Jesus coming toward him, and said, "Behold!
The Lamb of God who takes away the sin of the world!"

One of the most encouraging things you can receive from God is the hope that comes from being given a second chance. This is especially important when you have yielded to temptation or feel that you have fallen short of His plan and purpose for your life. The truth is that God never limits the opportunity for forgiveness.

Second chances encourage us to go on and not to give up even when the whispers of the world around us seem to say the opposite. After his denial of Christ, Peter was in need of a second chance, and Jesus, through His grace, provided this (John 21:15–17).

How many of us have longed for God's cleansing touch when we become trapped by our wrongful actions? The only cure for sin or failure of any kind is God's grace applied to our lives. This is what changes the stumbling sinner into a person living victoriously for Jesus Christ.

Even before you knew Him, Jesus knew and loved you. It was His love that saved you, and it is His love that will keep you throughout eternity. "God demonstrates His own love toward us, in that while we were still sinners, Christ died for us" (Romans 5:8).

Are you struggling with the idea of grace and how it applies to your life? Realize that God loves you. He stands beside you and is pleased to call you His own. This grace is yours.

Lord, thank You for Your grace—Your love and kindness toward me
even when I don't deserve it. I accept Your extended grace.

THE MESSAGE OF THE CROSS

SCRIPTURE READING: MARK 15:33–39
KEY VERSE: MARK 15:39

So when the centurion, who stood opposite Him, saw that
He cried out like this and breathed His last, he said,
"Truly this Man was the Son of God!"

Two men of different faiths sat across from each other at a restaurant table. In an effort to understand the other's views, the first man asked, "Can you sum up the essence of Christianity in one word?"

Without pause, the second man replied, "Forgiveness."

Would you have given the same answer? There are so many words that could have been said: love, sacrifice, joy, assurance, eternity. Yet forgiveness seems to carry the most meaning and power. What other religion offers its believers the ability to be set free from sin with no penance to pay?

We can count ourselves among the most fortunate in the world. When we pledge our lives to God and accept the Lord Jesus Christ as our personal Savior, we are guaranteed forgiveness and eternal life.

Though none of us are exempt from the storms and trials of life, we can live with inner joy and peace. We will never pay the penalty of eternal death for our sins. That price was paid for us at the cross by a loving God who is merciful and longsuffering.

The blood that Christ shed upon the cross is truly the key to heaven for those who believe. Today, why not reach out to someone who may not be aware of the gift God gave to the world through the atoning death of His only Son?

Lord, Your blood shed on the cross spelled forgiveness for me. I cannot repay You, but I can share this key to heaven with others.

An Image of Hope

Scripture Reading: Psalm 98:1–13
Key Verse: Psalm 98:2

*The LORD has made known His salvation; His righteousness
He has revealed in the sight of the nations.*

How often do you see people wearing a pendant, charm, or ring in the shape of a cross? How many churches do you pass regularly that have a large cross perched atop the building or bell tower? Stained-glass windows, baptisteries, pulpits, choir robes—all of these things are commonly adorned with the image of a cross. We see this so often, perhaps we have begun to take the cross for granted.

From our modern-day perspective, we often fail to understand the utter shock value of the cross. If you were a citizen of first-century Rome, you would most likely live your entire life hoping never to see such an image. In that culture, the cross was the ultimate symbol of shame, horror, death, and curse. Crucifixion was so repulsive that the Romans would not allow any of their citizens to die by this method, regardless of the crime.

How did such a horrific symbol become an image of hope and mercy? By dying on the cross, Jesus Christ paid the penalty for mankind's sinfulness. Every sin was nailed to the cross with Jesus, and it all died there with Him. When He rose from the grave, our sins did not. Therefore, sin and death were defeated once and for all. In Christ, all men and women have the opportunity to share in that salvation.

Praise God today for the gift of salvation, and thank Jesus for bearing the punishment for your sin.

Lord, when You accepted the cross, You accepted its humiliation. Let me never treat it as a vague symbol, but as a terrible place where You went to save me.

THE MIRACLE OF THE RESURRECTION

SCRIPTURE READING: MARK 16:1–21
KEY VERSES: MARK 16:9–10

Now when He rose early on the first day of the week, He appeared first to Mary Magdalene, out of whom He had cast seven demons. She went and told those who had been with Him, as they mourned and wept.

When you read the account of Jesus' death and resurrection in the Bible, do you ever stop to wonder why He appeared to His disciples and friends after the Resurrection? They already knew that the stone had been rolled away and that His body was not there. He had already promised them that He would rise again on the third day.

It is common belief that Jesus' multiple appearances were to answer the questions that existed among them and to cast out disbelief. He appeared to Mary Magdalene to rule out the possibility of His body being stolen and to expound upon the scriptural prophecies that were now fulfilled. He appeared to Thomas to prove that His broken, punctured body had indeed risen from the grave. He also appeared to Peter to reestablish His love, even after being denied.

These important visitations equipped the new messengers of the gospel with further knowledge and evidence of Jesus' true identity as the Son of God. If any had held the slightest doubts in their hearts before, they could not doubt now. Jesus suffered the death of a criminal to rise as a King. He is alive, and His love is great enough to conquer doubt.

Meditate on the miracle of His resurrection as you lift your prayers to Him today.

Lord, just as You appeared to Your followers to equip them for ministry, so, too, help my finite mind grasp the wonder of Your death as a criminal, and resurrection as a King.

POWER OF THE RESURRECTION

SCRIPTURE READING: ISAIAH 53:1–5

KEY VERSE: ISAIAH 53:5

But He was wounded for our transgressions,
He was bruised for our iniquities;
The chastisement for our peace was upon Him,
And by His stripes we are healed.

When a dear and faithful servant of the church learned of his terminal illness, he requested that the headstone upon his grave bear the words of 1 Corinthians 15:55: "O Death, where is your victory? O Death, where is your sting?" (NASB). This man's faith allowed him to claim these words before he passed away.

The verses following this passage explain his confidence: "The sting of death is sin, and the power of sin is the law; but thanks be to God, who gives us the victory through our Lord Jesus Christ" (1 Corinthians 15:56–57 NASB).

Not only did Jesus bear the weight of our sins upon the cross, He also accepted and withstood the pain of death. In one miraculous event, He changed the process of dying. No longer would His creation have to experience the fear, anguish, and pain associated with death. His sacrifice established a choice for us all—eternal life or eternal death.

Why would someone choose eternal death? We cannot know. Is it so difficult to believe in the power of God and the event of Jesus' resurrection? For some, it must be.

As you consider the specific events that occurred upon the cross, thank Jesus for freeing you from the pain of death, and pray for those who refuse to acknowledge Him.

Thank You, Lord, that Your resurrection quieted the sting of death and that I have been set free because of Your sacrifice.

THE MIRACLE OF RESTORATION

SCRIPTURE READING: ISAIAH 53:6–9

KEY VERSE: ISAIAH 53:6

All we like sheep have gone astray;
We have turned, every one, to his own way;
And the LORD has laid on Him the iniquity of us all.

Salvation is eternally linked to Jesus Christ. It was His death on Calvary's cross that paid the penalty for our sin. Nothing we can do equals what Jesus did for us. This is why the apostle Paul wrote that salvation is a gift.

The word *grace* is also linked to the message of salvation. The grace of God is His goodness manifested toward us. No one, on his own, is worthy of God's salvation. "All of us like sheep have gone astray, each of us has turned to his own way; but the LORD has caused the iniquity of us all to fall on Him" (Isaiah 53:6 NASB).

We are saved by God's grace—His goodness demonstrated toward us. And those God saves, He keeps. He will not cast us away or refuse us the love that He so willingly gives. However, believers need to be mindful that sin steals the joy that salvation brings.

Even if you have known Christ for many years, sin will darken your life and blind you to the wonder of God's grace. After his sin with Bathsheba, David prayed, "Restore to me the joy of Your salvation" (Psalm 51:12).

Joy is the evidence of God's work in our lives. Sin brings His displeasure and judgment, but obedience brings joy to our hearts. David did not ask God merely to make him happy. He prayed for the restoration of joy, which is more than an emotional expression. It is the evidence of a heart that found its contentment in God.

Lord, thank You for Your unchanging promise—eternal life through Jesus Christ. Thank You for the gift of salvation secured at the Cross.

THE HEART OF THE CROSS

SCRIPTURE READING: MATTHEW 27:45–54
KEY VERSE: EXODUS 34:6

And the LORD passed before him and proclaimed, "The Lord, the Lord
God, merciful and gracious, longsuffering, and abounding in goodness
and truth."

Could not God have come up with a better idea for the salvation of man
than the Cross?" This question is sometimes posed during debates
regarding the purpose for the brutal punishment Jesus endured at Golgotha.

Yet, apart from our human understanding, and in His infinite wisdom,
God had a perfect plan for the Cross. The circumstances of the day were
never out of His control or in conflict with His will. Instead, the Cross
revealed who God is and what He is like—compassionate and gracious, slow
to anger, and abounding in lovingkindness and truth (Exodus 34:6).

The Cross also exposed Satan for what he is and, at the same time, took
away his power. Though Satan's final defeat will occur at the end of time, the
Cross invalidated the need for a physical payment for sin for those who
would accept Christ's ultimate atoning sacrifice made for us all.

Finally, the Cross unveiled a new covenant relationship with God, which
gives all people the opportunity to experience eternity through Jesus Christ.
Matthew 27:51 tells us that at the moment of Christ's death, the temple veil
(which had allowed only high priests access to God) was torn in half from
top to bottom. This act signified the beginning of a new type of access to
God through Jesus Christ, our Intercessor. Was God's perfect will carried out
at the Cross? Yes. Even in death, His love was demonstrated to the world He
created to receive His blessings.

Lord, I embrace with my whole heart the covenant that was unveiled
at the Cross and signed with Your shed blood.

A Personal Message from God

SCRIPTURE READING: ISAIAH 53:10–12
KEY VERSE: ISAIAH 9:6

For unto us a Child is born,
Unto us a Son is given;
And the government will be upon His shoulder.
And His name will be called
Wonderful, Counselor, Mighty God,
Everlasting Father, Prince of Peace.

The cross of Jesus Christ is a sacred symbol to Christians, as it represents everything in which we believe. To truly understand the message of this symbol, we must increase in knowledge about the purpose of the Cross, which leads to a question: What personal message from God can be found in the event of Christ's death on the cross?

- The Cross reveals God's unconditional love for you. Though it was the collective sin of the human race that deserved punishment, God chose to lay this great debt upon one Man—His own Son. He did this as an act of love for you.
- The Cross exemplifies God's awesome power. Jesus' death and resurrection symbolize His ultimate triumph over eternal condemnation. His blood established a new covenant and a chance for all people to spend eternity in the presence of God.

As you meditate upon the event of the Cross, consider God's love, righteousness, faithfulness, and power. In one time-altering moment on the cross, His greatest blessing was poured out to a world thirsty for the saving grace of the one, true God.

Father, thank You that the cross links humanity from Genesis to Revelations and that in doing so it exemplifies your righteousness and faithfulness.

After the Cross

Scripture Reading: John 14:16–19
Key Verse: John 14:6

*Jesus said to him, "I am the way, the truth, and the life.
No one comes to the Father except through Me."*

It is possible that we can walk away from the Holy Spirit's control and endure a life that is less than Spirit filled. This is one of the reasons many believers endure defeated lives even after experiencing great joy for a period after salvation.

The Spirit-filled life is not about how much of the Holy Spirit a believer can gain. At salvation, God indwells you fully, forever, with His Holy Spirit. The Spirit-filled life is about how much of you the Holy Spirit can gain.

Many believers are defeated because they have not been properly taught about the Holy Spirit. Some refer to the Holy Spirit as an "it" and fail to recognize Him as a person. He is a person of the Trinity who comes into the life of the believer at the moment of salvation. There doesn't have to be an accompanying experience, feeling, or manifestation.

The Bible clearly states that the Holy Spirit is a person, and God is not going to equip you with a partial person or with a person who darts in and out of your life based on your successes or failures in the Christian walk. But if we are not taught properly, or if we burn out by attempting to walk and serve in our own power, we naturally are going to become discouraged and defeated.

Praise the Lord that the role of the Spirit is to enable us to live as God desires, after our lives are changed at the Cross.

Holy Spirit, help me to seek not what I can get from You, but what Your power can enable me to do for You.

Our Great Salvation

Scripture Reading: Luke 7:44–48

Key Verse: Luke 7:47

Therefore I say to you, her sins, which are many, are forgiven, for she loved much. But to whom little is forgiven, the same loves little.

Did you ever make a decision that proved to be full of unforeseen consequences? Things can snowball until the final product is far beyond what we could ever have imagined. Sometimes this can be positive and sometimes negative. So it is with Jesus. To accept Him introduces us to unimaginable glories, while to reject Him dooms us to unthinkable misery.

When we first get saved, we have little idea of the scope and depth of our salvation. As we progress to Christian maturity, however, we begin to discover the astonishing power of the gospel. This discovery is facilitated by a genuine understanding of how totally lost we were before Jesus found us. Jesus said that he who is forgiven much loves much (Luke 7:47).

The point is that, through the Cross, we have all been greatly forgiven, but few of us realize how much. If your unsaved heart were put under a divine microscope and you were allowed to fully view its desperate wickedness, you would have little trouble appreciating your great salvation. Any remedy that can present you blameless before the presence of His glory is a remedy that demands our entire life's devotion.

The Bible says that God made us alive together with Christ so "that in the ages to come He might show the exceeding riches of His grace in His kindness toward us in Christ Jesus" (Ephesians 2:7). Apparently these riches are so unsearchable that it will take ages to properly display and understand them, but our gratitude can begin here and now.

Lord, through the Cross You have forgiven me of so much. Thank You for the divine remedy of the Cross that presents me blameless in Your presence.

THE POWER OF THE GOSPEL

SCRIPTURE READING: 1 THESSALONIANS 2:1–12
KEY VERSE: 1 THESSALONIANS 2:4

*But as we have been approved by God to be entrusted with the gospel,
even so we speak, not as pleasing men, but God who tests our hearts.*

By itself, knowledge of the gospel—the power that saves us from our sins by Jesus Christ's death and resurrection—is powerless. In fact, many people have heard the gospel but refuse to believe its truth. It's not until we see the gospel at work in our lives or in the lives of those around us that we realize the power it possesses.

In Paul's letter to the church in Thessalonica, he wrote openly about the gospel and its potential impact in their lives. Just like Paul, we also are entrusted to deliver the message of the gospel. Whether with our mouths or through our actions and deeds, we should always be a witness of the power of the gospel. And here are four points we need to remember about the power of the gospel:

1. It's a superior message. The gospel is more important than anything we've ever heard, because the mind of God is in it.
2. It's a simple message. We can never fathom all the wisdom of God, yet His saving message is easy enough for a child to comprehend.
3. It's a sure message. Anyone from anywhere can be saved when they embrace the gospel.
4. It's a sufficient message. The Bible contains an answer for every trial or situation we encounter.

Lord, thank You for the power of the gospel—that it is superior, simple, sure, and sufficient for all my needs.

THE HEART OF GOD

SCRIPTURE READING: JOHN 3:1–18
KEY VERSE: JOHN 3:17

For God did not send His Son into the world to condemn the world,
but that the world through Him might be saved.

Have you ever wanted to peek into someone's heart—his very spirit—to see what is really going on in there? We all desire this at times; in fact, the more we are able to get glimpses into a person's heart, the better we can determine what kind of man he is. That is a basic way we grow to trust and love other people.

If we want to apply this concept to our relationship with the Lord, we need to look only one place: the Cross. There we can see a perfect picture of God's heart and His view of sin, love, and mankind. The most overwhelming image of the cross is the complete justice of God. The Lord's justice simply means He does the right thing—the righteous thing—in every situation.

When it came to dealing with mankind's sin and wickedness, a problem arose that needed an eternal solution. The issue was the fact that God's perfect holiness stood in complete opposition to man's sinfulness. Because of His unwavering justice, He could not simply ignore our sin. Therefore, He had only two options: either abandon man to his sinfulness or provide a perfect sacrifice to atone for the sin of the world. In His love, He chose the latter.

The cross of Jesus represents the only answer to a cosmic problem. Despite the great cost—His only Son—God worked to bridge the gap caused by sin. With His justice satisfied by Christ's sacrifice, God's eternal love can now welcome us into His holy presence.

Have you trusted Jesus as Savior and acknowledged the sacrifice He made on your behalf?

Lord, I am so grateful for the perfect sacrifice made on my behalf.
Thank You that You did not abandon me in sin.

GOD'S WISDOM REVEALED

SCRIPTURE READING: MATTHEW 28:1–8
KEY VERSE: MATTHEW 28:6

He is not here; for He is risen, as He said.
Come, see the place where the Lord lay.

The message of the Cross doesn't seem to make sense to the world, does it? It is difficult to explain the sheer power of the Cross to an unbeliever simply because that person is on the outside looking in. It is not until we see the issue through the eyes of the Holy Spirit that we begin to fully grasp the wisdom in it.

The apostle Paul explained that the message of the Cross seems like foolishness to the world, but for those of us who are in Christ, it is the very wisdom of God (1 Corinthians 1:18–25). Essentially, God's wisdom reveals how backward thinking the world really is!

The world thinks it has a firm grasp of wisdom, and it also regards Christians as wasting their time going to church and talking about "getting saved." However, these are the very things that can lead the lost into a saving relationship with the heavenly Father.

If it were up to us, we would have done it another way. In fact, every other religion on earth points toward good works as the means of salvation. However, God knew that no amount of good deeds could overcome the debt left by sin. So He acted on our behalf, doing what only He knew was necessary to save our souls.

We may not like to admit it, but God is a lot smarter than we are. He knows what we need before we even ask Him. Therefore, let us thank Him for taking this matter out of our hands and providing that which we could never earn: salvation, forgiveness, and eternal communion with our heavenly Father.

Father, thank You that through the Cross, You provided salvation,
forgiveness, and eternal communion with You.

HE IS ALIVE!

SCRIPTURE READING: MATTHEW 28:9–15
KEY VERSE: MATTHEW 28:10

Then Jesus said to them, "Do not be afraid. Go and tell My brethren to go to Galilee, and there they will see Me."

What must it have felt like for the disciples when Jesus died? They had left everything for this man, followed Him for three years, and built all their hopes and dreams on His ideas. Not only that, but they had heard all the incredible things He said. He told them that He "was" even before Abraham lived. He said that He and the Father were one. He declared He was the only way to God. He had told them such amazing things, but now there He was, hanging on a cross, dead. How could this be?

The disciples were confused, scared, mournful, and completely distraught. Only one thing could have turned them around. Only one thing could have breathed new life into their downtrodden spirits. Praise God, that one vital thing came in the cry of an excited friend running toward them, shouting, "He's alive! He's alive!" Jesus had conquered death.

Believers oftentimes take this news for granted. It seems so commonplace today to speak of the resurrection of Jesus. Our familiarity, however, must never lessen the impact of the declaration, "He's alive!"

For mankind, death had always been the final word, the inescapable end. By achieving victory over death, Jesus proved He was whom He claimed to be. By demonstrating His power over man's greatest fear, He showed Himself to be mankind's greatest friend, Savior, and Lord.

Does your heart leap when you hear the proclamation of the living Lord? Take the clouded church lenses from your eyes and see the story fresh and new: Jesus is alive!

Lord, my heart leaps with joy when I hear the proclamation of Your resurrection. I rejoice that You died for my sins and that You arose again. I declare to a lost world, You are alive!

MAY
Pathway to Prayer

But you, when you pray, go into your room, and when you have shut your door, pray to your Father who is in the secret place; and your Father who sees in secret will reward you openly.

—Matthew 6:6

THE PRIORITY OF PRAYER

SCRIPTURE READING: MATTHEW 6:5–8
KEY VERSE: PROVERBS 15:29

The LORD is far from the wicked,
But He hears the prayer of the righteous.

A few words offered up without much thought—that is what many Christians regard as their "prayer life." Only in times of desperation or great tragedy is any thought put into the words spoken to the God of the universe.

Prayer is so much more than that. It is when we communicate with God, sharing with Him our hearts as He shares His with us. And then we respond to what He says, walking in the direction that He desires for us to go.

Instead of being an afterthought to our busy days, prayer should be a constant. It should be the element of our lives that we establish and maintain with as much diligence as we do getting up in the morning.

Not only did Jesus spend a large portion of His teaching ministry talking about the importance of prayer, He also modeled a life of prayer, escaping often to the mountaintop to commune with God. In our desire to become more like Christ, we can imitate His actions as much as His words. And His actions speak much louder than words in this case.

Jesus realized it was imperative to maintain a constant relationship with His heavenly Father if He was going to obey Him. And He knew that no matter what happened, God would hear Him. "He hears the prayer of the righteous" (Proverbs 15:29).

Lord, I have been careless with my prayers. Help me to take more seriously these conversations with You, so that I can better understand Your will.

WHY PRAY?

SCRIPTURE READING: MATTHEW 6:9–13
KEY VERSE: LUKE 6:12

*Now it came to pass in those days that He went out to the mountain
to pray, and continued all night in prayer to God.*

Have you ever felt like asking God why you should pray? Your world seems to be hanging by a thread. Emotionally, you feel empty. The future looks dim, and just when you think it cannot get any worse, it does. How could prayer help your situation? It is in prayer that we find hope and a solution for every problem we face:

- Prayer readjusts the focus of our hearts and minds. In times of crisis, it is easy to focus on the darkness of the prevailing situation. Prayer causes us to look to a source of help that will never fail us. When we focus our minds on Christ and His ability, our hearts will cease to be anxious. Peace will reign.
- Prayer gives us an opportunity to witness God's involvement in our lives. His greatest desire is to build a personal relationship with each one of us. As we worship Him through prayer, He draws near to us and offers us His assurance and acceptance.
- Prayer helps us understand the love of God. Prayer is our direct line of communication to God. True prayer begins with confession of any sin, and repentance.

There may be times when you wonder, *Why pray? My world is crumbling all around me.* This is the time when you need to pray the most. Prayer is your greatest avenue of hope, because it leads you straight into the throne room of God.

*Lord, I thank You that prayer leads me straight to Your throne room.
I have total access in time of need.*

COMMISSIONED BY PRAYER

SCRIPTURE READING: COLOSSIANS 4:1–4
KEY VERSE: COLOSSIANS 4:2

Continue earnestly in prayer, being vigilant in it with thanksgiving.

In this high-tech world of data and progress, it is important to have fast, clear communication so that mistakes are avoided and redundant operations are kept to a minimum. Bases of operations send out armies of workers to complete specific tasks that work toward a predetermined goal. However, the need for communication is not a new phenomenon. In fact, it was an important concern for the apostle Paul.

The task of spreading the gospel is immense, which is why Paul wrote to the Colossians, "Pray for us, too, that God may open a door for our message, so that we may proclaim the mystery of Christ, for which I am in chains. Pray that I may proclaim it clearly, as I should" (Colossians 4:3–4 NIV). Paul needed to be in touch with the base of operations: the Lord God. Paul knew who gave him his marching orders. Paul understood who had the best view of the plans. He also knew who provided the ability, power, and resources to complete the mission.

Be devoted in prayer so that the gospel may be communicated all over the world. E. Stanley Jones writes, "Prayer is commission. Out of the quietness with God, power is generated that turns the spiritual machinery of the world. When you pray, you begin to feel the sense of being sent, that the divine compulsion is upon you."

Thank You, Lord, for the divine commission of prayer that provides the ability, power, and resources to complete my mission and achieve my destiny.

DEVOTED TO PRAYER

SCRIPTURE READING: PSALM 42:1–11
KEY VERSE: PSALM 42:1

As the deer pants for the water brooks,
So pants my soul for You, O God.

The Lord tells us in His Word that when we seek Him, we will find Him (1 Chronicles 28:9; Jeremiah 29:13). But have you ever thought about what is actually involved in seeking God?

It is not a matter of just attending church or following a certain religious tradition. Seeking God is a matter of the heart. This one activity leads us to cross over from just being a "churchgoer" to becoming a follower of "the way of Christ." We seek Him, not in a mysterious, mythical sense, but through intimate devotion.

In our seeking, we thirst after God, much like the psalmist who wrote, "As the deer pants for the water brooks, so pants my soul for You, O God" (Psalm 42:1). There is a longing to our seeking that ushers us into the presence of God, where we experience the fullness of His love and undivided care for our souls.

Jesus was quick to ask those who followed Him, "Why do you seek Me?" Was it the miracles He performed, or was it the closeness of His presence that drew them? Why do you seek the Lord? Is He an emergency switch you push in times of crisis, or are you truly longing to experience His presence on an intimate level?

God desires your love and devotion. By itself, memorizing amounts of Scripture will not draw you closer to Him. The thing that grabs God's heart is the humble, abiding love of someone who seeks Him above everything else.

Father, I seek You today above all else. My soul pants for You. Usher me into Your presence as I wait before You.

CHRIST–CENTERED PRAYER

SCRIPTURE READING: 2 CHRONICLES 20:1–12
KEY VERSE: 1 THESSALONIANS 5:24

He who calls you is faithful, who also will do it.

Jehoshaphat had admonished Israel to return to the Lord, reminding a rebellious nation of the God who had freed it from bondage in Egypt and sustained it through much adversity. Then came the report that three tribes were mounting an attack on Israel.

Jehoshaphat's response was a godly example not only for Israel but also for us today. The king's first act was to immediately seek the Lord. By doing so, Jehoshaphat inherently demonstrated the knowledge that God is interested in all of man's problems and that nothing is bigger than God.

Becoming a Christian does not give us a free ride from the problems of life. When we encounter trouble, our first response always should be to seek the Lord. God will give us a solution to the problem in His timing. We may have to wait for His answer. The wait may be long. He often uses such times to mold our character and to teach us principles He knows we lack. Sometimes, we're not ready for His perfect answer, so He has to prepare us. Finally, God's answer to our Christ-centered (not problem-centered) prayers usually requires an act of faith on our part.

Sometimes, as with having a choir lead an army into battle, His plans won't immediately make sense. But they are perfect. "He who calls you is faithful, who also will do it" (1 Thessalonians 5:24).

You are faithful, Lord. You will do it in Your timing as You promised.

LEARNING TO PRAY

SCRIPTURE READING: JOHN 17:1–26
KEY VERSE: JOHN 17:20

*I do not pray for these alone, but also for those who
will believe in Me through their word.*

Do you have a friend upon whom you call when you are discouraged or
when you have good news to share? Do you have someone with whom
you can converse and confide?

Think about this person for a moment. When you speak with him or
her, you probably discuss specific information about the concerns, needs, and
victories in your life.

This type of pointed conversation with someone who cares about you is
not frightening or difficult, is it? Of course not. Unfortunately, many people
approach conversation with God with unnecessary apprehension.

Praying to God does not require the use of eloquent language or carefully
constructed dialogue. Rather, God simply wants to communicate with you.
Prayer should be a natural expression of the feelings, thoughts, and emotions
you experience throughout your day.

If you truly desire to develop or enhance your prayer life, begin by talking
to God as you would to your trusted friend. He loves to hear from you and is
pleased when you reach out to Him. Bring your praises to Him and await His
response. Present your concerns and ask for His advice. Lift up your inquiries
before God today and seek His wisdom.

*Lord, would You teach me to make prayer more of a conversation
and less of an exercise? Help me to get past the language part of it
and communicate with the heart.*

PURSUING GOD

*Ask, and it will be given to you; seek, and you will find;
knock, and it will be opened to you.*

As youngsters, many of us learned to recite one or more "children's prayers." Believers and nonbelievers alike can easily recall the familiar verses of "Now I lay me down to sleep" and "God is great, God is good." In our formative years, it is vitally important to grasp the concept of communication with God. However, as we mature in our spiritual lives, these elementary, repetitive prayers seem to lose their value.

What, then, is the best way for a growing Christian to speak with God? Examine the text of Matthew 7:7–11. These encouraging words are meant to inspire prayer. Verses 7 and 8 advise us to ask, seek, and knock in order that we may receive, find, and have doors opened to us. Verses 9–11 reassure us that God's intent is never to harm us, but rather to give us things that are good for us.

What can we learn from this passage? Clearly, God wants us to pursue Him in our prayers and our actions, with confidence in His ability to meet our needs. Yet pursuing God (asking, seeking, and knocking) requires active participation. Our heavenly Father wants to be known. To truly know Him, we must seek His countenance, wisdom, character, and will for our lives. As you seek God, pray with originality and zeal. Pray actively from your heart, instead of passively from your memory.

Lord, help me to seek all that You are, in my prayers. In asking, seeking, and knocking, may I pursue You and Your will.

IN JESUS' NAME

SCRIPTURE READING: JOHN 14:11–14
KEY VERSES: JOHN 14:13–14

And whatever you ask in My name, that I will do, that the Father may be glorified in the Son. If you ask anything in My name, I will do it.

In Jesus' name. These powerful words are often used to close the prayers of the faithful and the obedient. There is power in the holy name of Jesus, and we are clearly instructed to use it in prayer.

As Jesus prepared to depart from earth, He gave this instruction: "Whatever you ask in My name, that I will do, that the Father may be glorified in the Son. If you ask anything in My name, I will do it" (John 14:13–14). This passage, however, is often misinterpreted. Simply tacking on the name of Jesus to the end of any prayer will not guarantee a desired result. When we carefully examine these verses, we find two qualifying situations: "that the Father may be glorified" and "in My name."

Essentially, prayers in Jesus' name must glorify God and parallel the things Jesus Himself would ask. Think of attaching the name of Jesus to your prayers as making a request on behalf of someone you love. For example, if your mother would not approve of a decision, would you make it in her name? Most likely not.

As you seek to strengthen your prayer life, carefully examine your requests to God. Do they bring glory to Him? Are they based upon ideals, values, and principles that Jesus would support?

Lord Jesus, when I ask for things in Your name, help me to understand that it is only in Your name when it is also the Father's will.

PRAYERFUL PLANNING

SCRIPTURE READING: LUKE 14:26–33
KEY VERSE: LUKE 14:28

For which of you, intending to build a tower, does not sit down first and count the cost, whether he has enough to finish it?

Have you made a financial plan for your future? Whether you are young or old, married or single, it is important to establish security for the years ahead.

As we examine today's Scripture passage, we find that there is biblical basis for wise planning. As Jesus spoke poignantly to the crowds around Him, He questioned, "Which of you, intending to build a tower, does not sit down first and count the cost, whether he has enough to finish it?" (Luke 14:28).

Jesus, along with His followers, was familiar with the ridicule persons could receive from failing to complete a project due to poor planning. With this in mind, He encouraged His listeners to include careful calculations in their future plans.

How can you incorporate this advice into your own life? First, realize that God expects us to not only trust Him but also actively make plans under His counsel. Second, we should study the Scriptures to develop a Christ-centered strategy of financial protection. Finally, we must subject our financial matters to the lordship of Jesus Christ.

Praying over decisions that will affect your future, and possibly the future of your children, is essential. "Be anxious for nothing, but in everything by prayer and supplication, with thanksgiving, let your requests be made known to God" (Philippians 4:6).

As you plan with God's will in mind, He will honor your diligence and obedience.

Lord, be at the heart of my planning so that I may be wise with my resources, but follow the leadings of Your will.

READY TO RECEIVE

SCRIPTURE READING: 1 PETER 5:5–9
KEY VERSES: 1 PETER 5:6–7

*Therefore humble yourselves under the mighty hand of God,
that He may exalt you in due time, casting all your
care upon Him, for He cares for you.*

Your morning begins with a problem. You turn on the shower but no water comes out. In frustration, you pick up the phone to call the repairman. However, when you dial the number, no one answers the phone. Now you have reached your breaking point. But your anger is justified, isn't it? After all, you need a solution to your problem, and you need it right now.

In our fast-paced world, we have become accustomed to receiving messages, money, packages, and answers almost instantaneously. This may be why it is difficult for so many Christians to wait upon the Lord. When we lift our prayers to Him, we oftentimes treat God like the faucet repairman— He should be ready and waiting to fix our problems in a moment's notice.

Though God is always with us through the presence of the Holy Spirit (John 14:16), He answers our prayers in a time frame determined by His divine will and plan for our lives (1 Peter 5:6–7).

Why does He do this? It is not to make our lives more difficult. Instead, it is to encourage us to trust Him and to rely upon Him completely. God is faithful to answer our prayers, but His answers come when we are truly ready to receive them.

When you feel anxious about an unanswered prayer, don't give up or get angry. Rather, seek God with a patient heart, and trust His timing.

Lord, I am finite and impatient. I am used to instant responses. Help me to wait on You, and in the waiting, understand that You operate outside our time frame.

SPIRITUAL BENEFITS OF PRAYER

SCRIPTURE READING: PSALM 69:13–18

KEY VERSE: PSALM 69:13

But as for me, my prayer is to You,
O LORD, in the acceptable time;
O God, in the multitude of Your mercy,
Hear me in the truth of Your salvation.

Perhaps your conversations with the Lord began as bedtime prayers when you were a child. Maybe you learned the Lord's Prayer in Sunday school. Throughout your life, the Bible, your pastor, and Bible teachers have stressed the importance of praying to God.

But how do you really feel about prayer? Is it something you do hurriedly out of obligation, or do you truly enjoy conversing with your heavenly Father many times throughout the day? Discovering the spiritual benefits of prayer may help you to understand the great things that can be accomplished by talking to God:

- Prayer deepens our relationship with Jesus Christ. It helps us to understand the character of the loving God we serve.
- Prayer purifies our lives. By confessing our sins and leaving them at God's feet, we can be relieved of unnecessary guilt and shame.
- Prayer helps us to trust God as our provider. As life's pressures increase, we will anticipate our times of fellowship with Him.
- Prayer leads to spiritual growth and maturity. The more time we spend with God, the more equipped we will be to help others and to weather the storms in our own lives.

If you are currently a "dutiful" pray-er, reach out to God in a new way today. Ask Him to show you the joys of being a dedicated prayer warrior.

Lord, I surrender to You my sense of duty in my prayer life, and ask in return that You infuse it with the trust and purity that leads to maturity.

PRAYER IN DIFFICULT TIMES

SCRIPTURE READING: PHILIPPIANS 1:27–30
KEY VERSE: PHILIPPIANS 1:29

*For to you it has been granted on behalf of Christ, not only
to believe in Him, but also to suffer for His sake.*

Many people mistakenly believe that faith in Jesus Christ can and will free their lives from the painful rigors of this fallen world. The apostle Paul took the opposite stance. Rather than denying the fact that Christians face even more difficulties than unbelievers, Paul boldly proclaimed a guarantee that believers will suffer in various ways. He exclaimed, "For to you it has been granted for Christ's sake, not only to believe in Him, but also to suffer for His sake" (Philippians 1:29 NASB). At first glance, this statement may seem outdated or misinformed. However, there are two things that we must remember about living as a Christian in today's world.

First, it is important to realize that a Christ-centered faith is not the focus of modern society. Our self-centered world is suspicious of anyone who claims to "love" others unconditionally.

Second, we must remember that martyrdom is not a thing of the past. Many Christians around the world still are killed because of their faith. Our faith is not a shield from suffering.

However, most importantly, our faith does put us in contact with the One who is more than able to lead us through the difficulties. If you are experiencing a season of hardship, do not delay. Take your problems to the cross right now.

*Lord, if I face hardship in my Christian life, let it be because of my
faith in You and not because of bad behavior carried out in Your
name.*

SOLVING PROBLEMS THROUGH PRAYER

SCRIPTURE READING: GALATIANS 6:2–5
KEY VERSE: GALATIANS 6:2

Bear one another's burdens, and so fulfill the law of Christ.

Hi, Bill. How's your brother doing?" Tom asked.

Bill replied, "I suppose he is fine. I haven't heard otherwise."

We often overhear exchanges like this, but have you ever stopped to consider what they mean? The implication is that while good things in a person's life may go by without fanfare, problems will usually be known well by everyone around. People simply enjoy talking about hardships because they make such dramatic stories.

Why is this so? Could it be that others discuss our problems so much because that is what we emphasize in our lives? Are we quicker to discuss our trials than our joys? Within a loving family or church body, it is appropriate and natural to share our concerns with others (Galatians 6:2). We do this so that others may be aware of our circumstances in order to pray specifically for our needs. However, when we become best known for our worries, it is almost impossible for anyone to perceive our joy in Christ.

Jesus takes our hardships quite seriously, and so should we. However, we must view our problems through the lens of our saving relationship with Christ. If you are suffering beneath immense obstacles, make sure that you are discussing the matter with Him more than anyone else. Only He has the power to solve every problem, every time.

Lord, only You have the power to solve my problems. Let me turn to You first in prayer, instead of talking to others.

READY WHEN CALLED

SCRIPTURE READING: PSALM 55:1–9

KEY VERSE: PSALM 55:1

Give ear to my prayer, O God,
And do not hide Yourself from my supplication.

The toddler climbed to the top step of the plastic slide in the backyard and lifted one leg onto the top platform. It left him straddled, one leg on the top of the slide and the other on the top step. His coordination was still undeveloped enough that he was trapped. He couldn't move either leg.

"Daaaaaddyyyyy!"

The toddler knew exactly what to do next. In his moment of complete helplessness, with fear setting in as he was stranded several feet above the ground, he called for his daddy. Watching nearby, the dad moved in to save the day.

What child wouldn't immediately cry out to the nearest authority? What father wouldn't act quickly in such a situation?

When hit with a trial, or when bad news comes our way, our most effective response is to immediately say, "Father." Not only does this immediately stunt the problem from growing into something that overwhelms us, but it reminds us of our rightful position as children of God. Our Father says He will never leave us or forsake us. Armed with such a promise, we know that God is under His own divine obligation to provide us guidance and direction.

There will be many times when life will leave us stretched into an awkward position. We should always remember that our Father is watching nearby, ready to act when called.

Father, I praise You that You are always there. When life stretches me into awkward positions, You are ready to act when I call.

PRAYER IS ESSENTIAL

SCRIPTURE READING: PSALM 55:9–22
KEY VERSE: PSALM 55:22

Cast your burden on the LORD,
And He shall sustain you;
He shall never permit the righteous to be moved.

Prayer was a priority in Jesus' life. He communed with His Father continually. In fact, prayer is an essential priority in the life of everyone mightily used by God—every person who is walking in the Spirit and living a holy life.

When our time alone with God is no longer a priority, we open ourselves to discouragement, doubt, disillusionment, and eventually disaster. When we no longer fellowship with Him, we begin to feel the spiritual, emotional, and physical weight of our earthly circumstances.

Prayer lifts up our burdens so that we don't have to bear their weight. Whether they are given to us by the Lord in order to teach us, or self-imposed as a result of the decisions we make, God tells us to cast our burdens upon Him. Bearing the weight of burdens we were not intended to carry not only takes a spiritual toll on us but leaves us physically and emotionally beaten as well.

Satan knows that tired and weary Christians are prime targets for his attacks. First, he strikes with discouragement. When we lose hope, we are primed and ready for his next weapon—doubt. A doubting Christian can easily be pushed into discouragement. Listening to the devil's proclamations, "Where is God?" and "The Christian life doesn't work!" can breed disaster.

Therefore, prayer is not only a comfort in times of need; it is essential for your survival. It guided Jesus through His life. Let it guide you.

Lord, I am burdened by so many things. I am sorry for thinking I can carry these on my own. Please take them and walk me through each difficult situation.

THE PRICE OF PRAYERLESSNESS

SCRIPTURE READING: PSALM 102:1–17
KEY VERSE: JAMES 4:8

Draw near to God and He will draw near to you. Cleanse your hands,
you sinners; and purify your hearts, you double-minded.

Have you ever considered the fact that each one of us pays a price when we allow our prayer lives to fall by the wayside? Of course this is not a monetary price; instead, it is a spiritual price.

When we fail to make prayer a priority—essentially forfeiting our time alone with God—we will begin to feel an emptiness in our lives, accompanied by a strange sense of unrest and uneasiness. In contrast, when our prayer lives are active, the weight of these burdens will be lifted from our shoulders by the mighty hand of the almighty God.

With this in mind, why would anyone choose to cease praying? The sad truth is that many of us have become so accustomed to weariness and hardship that we feel lost or uncomfortable without it. Yet, if we continue to nurture this style of living, we will begin to rely upon ourselves instead of upon God, thereby making ourselves vulnerable and at risk for disaster.

The clear solution, then, to avoid these difficulties is to place high priority upon our fellowship and communication with God. After all, we must be in contact with our heavenly Father in order to hear His voice and to understand and follow His will for our lives.

If you have allowed distance to come between you and your heavenly Father, confess this to Him today. When you renew your prayer life—the most important piece of your Christian walk—you will once again be able to experience God's blessings and His best for your life.

Father, I have deliberately distanced myself from You by withdrawing
from my prayer time. I am sorry. I surrender this burden of walking
alone and seek again Your face.

LIFTING OUR LEVEL OF PRAYER

SCRIPTURE READING: EPHESIANS 1:18–23
KEY VERSE: EPHESIANS 1:18

. . . that you may know what is the hope of His calling, what are the riches of the glory of His inheritance in the saints.

Have you ever wondered why church prayer meetings tend to have low turnouts? Think about it: When the church holds a Bible study, concert, or picnic, many people show up. But prayer meetings often slip to the bottom of attendance records.

Perhaps it is because many of us assume in advance how the meeting will go. "It will be too depressing," we say to ourselves. "I can't handle hearing all of the heartbreaking prayer requests for sick children, terminally ill relatives, and church members in financial turmoil."

If you identify with these sentiments, you are not alone. Prayer meetings that support only one aspect of prayer are imbalanced and can quickly be awash in negativity. To correct this problem, we must embrace all aspects of prayer. In the first chapter of Ephesians, Paul provided a wonderful starting point. He reminded us of the motivation behind prayer—communicating with the One who is in control of all things. In Ephesians 1:18, Paul wrote, "I pray that the eyes of your heart may be enlightened, so that you will know what is the hope of His calling" (NASB).

Though lifting our troubles and needs to God is both acceptable and important, we should never forget to express our thankfulness, jubilance, and praise to Him in prayer.

The next time you participate in a group prayer session, speak up with a bold heart and give honor to the almighty God. Your prayer will likely be a welcome reminder to others.

Lord, help me to influence prayer time at my church so that it is a healthy representation of the full Christian life, from supplication to praise.

THREE ELEMENTS OF PRAYER

SCRIPTURE READING: COLOSSIANS 4:2–6
KEY VERSE: COLOSSIANS 4:2

Continue earnestly in prayer, being vigilant in it with thanksgiving.

How would you assess your prayer life in its current state? Do you pray regularly? Are your prayers answered by God? If you find that you are less than satisfied with your times of fellowship with God, do not become discouraged. Many believers struggle to maximize their prayer lives, but the Bible has many wonderful tips for improvement:

- We must devote ourselves to prayer (Colossians 4:2–4). We are to pray without ceasing, and with the expectation of seeing results. Devoting ourselves to prayer means making time for listening to the Father as well as for talking to Him.
- We must stay alert in prayer (Ephesians 6:18–19). This means we must be aware as we pray. What should we be aware of? The schemes of Satan. The enemy wants to distract you from prayer. He wants your mind to drift and your heart to be troubled. If we expect these things, we can counteract them by focusing more intently on the task before us—communicating with God.
- We should pray with a spirit of thanksgiving (Colossians 3:16–17). We should never forget to thank God for the goodness He has shown us, or for the goodness He will show us in the future. Thank Him for listening, for His faithfulness, and for the answer He will bring.

Begin incorporating these three elements into your prayer life as soon as possible, and wait in faith for God to honor your efforts.

Lord, give me a heart to pray without ceasing, the stamina to stay in focus, and a spirit of thanksgiving for Your faithfulness.

Results of Prayer

Scripture Reading: Luke 18:1–5
Key Verse: Luke 18:1

*Then He spoke a parable to them, that men always
ought to pray and not lose heart.*

Yesterday we discussed three elements that will make our prayers more effective. Today, let's talk about the results we can expect from our efforts toward improvement.

There are ten things that should accompany devoted prayer:

1. A growing relationship with Christ
2. A change in perspective: God's versus your own
3. A positive faith attitude
4. Peace in the midst of pressure
5. A purifying effect on you morally
6. Spiritual growth in every area of your life
7. A passion to obey God
8. Reliance upon God to meet every need
9. Power in your service for God
10. Productivity in every area of life

What do you think about this list? Are you seeing some of the results mentioned above? Whether you are gaining victory in one area or all ten, you can be certain that, as you devote yourself to prayer, God will allow amazing things to happen in your life. He will use you in ways you never thought possible, and you will discover a relationship with Him that is indescribable.

Prayer is so simple. Truly, it is the act of communicating openly with God. It is a matter of giving time to the Father to let Him do in your life what He chooses to do. Are you ready to take your prayer life to a higher level? God is listening because He loves you.

*Lord, help me to recognize that I can gain far more depth of character
from spending time with You that I ever will by reading how-to books.*

In Times of Trial

SCRIPTURE READING: PSALM 25:1–7

KEY VERSE: PSALM 25:1

To You, O LORD, I lift up my soul.

No matter whether you are saved or unsaved, you can be certain that you will face problems in life. Because we live in a fallen world, we can expect trouble. But once you become a child of God, you have the tremendous asset of a loving heavenly Father to guide you. He will strengthen you to face any problem you will encounter.

Since you do not know what the future holds, perhaps the best way to prepare for a crisis is to seek the Lord when your life is problem free. When you become accustomed to seeking God during the good times, then your first response to a problem will become, "Father . . ." Calling out to the Lord during both ups and downs reminds us of our position as children of God.

So many people make the mistake of deciding on a course of action before praying to discover the mind of God. Bad choices can be easily avoided by going to our heavenly Father first. We should never let anyone push us into moving forward until we have heard from God. And we can be sure that when we call upon the Lord, He will be faithful to answer.

Sometimes His answer will come in a personal revelation or through godly teaching. Or it could come in the form of advice from a Christian friend. But most often, God reveals His will to us through His Word.

Are you facing a trial? Release it to the Lord in prayer, and He will help you overcome it.

Lord, Your will is a mystery that becomes clearer when I spend time in Your presence. Help me to seek Your counsel in good times, so that I recognize it in difficult ones.

HAVE YOU TALKED TO GOD?

SCRIPTURE READING: PSALM 105:1–5
KEY VERSE: PSALM 105:1

Oh, give thanks to the LORD!
Call upon His name;
Make known His deeds among the peoples!

When problems face us, we frequently try to figure out the solution ourselves. If we can patch it up, glue it down, or tape it on, we attempt to do so. Other times, we'll call someone to ask for a solution, but we are actually seeking sympathy and support to make ourselves feel better. Sometimes what we really need is for somebody to say, "Well, I appreciate you calling me, but have you talked to God about it? Have you prayed?"

Solving problems should begin with seeking the Lord before there is a crisis. In times of peace, we will experience the joy and contentedness that comes from worshiping God, reading His Word, and communicating with Him. When we set our hearts toward the Lord, our faith is strengthened, and we develop godly habits that sustain us through trials. We will awaken each morning thinking about God and talking to Him. We will ask God throughout the day about His plans for us and will act accordingly. Prayer will become our customary response.

Then, whenever we face any kind of problem, our first thought will be, "Father." In that one word, we acknowledge our relationship with Him, our awareness of His presence, and our dependence upon Him. God loves to hear His name on our lips, and He promises to respond to the prayer that follows.

But what if you are presently in the midst of trouble but haven't been seeking Him consistently? Begin now by humbly confessing this to God. Receive His forgiveness and then take every situation to Him in prayer.

Father, forgive me for trying to solve my problems without first seeking Your wisdom. Write Your name on my lips so that I may call on You first.

Requirements for Answered Prayer

SCRIPTURE READING: PSALM 66:1–18
KEY VERSE: PSALM 66:18

If I regard iniquity in my heart,
The Lord will not hear.

Is there something in your life that you have prayed for repeatedly? Perhaps your prayers are for a mended relationship, a job offer, or healing. Whatever your need may be, the Bible provides us with five requirements for answered prayer.

1. Complete dependence on Christ as the only grounds upon which we can claim blessing (John 14:13–14). We cannot rely on our personal merit for answered prayer. Instead, we must trust in Jesus alone.
2. Separation from all known sin (Psalm 66:18). If we continue in sin, God will not answer our prayers. To do so would be to condone our sinfulness.
3. Faith in God's word of promise (Hebrews 11:6). It is important to understand the difference between God's unconditional and conditional promises, and which ones are affected by our obedience.
4. Asking in accordance with His will (1 John 5). We must pray in God's will for our prayers to be answered. To know His heart, we must consult His Word and pray.
5. Persistence in our request (Luke 18:1–8). God wants us to continue in prayer until our request is answered or until He says, "I have something better." God is willing to answer our prayers, and He asks us to come boldly before the throne.

Cleanse my heart, Lord, of wrongdoing, so that I can surrender to Your will in prayer and depend completely on Your grace.

A Matter to Pray About

SCRIPTURE READING: ISAIAH 58:11–12
KEY VERSE: 2 PETER 1:3

*. . . as His divine power has given to us all things that pertain
to life and godliness, through the knowledge of Him who
called us by glory and virtue.*

Have you evaluated your spiritual life lately? If you did a thorough assessment of your perspective of God, you might be surprised by what you find.

Millions of Christians have received Christ as their Savior, but still give in to the allure of sin. Faith becomes merely a habit or an accessory, rather than a heart conviction and a way of life. When pulled in two directions, such people compromise themselves because they are convinced that they can't live the way Christ did.

There are several reasons for this kind of erroneous thinking:

- They are probably ignorant of God's Word and the power He gives us to live out authentic Christianity.
- They may think that their behavior is acceptable because they see other Christians living the same way—they are looking at their friends, not at Christ.
- Those who refuse to surrender completely to the Lord will never know the power of His Spirit to overcome sin.

If you struggle with any of these issues, remember that you are a new creation in Christ. You can draw strength from God's divine nature, which lives in you (2 Peter 1:3). It is available for the asking.

When you pray today, ask God to extinguish your love for the world and to replace it with a love for Him and His Word. Pray for Him to fill you with His Spirit so that you can discern wisely. "You will be . . . like a spring of water whose waters never fail" (Isaiah 58:11 NIV).

Father, extinguish my love for the world. Replace it with a love for You and Your Word. Fill me with Your Spirit so I can discern wisely.

How to Talk with God

SCRIPTURE READING: PSALM 116:1–19
KEY VERSE: PSALM 116:1

I love the LORD, because He has heard
My voice and my supplications.

Some people are afraid to ask God for the "little things." They think that somehow He is too big and too busy to care about the trivialities of their lives. Nothing could be further from the truth.

Catherine Marshall explains in her book *Adventures in Prayer*:

Oddly, we who are afraid to ask that the pain of rheumatism be removed or a lost contact lens be found often do not hesitate to pray for world peace or the salvation of souls or a revival to change the face of our time. It never occurs to us that if God's power is lacking for these everyday prayers, His power to handle big, all-inclusive petitions will be lacking too.

In order to make sure that we are not retreating from the tension of faith, it is helpful to ask ourselves as we pray, "Do I really expect anything to happen?" This will prevent us from going window-shopping in prayer. At times window-shopping can be enjoyable—but there it ends. . . .

So we decide to ask His help with some small immediate need. Our asking is like stepping into a tiny anteroom. Taking a hesitant step forward, we discover that the anteroom leads into the King's spacious reception hall.

To our astonishment, the King Himself comes forward to meet us, offering a gift so momentous as to be worthy only of the King.

Lord, thank You for being present in the small details of my life, for it is in finding You in the little things that I find courage to bring You the large ones.

Does Your Prayer Honor God?

Scripture Reading: 1 Thessalonians 5:16–22
Key Verse: 1 Thessalonians 5:17

Pray without ceasing.

The believer's two most important spiritual disciplines are Bible study and prayer. It is impossible to grow continually in Christ without practicing both. Prayer is the primary means by which we talk to God, and also a way He grows us: it is through prayer that we petition the Lord and trust Him for the answer. In this way, we learn to listen to Him, just as we learn to wait for His answer. And He loves for us to put Him in His proper place of honor through the spiritual act of worship called prayer.

Indeed, prayer is one of the best ways in which we can honor God. When we pray to our heavenly Father, we are acknowledging that He is God, that He truly is the high and exalted One who lives forever and whose name is Holy. God alone deserves glory, and we ascribe honor to Him when we pray continually—that is, maintain a God-ward attitude throughout the day, asking Him to govern every detail of our lives (1 Thessalonians 5:17).

Our heavenly Father dwells both on a high and holy place and also with the contrite and lowly in spirit. This means that our motives and the condition of our hearts are very important in prayer. Simply wanting to "get our way" is not the spirit of prayer that honors God. Furthermore, it does not produce prayers that God will answer. The Lord longs for an intimate relationship with us, and time spent in communication is the best way to grow close to Him.

Lord, examine the motives and condition of my heart. I want to exalt You in Your proper place of honor. Make me lowly in spirit.

Ask, Seek, Knock

Scripture Reading: 2 Timothy 2:11–13
Key Verse: 2 Timothy 2:13

If we are faithless, He remains faithful; He cannot deny Himself.

Those who ask will receive answers. Those who seek will find. Those who knock will find the door opened for them. It is God's acrostic: A-S-K: Ask, Seek, Knock.

The Lord wants us to pray to Him, not only because it honors Him, but also because it helps us to grow in Him. Furthermore, prayer taps us into His work in the world. At any given moment, you can pray for anyone anywhere on earth and have confidence that the Lord of the entire universe will hear you and respond in the most effective fashion.

For this reason, prayer is one of the best ways to get involved in God's mission. What a wonderful privilege it is to be able to participate in the expansion of God's kingdom by asking the Lord to help His children and impact His creation.

Another reason the Lord bids us to pray is to build our faith in Him. Even sinful men give gifts to their children. How much more does the holy God enjoy giving good gifts to those who ask Him? (Matthew 7:11). He enjoys helping us along in our faith as we learn His Word, practice His presence, and stay so close to Him that His thoughts become our thoughts. He also loves to answer our prayers and see us become bolder in our walk and witness.

God's Word tells us that He is faithful because He cannot deny Himself (2 Timothy 2:13). Be certain to set aside time daily to talk to Him, and you will learn this truth firsthand.

Father, teach me to ask, seek, and knock—to persevere in prayer until I receive an answer.

ANSWERED PRAYER

SCRIPTURE READING: JOHN 16:23–27
KEY VERSE: JOHN 16:24

Until now you have asked nothing in My name. Ask,
and you will receive, that your joy may be full.

We can be assured that God will answer our prayers in Jesus' name because of our

- Association: After salvation, we have a new relationship with God through His Son Jesus. Our association with Christ makes it possible to have intimacy with God the Father.
- Access: We can come to God's throne of grace with boldness and confidence. The reason is that Jesus' death and resurrection blotted out our sin problem and cleared the way for us to have unhindered access to God the Father.
- Authority: Because of the shed blood of Jesus, believers are coheirs with Him (Romans 8:17), identified eternally with God's holy Son. As such, we are delegated His authority and have the right to pray in Christ's name. Jesus, who sits at the right hand of the Father, gives us this privilege.
- Agreement: To pray in Christ's name, we not only must have His authority but also be in agreement with Him. If we ask for something outside of God's will, we can be assured that it will not be granted. Our request must be in keeping with the character of God and the content of His Word. Essentially, when we ask something in Jesus' name, we are saying that we believe Jesus Himself would make the same petition, were He in our situation.
- Assurance: Asking "in Jesus' name" means praying in confidence. Jesus meant it when He said He would give us what we ask—as long as we are in association and agreement with Him.

Lord, thank You for answered prayer! I claim the access, authority, agreement, and assurance that makes this knowledge a reality.

THE CONTENT OF PRAYER

SCRIPTURE READING: COLOSSIANS 1:9–13
KEY VERSE: COLOSSIANS 1:9

*For this reason we also, since the day we heard it, do not cease to pray
for you, and to ask that you may be filled with the knowledge of His
will in all wisdom and spiritual understanding.*

While reading today's Scripture passage from Colossians, ask yourself:
What specific things about Paul's prayer life made them worthy of
inclusion in God's Word? As you study, you may want to consider this out-
line of five elements Paul used to keep his prayer life active and fresh:

1. Paul made specific requests. Instead of using phrases like "God,
   bless everyone in the world," Paul prayed for tangible, measurable
   things, such as patience, strength, and wisdom for specific people.
2. Paul asked for big, "God-sized" things. Nothing was out of the
   question for the God of the universe.
3. His prayers were always Christ-centered. Never selfish, Paul
   petitioned God with a servant's heart, demonstrating submission
   and humility.
4. His prayers were kingdom-related. Paul's ultimate goal in prayer
   always centered on God's kingdom being increased.
5. Paul's prayers brought glory to God. Paul remembered to recognize
   and give thanks to God for His faithfulness.

How does your prayer life compare with the attributes on this list? Is
there an area in which you need strength or improvement? If you are unsure,
take time to ask God for specific insight and guidance today.

*Lord, I need courage to trust You with the specifics of the needs that
are laid on my heart. In sharing the details, let me also seek Your
will, not mine.*

A LIFE-CHANGING PRAYER

SCRIPTURE READING: 1 CORINTHIANS 3:10–15

KEY VERSE: 1 CORINTHIANS 3:13

Each one's work will become clear; for the Day will declare it,
because it will be revealed by fire; and the fire will test
each one's work, of what sort it is.

The prayer that the apostle Paul offered for the church is a powerful model for any believer to follow on behalf of others. This life-changing prayer will impact you as well as those whom you lift to the Father, asking that they

- May be filled with the knowledge of God's will. One of the major steps of knowing God's will is knowing His Word, which provides guidance in every imaginable situation. You are asking God to make clear His perfect and precise will for every decision. He numbers the hairs of our heads, so He certainly has an interest in the details of our lives, including every decision we make.

- May walk in a manner worthy of the Lord. First Corinthians 3:10–15 details the believer's judgment, when Christ will determine whether the weight of the believer's life was more eternal than temporal. When you ask the Lord to help someone walk in a manner worthy of Him, you are asking Him to help make that person's life count for eternity. Refined gold, silver, and precious stones— whatever we have done in the Spirit—are worth exponentially more than the ashes produced by a life of wood, hay, and straw.

- May bear fruit in every good work. When Christ is the center of your life, then your character, conduct, and conversation should bear fruit unto His kingdom. Asking God for His Holy Spirit's assistance is an indication of a sincere desire to live for the Lord and obey His Word.

Lord, I want to be filled with the knowledge of Your will. I want to walk in a manner worthy of You. I want to bear fruit in every good work.

ASK FOR THESE!

SCRIPTURE READING: PSALM 5:1–12
KEY VERSES: PSALM 5:1–2

Give ear to my words, O LORD,
Consider my meditation.
Give heed to the voice of my cry,
My King and my God,
For to You I will pray.

As we continue to learn about prayer, there are three important elements that we should incorporate into our intercession. We all should ask that we and other believers

- may increase in the knowledge of God. By knowing more about Jesus and drawing closer to Him, we will catch a greater vision of God, and as a result, will love Him. This passage is essentially a prayer to help us obey His Word, because those who love Him keep His commandments (John 14:15).
- may be strengthened and sustained with the power of God. The church is weakened any time we attempt to do something in our own strength. Our most successful efforts come not by power or might, but by God's Holy Spirit (Zechariah 4:6). His peace and presence are required if we are to live victoriously, regardless of circumstances.
- may give thanks of His salvation. We have qualified as saints of God because—and only because—He has qualified us. He chose us. He sent His Son to die for us. He gave us the gift of faith. He forgave us. He redeemed us. He reconciled us. He justified us. He is sanctifying us. And He will glorify us. Our part is to thankfully obey Him and live for Him every single day.

Lord, I pray that I will increase in knowledge and be strengthened and sustained by Your power . . . I thank You for my salvation.

PREPARATION BY PRAYER

SCRIPTURE READING: PSALM 31:1–5
KEY VERSE: PSALM 31:1

In You, O LORD, I put my trust;
Let me never be ashamed;
Deliver me in Your righteousness.

When you hear the word *preparation*, what comes to your mind? Do you think about life insurance, studying for a test, or maybe even packing all the necessary equipment before a camping trip? Of course, all of these things are acts of preparation.

When we prepare beforehand, we consider all possible outcomes and make sure that we will have what we need when the time comes. We explore any potential problems and arrive at a solution "just in case." After all, no one wants to be caught up in an unexpected situation with no idea of what to do.

Yet do we approach our spiritual lives with the same forethought, or do we tend to take more of a haphazard approach? All too often, we overlook "gearing up" before heading into unknown territory. If it makes sense to prepare for a simple camping trip, how much more important it must be to prepare for our very lives!

We make this preparation by spending time with the Lord. Too many people call upon the name of God only in times of stress; however, if you want to be ready for crisis, then you must seek the Lord when there is no problem at all. In these precious moments of prayer and reflection, we have the opportunity to calmly dwell in the Word, focusing on an intimate relationship with our heavenly Father. These are the occasions for girding up our strength and laying a solid foundation in the Word that will provide sure footing later on, when troubles come our way.

Lord, help me to draw aside each day to spend time with You. I want to be prepared for this life and eternity.

JUNE
Pathway to Faith

By faith Abraham obeyed when he was called to go out to the place which he would receive as an inheritance. And he went out, not knowing where he was going.

—Hebrews 11:8

THE PATHWAY OF FAITH

SCRIPTURE READING: GENESIS 12:1–9
KEY VERSE: GENESIS 12:1

Now the LORD had said to Abram: "Get out of your country, from your family and from your father's house, to a land that I will show you."

No one would have blamed Abram if he immediately began making to-do lists upon hearing the Lord's command to leave his country. After residing in Haran for seventy-five years, Abram would have had extensive details to care for and many ties to resolve.

The task for both Abram and Sarai must have been dizzying. Not only was the overall mission overwhelming, but they were also responsible for the daunting duty of caring for their entourage.

Great missions and trials are always accompanied by mountains of details. In fact, sometimes it is the smallest issue that is the most devastating discouragement to the believer. However, God cares for everything in our lives. R. A. Torrey counsels, "If our troubles are large enough to vex and endanger our welfare, they are large enough to touch God's heart of love."

You may believe that your situation is too small to bring before God. However, the pathway of faith is trusting God for every facet and feature of your life. Have confidence that He cares for you even in the smallest issues, and you will find how abundant His great love for you really is.

Lord, thank You for caring about the small details of my life. I get lost in all the miniscule tasks, but You have room in Your heart for all of them.

WALKING BY FAITH

SCRIPTURE READING: PSALM 27:11–14
KEY VERSE: PSALM 27:14

Wait on the LORD;
Be of good courage,
And He shall strengthen your heart;
Wait, I say, on the LORD!

In our excitement to see God work in our lives, we oftentimes forget that He knows the big picture, and He also knows what is best for us. Our zeal, apart from His divine knowledge, can send us racing into the unknown, when it's best for us to wait upon Him for guidance.

However, learning to walk by faith teaches us to stand firm while awaiting God's direction. Our mentality that places a disproportionate amount of emphasis on works can incite us to go forward. We forget that some of our greatest personal growth as believers, and the preparation necessary for God's next step in our lives, takes place in the stillness of our hearts.

David believed strongly that waiting upon God was vital to walking in His ways. In fact, twice in one verse, he implored us to wait: "Wait for the LORD; be strong and let your heart take courage; yes, wait for the Lord" (Psalm 27:14 NASB).

While we are anxious to tackle the next obstacle thrust in our path, God knows that we need time to grow—time learning to trust in Him—in order to conquer that obstacle. As we discover that our strength truly comes from God alone, we will wait patiently; for we understand that a deep faith in Him trusts that, with Him alone, we will succeed in walking victoriously by faith.

Lord, thank You for being there in the still, quiet places. Please calm my racing heart so that I may have the patience to wait and hear Your voice.

THE FIRST COMPONENT OF FAITH

SCRIPTURE READING: 1 SAMUEL 3:1–10

KEY VERSE: 1 SAMUEL 3:10

Now the LORD came and stood and called as at other times, "Samuel! Samuel!" And Samuel answered, "Speak, for Your servant hears."

Our desire to walk by faith, stepping solely within the will of God for our lives, begins with a desire to hear what He is saying. When we have no idea where God is leading us or what He wants to change in our hearts, listening is the first and most crucial component to a greater faith.

Samuel was a young boy when he first heard God speak to him. The first sounds of God's voice were difficult for him to discern. Yet through some gentle guidance from Eli, Samuel's faith began to blossom. Listening for God's voice became a pattern for Samuel's life. Countless times throughout his leadership in Israel he heard and obeyed the voice of the Lord.

As we deepen our relationship with the Lord, we can improve our hearing in relation to God's voice through the following:

- Meditate upon God's Word. If we know the Word of God already spoken, discerning His voice clearly will be easier.
- Establish a time to listen to God. Our prayers become more effective when we are willing to hear God's heart.
- Expect God to speak. If we don't believe that God does and desires to communicate to us today, we won't be as inclined to listen. However, when we do believe the truth—that He does want to speak to us—we hear Him loud and clear.

Lord, open my heart to discern Your voice. Give me the discipline to listen for You and the faith to believe You want to speak to me.

FAITH DEFINED

SCRIPTURE READING: 2 CORINTHIANS 5:1–8
KEY VERSE: 2 CORINTHIANS 5:7

For we walk by faith, not by sight.

So much is written about faith these days. We think and talk about trusting God, and try, even though we stumble at times, to walk by faith. Many times, it is our trying that trips us up. God wants us to learn to live by faith and not by sight (2 Corinthians 5:7). This means living with the idea that He is able to do what we cannot do for ourselves. What a victorious thought! It is also a marvelous invitation to experience freedom from doubt, worry, and disbelief.

Before we can trust God fully, we must come to a point of helpless dependence. It is here that we realize we simply cannot do it all, be all that is needed, and have all the answers. If we could, there would be no need for God. We would be in total control and very proud of it. While God gives us the ability to solve many of the problems we face, His greater desire is for us to live our lives dependent on Him. Godly dependence is not a sign of weakness but one of immeasurable strength and confidence. There are problems in life that only God can solve, tasks only He can perform, and solutions that can only be discovered through the wisdom He gives.

The basic foundation to faith is this: trust God more than you trust yourself. When you do this, you gain wisdom and hope for every area of life.

Dear Lord, help me to trust You more. Give me a confident conviction that You keep Your promises.

A PERSON OF FAITH

SCRIPTURE READING: 1 CORINTHIANS 2:1–5
KEY VERSE: 1 CORINTHIANS 2:5

*. . . that your faith should not be in the wisdom
of men but in the power of God.*

Today, let's take a look at the characteristics of someone who is walking in faith. What will his or her life look like? God's Word suggests that this person will generally be

- Firmly rooted in Him. A person walking in faith knows and trusts God.
- Built up in Him. This person will allow God to provide strength and inspiration for daily living.
- Established in faith. Knowing what he or she believes—based on truth of God's Word—will provide stability and security.
- Open to instruction. Someone walking in faith will demonstrate a willingness both to be taught and to weed out false teaching or flawed ideas.
- Overflowing with gratitude. One who walks in faith will consistently demonstrate an attitude of thankfulness and praise for what God has done and continues to do.

How does your life compare to this list of qualities? As you read each one, did the Holy Spirit allow a twinge of conviction to enter your heart?

Although the process of walking in faith is a continual journey, we should seek to become stronger with each step. If you felt conviction today, allow God to use it in a constructive way. When you humble yourself before Him, He will provide His wisdom to equip you to serve Him.

Lord, I want to walk in faith, rooted and built up in You. I am grateful for Your guidance. Instruct me and lead me.

Faith Versus Reason

Scripture Reading: 1 Corinthians 2:12
Key Verse: 1 Corinthians 2:12

*Now we have received, not the spirit of the world, but the Spirit
who is from God, that we might know the things that
have been freely given to us by God.*

The wisdom of God was to make the way of salvation easy and simple. True to His Word, He has confounded the wise. Many "intellectuals" consider the Cross foolishness, but they should consider God's wisdom for a moment. If you were God, separated from the people you created because of their sin, what would be the easiest method by which you could restore them to your eternal forgiveness and fellowship?

Would it be a hard and fast list of certain physical or intellectual requirements? Wouldn't that cheapen the salvation and build no lasting covenant or meaningful relationship?

No, the simplest way was for God to send His own Son in the form of a sinless Man to serve as a sacrifice for sin. The best and simplest plan would call for man's salvation to therefore be attained in one word. Just one word. Faith.

Is it not immeasurable wisdom that forges a salvation plan so simple that even a five-year-old can grasp it? But the wisdom of the true God befuddles the wisdom of the world. He sacrificed His Son as a free gift to all who would believe in Him.

"Now we have received, not the spirit of the world, but the Spirit who is from God, that we might know the things that have been freely given to us by God" (1 Corinthians 2:12).

Lord, the message of the gospel is so clear and so puzzling to the human mind. I embrace it in its simplicity and pray for Your wisdom that I might increase in faith.

THE BASICS OF FAITH

SCRIPTURE READING: HEBREWS 11:1–6
KEY VERSE: HEBREWS 11:6

*But without faith it is impossible to please Him, for he who comes
to God must believe that He is, and that He is a rewarder
of those who diligently seek Him.*

Until we discover what it means to have faith, we cannot begin to walk by faith. Faith in God is more than just believing He exists; it is living with confidence that He will fulfill all His promises and bring salvation to us. We must discover whether we have placed our faith in God or if we only are wishing His Word is true. As our faith is tested, the true spiritual state of our hearts is revealed.

A situation is presented before us where we can act within our own strength, doing whatever we can to manipulate the outcome, or we can trust in God's strength, taking our hands off the problem and allowing Him to enter the scene.

As we begin to walk by faith, there will be times when we stumble and fall. However, falling and getting up is part of learning how to walk. Once we get up and dust ourselves off, we take our next step with more wisdom, more strength, more faith.

Walking by faith is a lifestyle, a way in which we conduct ourselves. As God molds and shapes us more into His image, He desires for us to live a life of faith, a life that relies upon Him for everything we need. Paul wrote, "For we walk by faith, not by sight. . . . Therefore we also have as our ambition, whether at home or absent, to be pleasing to Him" (2 Corinthians 5:7, 9 NASB).

Lord, guide me to that place where I go beyond just believing You are real but, rather, rely on Your wisdom for every detail of my life.

TESTED FAITH

SCRIPTURE READING: JAMES 1:2–8
KEY VERSE: JAMES 1:6

*But let him ask in faith, with no doubting, for he who doubts is
like a wave of the sea driven and tossed by the wind.*

Losing faith in God in the midst of difficult circumstances undermines what we claim to believe about Him. However, a faith tested and proven yields immeasurable fruit in the kingdom of God.

God's desire is to mold and shape us into His image so that we reflect His beauty, love, and grace to a dying world. He allows certain situations to touch our lives so that our faith in Him will be strengthened.

The testing of our faith gives us an answer to questions like these: Do we really say what we believe? Or are we spouting off biblical truths without trusting them in our hearts?

James wrote, "The testing of your faith produces endurance. And let endurance have its perfect result, so that you may be perfect and complete, lacking in nothing" (James 1:3–4 NASB).

When our faith goes on trial, we should slow down and set our focus on Christ. Attempting to get to the other side of adversity too quickly will sometimes prevent us from learning the lesson God wants to teach us.

Learning to endure such hardships will benefit us, maturing us as believers and strengthening the foundation of our faith. Instead of allowing ourselves to be swayed by our emotions in the moment, we can live victoriously by faith when we refuse to let our faith be shaken. God always brings to completion the works He begins.

Lord, in the midst of my asking You to be present in my difficult times, let me accept Your shaping and molding. Grant me an unwavering faith.

JUNE 9

SUFFERING A FAITH FAILURE

SCRIPTURE READING: NUMBERS 13:27–33
KEY VERSE: HEBREWS 3:19

So we see that they could not enter in because of unbelief.

By nature, we are people of belief because faith is the foundation of our relationship to God. But every once in a while, we experience what can be called a faith failure. Often, these failures happen when we hesitate or cease to trust God during challenging times. Yet there are many other causes for faith failures:

- Fear of being unsuccessful
- Failure to understand the nature of God
- Forgetting God's power
- Focusing on our obstacles

As you read through today's Scripture passage from Numbers, ask yourself this question: Which of these factors do you think played a role in the Israelites' hesitance to enter the land of Negev?

Actually, it can be argued that a combination of all these issues suddenly caused the Israelites to doubt God and become fearful. This massive faith failure then led to a crisis among the people.

So, how do we avoid faith failures? Truthfully, we will all experience doubts from time to time. But we can be prepared for these episodes by filling our minds with God's truth. When we know the character of our heavenly Father, we will be prepared to respond with spiritual maturity when our faith is tested.

As you spend time with God today, focus on His true nature. Which of His characteristics has He shown you: faithfulness, goodness, mercy? The Lord longs for you to know and trust Him so that His perfect will may be carried out in your life.

Lord, there are lands of the Negev in my life—places where I fear to go. I want to immerse myself in Your truth so that my bolstered faith will carry me through.

The Stages of Faith

Scripture Reading: Romans 4:16–21

Key Verses: Romans 4:20–21

He did not waver at the promise of God through unbelief, but was strengthened in faith, giving glory to God, and being fully convinced that what He had promised He was also able to perform.

Making the decision to follow Christ takes faith. No matter how weak our faith begins, salvation only comes through belief in Christ. Once we accept Jesus as our Savior, God begins the process of stretching and increasing our faith. When facing a challenge, a person with small faith might say, "I know He can, but I am not sure He will." We all begin our journey unsure about many things, yet we are sure enough to take the first step.

At this point, our emotions play a big role in whether or not we believe God is going to hear and answer our prayers. We give up and doubt, and our faith remains restless. However, God wants us to continue on past that point to a place of great faith where we say, "I know He can, and I know He will."

It is there that we begin to ignore the circumstances surrounding us. We trust in Him, meditating on His promises and seeking understanding. We remember what He has done in the past, and we refuse to give up.

Abraham "did not waver in unbelief but grew strong in faith, giving glory to God, and being fully assured that what God had promised, He was able also to perform" (Romans 4:20–21 NASB). Through difficult times, our faith is tested, seasoning us as believers and teaching us that trusting in God alone is vital to keeping our confidence in Him.

Father, just as Abraham, in all his human weakness, followed You without wavering, I, too, claim Your promises and want to stand firm in my faith.

REASONS TO TRUST GOD

SCRIPTURE READING: PSALM 37:1–9

KEY VERSE: PSALM 37:3

Trust in the LORD, and do good;
Dwell in the land, and feed on His faithfulness.

There are many reasons why we can trust God:

- He is the one, true God (2 Samuel 7:21–22). From the beginning of time, those who seek God have found Him. No other god has revealed himself to man in this way.

- He is the essence of truth (Hebrews 6:17–18). God cannot lie, and He will never lead you astray. However, He has told us that there is one who deceives us, and that is Satan. Jesus called him the "father of lies" and rightly so (John 8:44).

- He is absolutely faithful (Lamentations 3:23). When was the last time God let you down? He never has, and He never will. No matter what you are facing, God knows about it, and He is near to show you how to resolve your dilemma.

- He has all power (Matthew 28:18). Henry Thiessen writes, "God can do what he wills to do, but he does not necessarily will to do anything. . . . To the Christian the omnipotence of God is a source of great comfort and hope."

- He loves you unconditionally (John 15:9). God will never stop loving you. Even when you are unlovely, He loves you. And it is His love that draws you away from sin and into His arms of infinite care.

- He never changes (Hebrews 13:8). God is immutable. Thiessen writes: "He is exalted above all causes and above even the possibility of change."

You are the one, true God and the essence of all truth. You are faithful, You have all power, You love me unconditionally, and You never change!

REBUILDING YOUR FAITH

SCRIPTURE READING: MATTHEW 17:15–21
KEY VERSE: MATTHEW 17:20

So Jesus said to them, "Because of your unbelief; for assuredly,
I say to you, if you have faith as a mustard seed, you will say to this
mountain, 'Move from here to there,' and it will move;
and nothing will be impossible for you."

When circumstances appear to take an unexpected turn, sometimes our faith can be rocked. We wonder how we will ever endure the tragedy or injustice unfolding before us. However, adversity should never be the end of our faith; it should be the beginning. No matter the adversity, a strong faith will enable us to endure life's toughest hardships.

But what should we do when we discern that our circumstances are indeed rattling our faith? How do we regain our footing?

- Make a decision to choose to believe that God is trustworthy and faithful. God always keeps His promises. He desires the best for our lives. At times, what we think is the best and what He knows is the best may be conflicting. However, God's ways always produce the most spiritual fruit, the strongest character, and the unimaginable perfect result.
- Refuse to doubt God. The enemy hopes to thwart us by infusing doubt into our minds that will lead us to question our faith. When we refuse to look at our circumstances through worldly eyes, God gives us a sense of peace and rest.
- Read God's Word and meditate on His promises. Searching the Bible for God's promises is one way we can quiet the wavering of our faith, standing on all His promises with the deep assurance that God always keeps His Word.

To you, Lord, who created the universe and the mountains, the obstacles in my life are comparably the size of tiny stones. I trust You to help me step over these challenges.

PASSING ON YOUR FAITH

SCRIPTURE READING: 2 TIMOTHY 1:3–7
KEY VERSE: 2 TIMOTHY 1:5

When I call to remembrance the genuine faith that is in you,
which dwelt first in your grandmother Lois and your mother Eunice,
and I am persuaded is in you also.

The world always keeps a keen eye on believers. So desperate to find something genuine and true, they will watch to see if our talk measures up to our lifestyle. Many times, their motives are just to confirm their growing suspicion that nothing true and genuine exists.

In passing along our faith, nothing is stronger than the way we live our lives. We can espouse all the Christian rhetoric we know, but if it does not match our actions, our true hearts are exposed.

Jesus gave everything He had before He left earth, including His life. While His primary purpose in coming to the world was to save it through His death and resurrection, He also longed to impart to us a solid faith. And to those whom He gave special attention in teaching them the ways of the heavenly Father, Jesus asked that they do the same to others. After His resurrection, He asked this of Peter: "Do you love Me? . . . Feed My sheep" (John 21:17).

Passing on our faith often consists of thoughtful encounters where we verbally express what God means to our lives. But people hear more through what we do than what we say. Living a life that reflects the true nature of our love for Christ is a way we can pass on our faith to the world around us.

Lord, bathe me in Your all-knowing presence so that my simple life may be a beacon to those who no longer believe in the light. Make my life serve as an example.

Faith Worth Imitating

SCRIPTURE READING: PROVERBS 3:1–12
KEY VERSE: PROVERBS 3:5

Trust in the LORD with all your heart,
And lean not on your own understanding.

When we make the decision to follow Christ, we begin the journey of a lifetime, a journey that is unknown as to what path it will lead us down but certain as to where we will arrive. It is our commitment to follow Christ that reflects to everyone around us exactly where we place our faith.

Although our circumstances might suggest we search for our own course of action, God's Word tells us that a committed heart results in the best pathway: "In all your ways acknowledge Him, and He shall direct your paths" (Proverbs 3:6).

To pass on our faith, we must have faith. We must realize that when difficult times arise in our lives, running *to* God—not *from* Him—results in victory. It is when we experience victory in Christ that our faith swells.

As a result of our victories in Christ, no longer can we contain ourselves when it comes to sharing our faith. We recognize just how much God has done for us and how much He has intervened in our impossible situation when we trusted Him alone. We cannot keep that to ourselves.

Passing on our faith occurs when we demonstrate openly those truths that we clutch in our hearts. To remain dedicated to the cause of Christ, even when it is difficult, shows that our faith is more than just a passing fancy or another religion. It shows it is faith worth imitating.

Lord, help me to remain dedicated to You even when it is difficult. I want to have faith that is worth imitating.

HEALTHY FAITH

SCRIPTURE READING: PSALM 100:1–5
KEY VERSES: PSALM 100:3–4

Know that the LORD, He is God;
It is He who has made us, and not we ourselves;
We are His people and the sheep of His pasture.
Enter into His gates with thanksgiving,
And into His courts with praise.
Be thankful to Him, and bless His name.

In Psalm 100:3–4, words of praise flowed from David's heart like a river pulsing down a mountain. David truly adored God. We know this because Matthew 12:34 teaches, "The mouth speaks out of that which fills the heart" (NASB). If David's heart were not filled with immense love for God, he would not have been able to express himself so eloquently.

Even when David faced immense pressures, he was able to place his hope in God. It was through small steps of worshiping God in the difficulties that his adoration of the Lord grew to overflowing.

When you speak about the Lord, do you praise Him with all your heart? What flows from your mouth may be an indication as to the health of your faith. Are you able to proclaim gladly that the Lord is God?

Is there a flaw in your faith? Then praise Him. Once you allow the spring of praise to course in your heart, it will continue to grow until it overflows through you. Enter His gates with thanksgiving and His courts with praise and watch Him bring something truly beautiful from your faith.

Lord, I often forget that the words from my mouth are the first place some people hear evidence of You at work. Let it be a receptacle of praise for You.

The Faithfulness of God

Scripture Reading: Lamentations 3:19–26
Key Verses: Lamentations 3:22–23

Through the LORD's mercies we are not consumed, because His compassions fail not. They are new every morning; great is Your faithfulness.

The first verse of the hymn "Great Is Thy Faithfulness," by Thomas Chisholm, speaks to God's faithfulness:

> Great is Thy faithfulness, O God my Father!
> There is no shadow of turning with Thee;
> Thou changest not, Thy compassions, they fail not:
> As Thou hast been Thou forever wilt be.

These famous words summarize a foundational truth: God is faithful, and He does not change (Hebrews 13:8). Theologians call this God's "immutability." Have you ever thought about why it is so important to understand this aspect of God's character? God's unchanging nature is the basis for everything we believe about Him.

If God could change on a whim, then every promise He made in Scripture would be invalidated. He would be untrustworthy. He loved you unconditionally yesterday, but what about tomorrow when you really blow it? That is why God emphasizes His absolute, uncompromising faithfulness throughout His Word. We need that assurance in order to know Him as God and to place our faith in Him.

In 1 Corinthians 1:9 we read, "God is faithful, by whom you were called into the fellowship of His Son, Jesus Christ our Lord." Your salvation is guaranteed, because He sealed your redemption at the Cross. Let your heart rejoice and say, "Great is Thy faithfulness!"

Father, Son, Holy Spirit—triune God—You have ever been the same, unchanging. Thank You for Your faithfulness. I offer You my heart to mirror that faithfulness.

An Eternal Perspective

SCRIPTURE READING: MATTHEW 21:18–22
KEY VERSE: MATTHEW 21:21

So Jesus answered and said to them, "Assuredly, I say to you,
if you have faith and do not doubt, you will not only do what
was done to the fig tree, but also if you say to this mountain,
'Be removed and be cast into the sea,' it will be done."

Some of the most noble and valiant events in history were born out of hearts that had an eternal perspective.

George Washington, renowned Revolutionary War general and first president of the United States, demonstrated such a heart. From his earliest days, he was taught by his mother to put God first in his life. When he accepted a position of leadership in the war, he had no idea how much his faith would be put to the test.

One of the most precious documents Washington ever produced as a young man was a small prayer diary that he titled "Daily Sacrifice." Peter Marshall and David Manuel recount Washington's prayer in *The Light and the Glory*:

O most glorious God . . . I acknowledge and confess my faults; in the weak and imperfect performance of the duties of this day. . . . O God, who art rich in mercy and plenteous in redemption, mark not, I beseech Thee, what I have done amiss. . . . Cover my sins with the absolute obedience of Thy dear Son . . . the sacrifice of Jesus Christ offered upon the cross for me.

Washington made a habit of private prayer, and his faith inspired his men in the most brutal conditions. He is remembered for his great deeds, certainly, but it is his faith that made his impact lasting. Only when your focus is on the eternal will your work have eternal merit.

Father, like George Washington, I confess that I am often weak and imperfect. I praise You for Your mercy in covering my sinfulness with the blood of Jesus.

REINFORCING OUR FAITH

SCRIPTURE READING: JUDE 1:3–23
KEY VERSES: JUDE 1:20–21

But you, beloved, building yourselves up on your most holy faith,
praying in the Holy Spirit, keep yourselves in the love of God, looking
for the mercy of our Lord Jesus Christ unto eternal life.

We must be careful to reinforce our faith so that we can stand firm against the subversive pull of the world. But how can we build a stronger faith?

- We must saturate our minds with the holy, unchanging Word of God. Then the Holy Spirit will continually refresh our minds and bring new insights as we develop Christian maturity.
- We must commit to pray in the Holy Spirit (Ephesians 6:18). We can trust the Spirit to guide us in our prayers, leading us with regard to what, when, and how to pray.
- We must keep ourselves in the love of God. Of course, we can never fall beyond the scope of God's love, but we shouldn't ever take His amazing grace for granted. With that in mind, we need to closely guard our intimacy with Him and the time we spend in His presence.
- We must wait anxiously for the return of Jesus Christ. For Christians, the Second Coming is the most anticipated event in history, and we need to keep our eyes on this goal. The thought that Christ could return at any moment is a purifying and protective realization for the believer (1 John 3:2–3).

There is no "magic formula" for Christian growth, but these simple steps, laid out in Jude 1:20–23, can serve as a guide as we strive to protect our faith from the snares of the world.

Lord, saturate my mind with Your Word and fill me with Your Spirit. Keep me in Your love as I await Your return.

THE COMPANION OF FAITH

SCRIPTURE READING: 1 THESSALONIANS 1:6–10
KEY VERSE: 1 THESSALONIANS 1:6

And you became followers of us and of the Lord, having received the word in much affliction, with joy of the Holy Spirit.

God is continually molding believers to be more like Him. Often, transforming people into the image of Christ is a difficult process. It involves emptying a person of sins and filling him or her with Christlike characteristics. In 1 Thessalonians 1:6, Paul admonished, "You also became imitators of us and of the Lord, having received the word in much tribulation with the joy of the Holy Spirit" (NASB).

You are being molded by God. He teaches you through trials, and He guides you by the Holy Spirit. You endure this process so that you will understand God's Word and be His witness in the world.

D. L. Moody said, "I believe firmly that the moment our hearts are emptied of pride and selfishness and ambition and everything that is contrary to God's law, the Holy Spirit will fill every corner of our hearts."

Each of us needs help becoming all that God created us to be. This is why God has given us His Spirit. The frustrations we face help to refine us and mold our lives so that we reflect God's mercy and grace to others. It is through this molding process that God helps us fulfill His plan for our lives.

The Holy Spirit keeps you connected to the heart and will of the Father. The Spirit guides you through the toils and trials on the pathway to becoming more like Christ. He sustains you with joy as you conform to the image of your beloved Savior.

Holy Spirit, fill the corners of my heart. Show me the places where You cannot enter because of my own debris. Guide me in sweeping clean a pathway for You.

Fear or Faith?

SCRIPTURE READING: MATTHEW 14:22–34
KEY VERSE: MATTHEW 14:31

*And immediately Jesus stretched out His hand and caught him, and
said to him, "O you of little faith, why did you doubt?"*

When faced with a serious challenge, what is your first response? Do you run from the situation with fear in your heart, or do you stand and face the enemy with the shield of faith? God wants us to stand firm in our faith.

He has promised to contend with those who contend with us (Psalm 18). Therefore, we can face each situation with confidence and power knowing that He is with us and He is in control.

He provides the wisdom you need for the challenge, the strength you need to do what seems to be impossible, and the protection you need from the enemy's wicked plots and schemes. You never have a reason to feel fearful, because you are God's beloved, and He will fight for you.

Matthew 14 relates a story where the disciples had to face their greatest fear—loss of control on an open, storm-driven sea. Scripture tells us that Jesus made the disciples get into the boat and go on ahead of Him across the Sea of Galilee (Matthew 14:22).

The Lord did not make a suggestion to His disciples; He told them to go. Jesus knew His disciples would encounter a great storm and their faith would be tried. When He came to them walking on a storm-tossed sea, they thought He was a ghost.

Don't allow fearful thoughts to keep you from seeing the Savior. Whenever there is danger or a threat of any kind, He always makes His presence known.

*Dear heavenly Father, help me reject fear and embrace faith. I thank
You that in every situation, You make Your presence known.*

THE REWARD OF FAITH

SCRIPTURE READING: LUKE 4:35–41
KEY VERSE: MATTHEW 14:27

But immediately Jesus spoke to them, saying,
"Be of good cheer! It is I; do not be afraid."

Jesus had sent His disciples on ahead to Bethsaida. They had crossed the Sea of Galilee with trepidation. As skilled fishermen, they could tell that the cool air on their faces preceded a storm front. The volatile air currents would soon clash and a violent tempest would erupt—something they had learned to dread.

In the dead of night, the torrents of rain started. Even with their seasoned experience, the tossing seas and whipping winds were daunting. Just when it seemed as if they would die, a ghostly figure approached their boat by walking on the water.

When was the last time you were overcome with fear? Do you remember how you felt? Right now, you may be facing a fearful situation. Perhaps you feel as though you are barely surviving the tempest blows, and your faith is being confronted with a terrifying unknown. Matthew 14:27 reports that Jesus told them not to be afraid. This is Christ's message to you. Augustine writes, "Faith is to believe what you do not yet see; the reward for this faith is to see what you believe." You may not understand how God will deliver you, but you can be sure that He will.

Take courage! Believe that He will calm the raging storm surrounding you, and you will witness the clouds breaking apart.

I believe, Lord, even though I cannot see. Give me courage. Calm the raging storm around me.

Our Faithful Father

Scripture Reading: 2 Timothy 2:1–13
Key Verse: 2 Timothy 2:13

If we are faithless, He remains faithful; He cannot deny Himself.

How many times have you thought, *I just don't have the faith to go on?* Even though you have believed in Jesus Christ as your Savior, sometimes it becomes really hard to keep clinging to the hope you have been called to. Sometimes the effort it takes to believe that God will help you is more than you can handle, since your circumstances weigh so heavily upon your shoulders.

However, what you must understand is that your relationship with Jesus will not waver in concert with the strength of your belief. As 2 Timothy 2:13 promises, "If we are faithless, He remains faithful; He cannot deny Himself."

Once you accept Jesus as Lord and Savior, you enter into a new relationship with Him. You become part of His family, part of Him. John Calvin explains, "We have been adopted as sons by the Lord." The Lord welcomes you as His beloved child. And as a faithful Father, He looks after you, helps you, and protects you.

The purpose for your faith is to comfort you and help you in your times of suffering and trial. This is because faith finds its basis in the trustworthy character of the Savior and His promises. However, your lack of faith will not lock you out of a relationship with Christ. Trust your faithful Father. He loves you and will never let you go.

Thank You for Your faithfulness, dear Lord. I praise You that Your love will never let me go.

Unshakable Faith

Scripture Reading: Psalm 16:1–11
Key Verses: Matthew 6:33–34

*But seek first the kingdom of God and His righteousness,
and all these things shall be added to you. Therefore do not worry
about tomorrow, for tomorrow will worry about its own things.
Sufficient for the day is its own trouble.*

Clinging to your faith in times of trouble is not a casual undertaking. To stand strong in faith, unwavering in your stance, takes determination, purpose, and intentional action. In the life of David, we see the determination and resolve it took for his own mind to stay on the Lord rather than on the enemies that hotly pursued him. In Psalm 16:8, David shared, "I have set the LORD always before me . . . I shall not be moved."

That's determination. He purposed to concentrate on who the Lord is instead of on who was chasing him. He intentionally acted on faith rather than on fear. Did David ever experience moments of fear? He wouldn't be human if he didn't. Yet the key is, how did David respond? The key is, how do we respond?

If we believe God is truly in control, we need not worry about tomorrow (Matthew 6:33–34). The first step in responding to times of uncertainty is to focus on God. Get in His Word and learn about His character.

That sovereign character of the Lord Almighty is what will remind you that this life is all about Him. His purpose is always at hand. You will not experience any trial, hardship, or even loss of life on earth until the Lord has allowed it. Will you trust that the sovereign God knows what is best for your life?

Lord, help me be focused on Your kingdom, determined in my purpose, and intentional in my actions as I serve You.

Whom Shall I Fear?

Scripture Reading: Psalm 27:1–14
Key Verse: Psalm 27:1

The LORD is my light and my salvation;
Whom shall I fear?
The LORD is the strength of my life;
Of whom shall I be afraid?

No matter what kind of life you're leading, the issue of uncertainty will always be present. Especially in the wake of current world events, you're probably realizing the magnitude of how uncertain these times are. So the question arises: How will you respond in the face of uncertainty?

David responded by keeping his focus on the Lord. He didn't look about him and wonder where Saul was at every moment. To have lived a life with such fear and anxiety would not have been living at all. David knew that.

As we face possible economic hardship, adversity, and opposition, we can stand firm because of one thing: God is our defender. When fearful thoughts start to assail you, recite Scriptures like Psalm 27:1 over and over again. Basing your life on the confidence of David means barricading your mind with the Word of God.

Father, I am so thankful that You are with me in every situation. I rejoice that I have nothing to fear!

LETTING GO OF FEAR

SCRIPTURE READING: PSALM 55:1–8
KEY VERSE: HEBREWS 13:5

*Let your conduct be without covetousness; be content with
such things as you have. For He Himself has said, "I will never
leave you nor forsake you."*

When those around you are talking about fears and anxieties, how do you react? Do you let their fears influence your thinking, or do you hold tightly to what you believe? The Lord wants you to be sure of what you believe. What you believe—your faith—is based on what your focus is and whether you have a personal relationship with Jesus Christ.

When you're focusing on a God who is sovereign, you know that nothing in heaven or on earth is beyond His control. And when you're in a personal, daily relationship with God through acceptance of His Son, Jesus Christ, you have another anchor. That anchor is the unchanging nature of God. He promises that He will never leave you (Hebrews 13:5).

In Psalm 55:4–8, we read David's firsthand account of feeling overwhelmed. You may feel overwhelmed right now by difficulties surrounding you. Overwhelming emotions are not wrong; clinging to them is.

God wants you to tell Him how you feel and then let go of it. He wants you to know that because He loves you and is in control of your life, you do not have to live under a cloud of overwhelming doom or anxiety.

Will you trust His Word and let go of your fear?

*I trust Your Word, Lord. I let go of my fears. Help me to focus on You
today instead of my problems.*

SEEDS OF DISCOURAGEMENT

SCRIPTURE READING: 1 SAMUEL 17:28–32
KEY VERSE: 1 SAMUEL 17:32

*Then David said to Saul, "Let no man's heart fail because of him;
your servant will go and fight with this Philistine."*

Words are so powerful in the way they affect our actions. A simple word of caution may prevent us from ever setting foot on a path of destruction. A word of encouragement could give us the confidence we need to follow God's call on our lives. A trait of conquering faith is that it turns a deaf ear to discouragement. Instead of listening to—and believing—the words of the faithless, we need to hold fast to the promises God has given us.

As David listened to Goliath's threats, he wondered why no one would challenge this giant. Goliath was mocking God, yet no one seemed too concerned with putting an end to it. David's courage rose up within him, and he voiced that he wanted to fight Goliath. However, discouragement began bombarding him. David was determined to ignore it, resulting in a conquering faith.

Despite the discouragement, David was determined to triumph. Likewise, we need to remember the example of David and refuse to allow the seeds of discouragement to take root in our hearts. We must remember that God is on our side, and that He is the One who will conquer all our enemies as we place our faith in Him.

Heavenly Father, I refuse to allow the seeds of discouragement to take root in my heart. I believe You will conquer all of my enemies as I put my faith in You.

Conquering Faith

SCRIPTURE READING: 1 SAMUEL 17:1–11

KEY VERSE: 2 TIMOTHY 1:7

*For God has not given us a spirit of fear, but of power
and of love and of a sound mind.*

David put into practice several sound biblical principles when he faced one of the biggest challenges of his life—Goliath. These principles are effective for all of God's servants:

- Recall past victories: David immediately recounted his victories as a shepherd when he defeated attacking lions and bears. Recounting those times when the Lord has come to your aid will fortify you for your present challenge.
- Reexamine and reaffirm your motivations: David's love and devotion to the Lord and defense of His name superseded any of man's paltry rewards. We must be ever-vigilant to gauge our true motivations.
- Reject discouragement from others: David did not listen to his older brother or even King Saul. He listened to the Lord's voice. Well-meaning people sometimes can quench your faith if you heed the wrong voices.
- Recognize the true nature of the battle: God is involved in every aspect of the believer's life. This means that everything is spiritual in our lives—everything that touches us must come through Him first.
- Rely upon God's power for victory: From the beginning, David proclaimed that the battle was the Lord's. This isn't "psyching yourself up." It simply means that you trust the Lord so much that the victory already is decided in your mind. It is a settled issue.

Dear Lord, I am relying upon You in the conflicts of life. The battle is Yours! The victory is already decided in my mind. It is a settled issue.

STRATEGIES FOR THE FAITHFUL

SCRIPTURE READING: 1 SAMUEL 17:12–27
KEY VERSE: 1 SAMUEL 17:26

Then David spoke to the men who stood by him, saying,
"What shall be done for the man who kills this Philistine and takes
away the reproach from Israel? For who is this uncircumcised
Philistine, that he should defy the armies of the living God?"

A faithful child of God will reckon spiritual victory as sure and certain by applying the strategies David used against Goliath:

- Fight the battle before the battle. Get on your face before God and pray through the challenge. Let the Lord prune, sift, sand, and weed you as you hash over the situation with Him. Do this until you are certain that you know the will of God.
- Reaffirm in your heart that the battle is the Lord's. Only the Lord can work in your situation for good, and only He can bring about true victory.
- Declare the victory. David not only promised to slay Goliath but also said the Lord would destroy the entire Philistine army. His was the most ambitious of declarations, because he served the most certain, true God.
- Wait on God's timing. It wasn't until David declared what the Lord would do through him that the Lord brought about the victory. Sometimes He asks us to wait. Always His timing is perfect.
- Proceed in God's way. We are prone to rely upon the world's ways when we get into battles. We have to trust God always—even when He asks us to do something that doesn't make sense immediately.
- Trust God. Pray unceasingly. Fight with confidence. Believe God's promises. Take Him—at His Word. Wait for His victory.

The battle is Yours, Lord! I will wait for Your timing and proceed in Your way, trusting You to give the victory.

TRUTH IN ACTION

SCRIPTURE READING: 1 SAMUEL 17:34–51
KEY VERSE: 1 SAMUEL 17:45

Then David said to the Philistine, "You come to me with a sword,
with a spear, and with a javelin. But I come to you in the name of the
Lord of hosts, the God of the armies of Israel, whom you have defied."

At some point during our relationship with Christ, we have to plunge into the unknown with some measure of faith. The circumstances could vary—a new job, a new relationship, a battle with an illness—and we have no idea what the outcome will be.

Yet we put our faith to the test, trusting that God will bring about the best for our lives. As He works, transforming us into the image of Christ, our faith builds. Faith isn't merely a concept anymore. It is truth in action.

Conquering faith develops from faith that has been tested and has seen the faithfulness of God. And conquering faith never forgets past victories won by the Lord. When David approached King Saul about fighting Goliath, he went with great confidence. While Goliath was large and intimidating, David remembered from where he derived his strength: God. During his days as a shepherd, David battled a lion and a bear, defeating them both through the strength of the Lord. He knew that it had nothing to do with his own strength, just his faith. He believed God would deliver him again in a battle against Goliath.

In our desire to have a conquering faith, we must never forget where we have been with the Lord. It is necessary to get where we are going.

Lord, give me conquering faith. Help me remember where I have
been with You in the past so that I may arrive at my future destiny.

CONSISTENT FAITH

SCRIPTURE READING: COLOSSIANS 2:1–7
KEY VERSES: COLOSSIANS 2:6–7

As you therefore have received Christ Jesus the Lord, so walk in Him,
rooted and built up in Him and established in the faith, as you
have been taught, abounding in it with thanksgiving.

Having consistent faith is one area we all struggle in somtimes. We have faith in Jesus, but we often wrestle with our inability to walk consistently in faith.

So, as we examine Colossians 2:6–7, let's determine what walking by faith means. Keeping in mind that our "walk" represents our behavior as a Christian, what can we gather from the apostle Paul's teaching in this passage? He explained that, just as we received Christ by faith, we must also walk in Him. In other words, the believer should give Christ lordship over his or her life.

You can confidently submit to His lordship for two reasons:

- For who He is. Psalm 9:10 says that those who know God's name will put their trust in Him, because He will not forsake those who seek Him. Oftentimes, nonbelievers are hesitant to trust Jesus because they do not know Him. But when a person steps out in faith, His magnificent character will be revealed.
- For what He has done. When Jesus died on the cross, He paid the price and made us complete in Him. Never will we have to struggle to meet our own needs, because He is our ultimate provider. His love for you is beyond measure.

Will you walk with Him in faith? Will you trust Him to be true to His Word?

Lord, I want to be consistent in my faith. Help me to submit to Your lordship, remembering always the wonder of Your greatness and Your sacrifice for me.

JULY
Pathway to Freedom

Jesus answered them, "Most assuredly, I say to you, whoever commits sin is a slave of sin. And a slave does not abide in the house forever, but a son abides forever. Therefore if the Son makes you free, you shall be free indeed."

—John 8:34–36

Freedom from Sin

Scripture Reading: Psalm 25:8–18
Key Verse: Psalm 25:18

Look on my affliction and my pain,
And forgive all my sins.

Sometimes the sin in our hearts clutches us so tightly that we wonder if anyone sees the pain on our faces. We wonder if we must always mask the darkness beneath the surface. Despite confessing that our hope is in Jesus Christ, a sense of hopelessness can breed within us. But God wants to shatter the bondage of sin and shame into which our lives may have fallen.

We must take the first step in going to Him and asking Him to free us from the sin in our lives. Oftentimes, we fear going to God with our sins because we misunderstand the heart of our heavenly Father. He doesn't backhand us—He opens His hands to receive us back into His arms. No matter what particular sin we have committed or how many times we have done it, God's grace and forgiveness reaches deeper, desiring not only to cleanse us but to transform us. He wants to set us free.

The change may not always be instant, but as we commit to turning to Him during our moments of temptation—and times of failure—God will begin to bring freedom to our lives. The sin in our lives that once held us so tightly will be washed away as waves of the Lord's freeing forgiveness crash over us.

Lord, all I need to do when I have sinned is come before You. There is no sin deep enough to separate my repentant heart from You.

THE FREEDOM WE NEED

SCRIPTURE READING: 1 CORINTHIANS 1:18–25
KEY VERSE: 1 CORINTHIANS 1:18

For the message of the cross is foolishness to those who are perishing,
but to us who are being saved it is the power of God.

The mother wonders if her daughter will ever speak to her again. The father wonders if his relationship with his son can be restored. The young man wonders if the damage in his relationship with his best friend will ever be repaired.

When situations in our lives appear broken forever, despair can settle in our hearts if we don't turn to the source of ultimate freedom: our heavenly Father.

As Paul wrote to the church in Corinth, he explained that the word of the Cross—the death of Christ there and what that means to us today—is what brings power to our lives. Jesus' death and resurrection was the ultimate portrait of freedom from a life of despair.

The sin of the world seemed far beyond forgiveness, and the weight of all that sin rested on the shoulders of Jesus. Yet, through His death and resurrection, He not only paid the price for our sin, He brought us freedom, both for now and eternity.

It doesn't matter how desperate our situations appear to be here on earth now; we can always find hope in God. As we read Scripture and seek Him in prayer, we discover that He desires to free us from the bondage of despair, giving us the freedom we need to trust in Him.

Lord, I relinquish to You the sins that would own me. In Your forgiveness lies my power to overcome.

What Is Truth?

SCRIPTURE READING: JOHN 8:31–36
KEY VERSES: JOHN 8:31–32

*Then Jesus said to those Jews who believed Him, "If you abide in
My word, you are My disciples indeed. And you shall know the truth,
and the truth shall make you free."*

You may know when sin has a stranglehold on your life, but it is more difficult to discern the subtle traps of inferiority, inadequacy, and insecurity that the enemy may use to enslave you. Jesus said the truth will make you free. What is the truth? It can be found in His Word.

The truth is related to your position, person, and possessions in Christ. You will be made free when you stop living by perceptions and feelings and start living by fact. For believers, these are the facts:

- Position: As a child of God, you have been forgiven of your sins because of your acceptance of Christ. God has applied the righteousness of Christ to your account and sent His Spirit to live inside of you. Why should anyone feel inferior when God loved them enough to do all of that?
- Person: You have been redeemed and justified because of Christ's work. You are a child of God, the son or daughter of the King of the universe, a saint on the way to glory. You are worthy, no matter what anyone else says or thinks! God says so!
- Possessions: Paul summed it up in Philippians 4:13 when he said, "I can do all things through Christ who strengthens me." You should have a great sense of confidence to know that you have the Spirit of the living God inside of you, equipping you for whatever God requires of you.

Father, help me to stop living by perception and feelings and start living by fact. I am Your child. I have been redeemed and justified. I can do all things through You.

THE GIFT OF FREEDOM

SCRIPTURE READING: GALATIANS 2:16–21
KEY VERSE: GALATIANS 2:20

I have been crucified with Christ; it is no longer I who live, but Christ lives in me; and the life which I now live in the flesh I live by faith in the Son of God, who loved me and gave Himself for me.

Perhaps you thought you had conquered every sinful impulse. That was, until temptation or a new set of trials brought to light some area of your life that you thought had been conquered. This is when you wondered, *How could this happen? I am supposed to be free from sin.*

Oswald Chambers offers this explanation: "The Savior has set us free from sin, but this is the freedom that comes from being set free from myself by the Son. It is what Paul meant in Galatians 2:20 when he said, 'I have been crucified with Christ.' His individuality had been broken and his spirit had been united with his Lord; not just merged into Him, but made one with Him."

If you have accepted Christ as your Savior, then you are one with Him. His likeness and holiness are present within your life. However, there remains within you a sin nature that must be surrendered to God.

In Galatians 2:20, Paul said he lived by faith. The gift of freedom that Jesus gives requires faith. We must believe that He can root out the strongholds within our hearts and that He continuously works to make us free from all sin and bondage. Our responsibility is to say no to sin and yes to God as we trust Him to provide the all-encompassing liberty that our souls crave.

Lord, I praise You. You know the strongholds in my life where sin lies, and You have the victory over them.

No Condemnation

SCRIPTURE READING: JOHN 8:1–11
KEY VERSES: JOHN 8:10–11

When Jesus had raised Himself up and saw no one but the woman,
He said to her, "Woman, where are those accusers of yours? Has no one
condemned you?" She said, "No one, Lord." And Jesus said to her,
"Neither do I condemn you; go and sin no more."

Heaping condemnation upon our own heads rarely solves our problems. Perhaps our insensitivity toward someone was wrong. Or maybe we made a mistake, offending someone in the process. Guilty feelings—real or contrived—have a way of taking the life out of us.

They divide our minds, drain our energy, cause us to punish ourselves, and stir up feelings of insecurity. Following our rebirth in Christ, the guilt of our past sins is taken away. But guilty feelings—conviction from the Holy Spirit—return when we sin against God. However, we must learn to be a repentant people, understanding how to accept the forgiveness of God in our lives.

No matter how mired we are in our sin, God will cleanse us when we ask. There might be consequences associated with our actions, but the sin is not held against us. God has forgiven us, and we must accept it, refusing to condemn ourselves any longer.

Like the lady caught in the act of adultery, we must learn to accept God's forgiveness. Regardless of how dirty and guilty she felt, Jesus wiped away her sin. He simply told her to go and sin no more.

I stand before You free from condemnation. Thank You, Lord, for wiping clean my sins. I will not look back.

HOW TO HANDLE REJECTION

SCRIPTURE READING: JOHN 1:1–13

KEY VERSE: JOHN 1:12

But as many as received Him, to them He gave the right to become children of God, to those who believe in His name.

At some point, each of us will experience some form of rejection. And while we have to deal with it, we must keep in mind that we are not rejected.

God deemed our lives so precious and valuable that He sacrificed His only Son for us, guaranteeing acceptance by Him forever, should we choose to make Him Lord of our lives. Paul wrote, "And although you were formerly alienated and hostile in mind, engaged in evil deeds, yet He has now reconciled you in His fleshly body through death" (Colossians 1:21–22 NASB).

In combating feelings of rejection, we must remember what God says about us:

- We belong. We are His children, children who belong.
- We have worth. Regardless of what others tell us, God says we have worth because of Christ who lives inside of us. That's what counts!
- We are capable. With the Holy Spirit living inside of us, we have the power to accomplish whatever God calls us to do (Philippians 4:13).

The world is wrong! We are valuable. And we are valuable to God, who places great importance on our lives as He desires to see us enjoy His kingdom and fellowship.

Thank You, Father, for the sacrifice of Your Son for me. Because of that I am Your child. No one can take that away from me.

TOTALLY ACCEPTED

SCRIPTURE READING: 1 JOHN 4:1–10
KEY VERSE: 1 JOHN 4:10

*In this is love, not that we loved God, but that He loved us
and sent His Son to be the propitiation for our sins.*

While we would like to think that we can avoid rejection from the world, we cannot. However, it is not the world that will save us from ourselves—it is our heavenly Father. And His acceptance is eternal.

Perhaps we feel rejected because someone strongly dislikes what we thought was a good idea. Or maybe rejection comes from our kids or our parents. We struggle to understand why they refuse to accept us.

Whenever those feelings persist, we must recognize and refute them. Jesus understands our feelings of rejection. However, it was His death and resurrection that led to our eternal acceptance. Once we refute those feelings of rejection, it is important to affirm what God speaks over us. In His unfailing love for us, God says this:

- We are unconditionally loved. He never leaves or forsakes His children. He will forever stand by us.
- We are completely forgiven. God does not hold our sins over our heads. "This is love, not that we loved God, but that He loved us and sent His Son to be the propitiation for our sins" (1 John 4:10 NASB).
- We are totally accepted. Gaining God's acceptance is simple: accept His love and forgiveness for our lives. We are complete in Christ. Our searching ends once we enter into relationship with the Lord. Nothing else will ever satisfy us like He does.

Lord, I sometimes feel rejected by people in my life. But I know that in You I have received unconditional love and acceptance.

How to Handle Fear

SCRIPTURE READING: MATTHEW 14:26–32
KEY VERSE: MATTHEW 14:30

But when he saw that the wind was boisterous, he was afraid;
and beginning to sink he cried out, saying, "Lord, save me!"

Before we know it, fear strikes furiously. We fail to see a certain circumstance coming, but now that it has arrived; we have serious questions as to how we will avoid its impending consequences.

When we are grounded in our faith, confidence emanates from our lives. Then in the presence of confidence, there is no fear. When we exude certainty, the outcome is never in question. We know God will prevail.

The focus of our lives must be set upon God in order to defeat fear. Even removing our eyes from Him for a moment can send us trembling in fear, forgetting the power that rests with the One who loves us completely.

On the turbulent waters of the Sea of Galilee, Peter leaped over the side of the boat toward his Savior. While a sense of doubt existed in Peter's mind, he decided it would disappear if he, too, could walk on the water.

For a short period of time, Peter was right. He began walking on the waves just like his Savior. But then he began to focus on the whitecaps and wind instead of Jesus.

By placing our focus upon the Lord, we demonstrate where our faith rests—solely upon God, whose unconditional love gives us the confidence we need to be free from fear.

Lord, lift my eyes up to see You, my rock, my solid footing, when the
troubled waters pull me down and I become afraid.

FACING FEAR

SCRIPTURE READING: ISAIAH 41:10–20
KEY VERSE: DEUTERONOMY 3:22

You must not fear them, for the Lord your God Himself fights for you.

Many times, instead of facing our fears with courage, we cower. Somehow, we cannot imagine having the strength to overcome the many trials that come our way, but we have the strength we need to overcome the adversity within our lives.

Paul wrote to Timothy, who was faced with a tremendous task—maintaining a spirit of worship and Christian growth in the early church. If there were ever reasons for fear, Timothy had a few. However, Paul knew that if Timothy caved into his fears, then his ministry would be ruined. Therefore, Paul wrote to admonish his young protégé: "For God has not given us a spirit of fear, but of power and of love and of a sound mind" (2 Timothy 1:7).

God wants us to face fear with the knowledge that He will give us the ability to conquer fear's attempt to paralyze us. "Do not fear them, for the LORD your God is the one fighting for you" (Deuteronomy 3:22 NASB). We triumph over fear as we look to God for the strength to move forward, courageously pressing on because He is the One strengthening us.

Africans say that when a lion is stalking its prey, it will roar very loudly. You would think that the prey would run, but actually the roar paralyzes it with fear. Don't allow Satan's roar to paralyze you in your faith. Christ is your Savior, and He is your eternal strength.

Lord, when Satan roars and I am afraid, I know that You have already defeated him. I put my trust in You.

How to Handle Loneliness

SCRIPTURE READING: PSALM 40:1–8
KEY VERSE: PSALM 40:2

He also brought me up out of a horrible pit,
Out of the miry clay,
And set my feet upon a rock,
And established my steps.

Regardless of how many people surround us, we can feel lonely. Numerous friends and family are not always the answer to squelching those feelings of loneliness in our lives. While we need to be alone from time to time, there is a difference between being alone and loneliness. Being alone is purposeful, a time of self-discovery, healing, and calming. Loneliness, however, causes anxiety and cannot be ignored because of its consequences.

Many times in an effort to avoid feeling lonely, we enter into relationships that are not God's best for us. Whenever we compromise our convictions, trouble and loneliness increase. Looking to anyone other than God in the midst of our loneliness leads to disappointment and a greater sense of anxiety.

When God's people have a desperate need, He is quick to offer true hope. God desires to be your all in all, the One who fulfills your deepest needs and desires, including the desire to be loved, not lonely. Only He can love you the way you need to be loved.

Lord, I picture Your loving arms around me in times of loneliness.
No one but You can fill the void in my heart, and I turn to You.

SET FREE FROM LONELINESS

SCRIPTURE READING: JOHN 14:15–21
KEY VERSE: JOHN 14:6

*Jesus said to him, "I am the way, the truth, and the life.
No one comes to the Father except through Me."*

Sin is oftentimes the spark that fans the flames of loneliness in our lives. We believe we are unworthy of God's grace, so we stop seeking Him. God, however, is longing for us to run to Him, not from Him.

Whenever we feel loneliness beginning to settle on our lives, we can overcome its grip with these steps:

- Reconcile with God through Jesus. God's awesome plan of redemption for our lives restores our relationship with Him (Romans 5:10–11).
- Remember God's promises. No matter how lonely we feel, we are never alone—God is always there with us. Whatever we are experiencing in life, we cannot escape Him. Wherever we go, He goes there too (John 14:16–18).
- Respond to circumstances based on truth, not our feelings. Reacting to situations on the basis of how we feel can lead us down roads that are treacherous and dangerous. We must rely on God and what we know about Him, not how we feel in the moment.
- Refocus our attention off ourselves and on to someone we can serve. Instead of focusing on our needs, we should look to serve those around us. In the process, we will find great joy and blessing in showing them Christ. God does not desire for us to be lonely. He wants us to have an intimate relationship with Him. Loneliness will fade in the warmth of His love and friendship.

Lord, when my feelings turn my eyes on self, and I think I am alone, I rejoice that You are right there, waiting for me to recognize Your constant presence.

How to Handle Anger

SCRIPTURE READING: MATTHEW 6:43–48
KEY VERSE: EPHESIANS 4:26

"Be angry, and do not sin": do not let the sun go down on your wrath.

Like a sore festering on our bodies, so is unforgiveness in our hearts. The gaping wound left by someone angers us. Instead of attending to it, we leave it open. We want the world to see what was done to us. Each time we look at how mangled we are, our anger grows. Anger can destroy us from without and within. It quickly can turn into uncontrollable rage, or it can simmer quietly for years inside of us. Paul told us to not sin in our anger (Ephesians 4:26).

God created us with emotions. Anger is one. However, He does not want us to use it to hurt others or become embittered. Anger should be expressed sparingly—not for selfish purposes or to gain our own way. And always, anger needs to be dealt with immediately and not left to linger in our thoughts.

In teaching, Jesus emphasized the importance of forgiveness, especially when dealing with anger and personal hurts (Matthew 6:14–15). Realize that Satan looks for every possible avenue to thwart your Christian witness. Therefore, don't allow anger to become a place where he can build a stronghold in your life.

If you are struggling with feelings of anger, ask God to help you deal with it before it grows any further.

Lord, Creator of my emotions, I turn them over to You. When I am angry, give me the desire to rise above self, and the strength to forgive.

GETTING A GRIP

SCRIPTURE READING: EPHESIANS 4:26–32
KEY VERSE: EPHESIANS 4:31

Let all bitterness, wrath, anger, clamor, and evil speaking
be put away from you, with all malice.

We cannot believe someone would commit such an act against us—cut us off in traffic, gossip about us, or show another form of disrespect. We wonder, *What did I do to deserve this?*

Getting a grip on our anger is imperative, especially when we are in the company of others who have not offended us. If we allow our anger to explode, everyone around us will sense its fury. Nothing can be gained from this. When anger comes, step away from the situation and take time to calm down. Tell God what you are feeling, then ask Him to defuse the situation.

When we acknowledge to God that we are angry, then He will help us identify the source of our frustration. He will also teach us how to deal with the situation from a godly perspective. God has a lesson for us to learn in every circumstance of life. Frustrations will come, and we will feel angry. However, we can say no to anger and yes to God's ability to deal with our frustrations. Ask Him, "Lord, what do You want me to learn through this?"

When you pray this prayer, He will make His will clear. Anger will disappear once you know that God has a plan in mind that includes freedom and not frustration.

Lord, when I am angry, teach me to surrender my feelings to You and to ask, instead, what I am to learn. Make me willing to hear Your answer.

The Appeal of Temptation

SCRIPTURE READING: JOHN 8:43–47
KEY VERSE: JOHN 8:44

*You are of your father the devil, and the desires of your father you want
to do. He was a murderer from the beginning, and does not stand in
the truth, because there is no truth in him. When he speaks a lie, he
speaks from his own resources, for he is a liar and the father of it.*

Satan is so cunning that he was able to deceive Eve into sinning. Her
response to his question in the third chapter of Genesis reveals that she
knew exactly what God had told her.

Aren't we exactly the same today? We know precisely what God's Word
says. Still, we often fail to obey Him. Do you spend more time indulging
your desires—even if it sometimes means bordering on sin—than you do
meditating on God's Word and praying? We humans have finite minds and
all kinds of emotions; on our own, it is almost impossible to successfully
combat temptations thrown at us by an enemy who is supernatural.

Read Pastor John MacArthur's commentary on the ruthlessness of Satan
as expressed in today's passage:

Satan, emboldened by [Eve's] openness to him, spoke a direct lie. This lie
actually led her and Adam to spiritual death (separation from God). So,
Satan is called a liar and murderer from the beginning (John 8:44). His lies
always promise great benefits. Eve experienced this result. She and Adam
did know good and evil; but because of personal corruption, they did not
know as God knows in perfect holiness.

When Satan throws his darts, simply say, "Lord, thank You that I'm Your
child. Please protect me." Remember that He who is in you is greater than he
who is in the world (1 John 4:4). God is faithful. He will lead you to freedom
through the way of escape.

*Lord, thank You that I am Your child. Please protect me from the
fiery darts of Satan.*

FREEDOM FROM SIN

SCRIPTURE READING: ROMANS 6:15–23
KEY VERSE: ROMANS 6:22

But now having been set free from sin, and having become slaves of
God, you have your fruit to holiness, and the end, everlasting life.

All sin begins with a thought. Our minds are the enemy's targets. Not only does sin enslave us and bind us to destructive activity, it separates and isolates us from God's love.

This does not mean that God changes the way He loves us. His love is unconditional and eternal. However, in the Garden of Eden after Adam and Eve yielded to sin, they immediately "hid" themselves from God. God did not avoid or hide from them. They were the ones who ran from God. Is any sin too great for God to forgive? No. Nothing is greater than God. However, we must make the decision to turn away from sin and return to the Lord.

You may be in a situation where you feel totally out of control. You have given yourself to someone or something and now you are no longer in control of your feelings or emotions. Sin has a stranglehold on your life. What do you do?

Cry out to God—He knows where you are. He sees what sin has done to your life, and He promises to make a way of escape when you cry out to Him. Maybe you are not a believer and you wonder how you can receive true hope that does not fade. Cry out to God, and He will reach out to you and save you.

Make a commitment to say no to everything that does not line up with the Word of God. This will mean spending time studying His Word. Once you have tasted His goodness and learned His principles, sin will lose its appeal.

Lord, I realize that freedom from sin is the privilege and the power
to do what is right. Help me to do what is good in Your eyes.

APPLYING GOD'S WORD

SCRIPTURE READING: PSALM 51:1–19

KEY VERSE: PSALM 51:4

Against You, You only, have I sinned,
And done this evil in Your sight—
That You may be found just when You speak,
And blameless when You judge.

There is a sure way to deal with sin, and that is by applying God's Word to whatever temptation you are facing. If not dealt with, temptation will turn into sin, and sin will gain a stronghold in your life. From that point, it will permeate all you do.

People like to think that sin only affects them. For example, they deny the seriousness of adultery by thinking it won't hurt anyone else, but it always does! Sin destroys families and friendships, but, most of all, it destroys our fellowship with God. The aftershock of David's sin with Bathsheba was felt throughout his family and kingdom. It weakened his ability to rule Israel and cost him the respect of family and countrymen. However, the most dramatic result of his sin was how it clouded his fellowship with the Lord.

In Psalm 51, David pled with God for forgiveness. When we cry out to the Lord, He provides the strength and power we need to deal with our sin. He forgives and cleanses us from all unrighteousness. While there are consequences to sin, God will not cast us away. We may have to endure sorrow and embarrassment, but He will walk beside us and strengthen us in our walk with Him.

Father, I realize that sin is rebellion against You. I thank You that through Your Son, Jesus Christ, I can be set free from its entanglement.

FREEDOM FROM GUILT

SCRIPTURE READING: JOHN 10:7–10
KEY VERSE: JOHN 10:10

The thief does not come except to steal, and to kill,
and to destroy. I have come that they may have life,
and that they may have it more abundantly.

Once we enter into a relationship with Jesus Christ, our guilt vanishes. The sins that once haunted us are forgiven as we confess them before God. The penalty of sin was paid with the sacrificial death of Jesus.

However, many believers struggle with feelings of guilt when they instead should feel the freedom of God's love. As children of God, whenever we sin, we feel conviction—the Holy Spirit tugging on our hearts to resolve the sin against God. All other feelings of guilt should be devoid from our lives. Unfortunately, that is not always the case. Once we ask God to forgive us for sinning, we need to return to His calling for our lives. There are consequences for our actions, but His forgiveness restores us to do His good work again.

Jesus came to give us abundant life (John 10:10). Guilt steals us of our joy and robs us of that life. It holds us captive for the actions of our past. However, once we ask God for forgiveness of our sins, God atones us. The guilty feelings for things in the past—even things over which we had no control—are from the enemy. God loves us, and He desires for us to live in His freedom, free from the guilt of the enemy.

I acknowledge, dear Lord, that lingering guilt steals the abundant
life You have promised believers. I leave that guilt at the cross, where
it was crucified with You.

THE TOOL OF FRUSTRATION

SCRIPTURE READING: ROMANS 8:20–27
KEY VERSE: ROMANS 8:26

Likewise the Spirit also helps in our weaknesses. For we do not know what we should pray for as we ought, but the Spirit Himself makes intercession for us with groanings which cannot be uttered.

Frustration is defined as "a deep chronic sense or state of insecurity and dissatisfaction arising from unresolved problems or unfulfilled needs." Though frustration hardly seems like a tool God would use, Romans 8:20–21 reports that it is an avenue by which God teaches us how to enjoy the freedom He so graciously provides: "The creation was subjected to frustration, not by its own choice, but by the will of the one who subjected it, in hope that the creation itself will be liberated from its bondage to decay and brought into the glorious freedom of the children of God" (NIV).

Do you experience a deep sense of frustration that derives from problems or needs beyond your control? Remember, God is in the process of revealing a great lesson to you. He allows frustrations to build so you will be driven back to Him in prayer.

It is in times of quiet devotion that we hear the Savior whisper words of hope and peace to our confused and frustrated hearts. Only God can offer the freedom we need to survive our greatest frustrations. He is the One who knows how to satisfy perfectly our every need.

Are you feeling frustrated today? Rejoice! God is at work in your life. Ask Him how you should handle this frustration. Never allow feelings of doubt and confusion to rule your emotions. God has set you free!

Father, thank You that Your Holy Spirit lives in the center of my frustrations and gives direction to my prayers. Help me to remember that when I am most despairing, I am also brought closest to You.

FREE TO ENJOY GOD

SCRIPTURE READING: 1 TIMOTHY 6:1–8
KEY VERSE: 1 TIMOTHY 6:1

*Let as many bondservants as are under the yoke count their own
masters worthy of all honor, so that the name of God and
His doctrine may not be blasphemed.*

Paul understood being imprisoned. He knew what it was like to be under someone else's command and subject to another person's will: demoralizing and laborious. However, in 1 Timothy 6:1, Paul admonished all slaves to honor their masters *in order to* honor God.

This may be a difficult principle for you, especially if there is an authority in your life who is treating you unfairly, dishonestly, or cruelly. Though you wish to obey God, your adverse feelings toward the party in question get in the way.

Paul understood this, but he also realized that the only true freedom is through Christ. It is exercised by representing Christ's love to others. Whittaker Chambers explains, "Freedom is a need of the soul, and nothing else. It is in striving toward God that the soul strives continually after a condition of freedom. God alone is the inciter and guarantor of freedom."

Being free of the authority over you will not make you free, because your inherent need for freedom is that which only God can meet. Trust Him to make you free no matter what your circumstances. You represent Christ best when you show His love to all, regardless of how they treat you.

Father, there are times when I cannot abide the unkindness of people in authority over me. Thank You that I am not owned by earthly circumstances. You have set my spirit free.

FINDING YOUR FOCUS

SCRIPTURE READING: 1 TIMOTHY 6:9–21
KEY VERSE: 1 TIMOTHY 6:17

Command those who are rich in this present age not to be haughty,
nor to trust in uncertain riches but in the living God,
who gives us richly all things to enjoy.

Admiral Arthur Radford once wrote, "In the Bible, and particularly in Jesus' spiritual concepts of God and man, all men can find the key to victory, not only one evil system, but in the greater crusade against all falsehood. Mankind, however, appears to come slowly to the realization that freedom is not won and held solely by material means."

Think about the truth of that statement in your own life. You have the key to victory, to ultimate freedom and triumph over all falsehood. Are you clinging to the hope of some material means to open the gates of freedom for you?

If you are, 1 Timothy 6:17 has a word for you: make sure that nothing becomes a stumbling block for you. True freedom comes when you fix the focus of your heart on Christ alone. Wealth, power, intelligence, beauty, status, politics, or even religious piety can lead quickly to bondage, especially when we desire these more than we desire Christ.

Turn to God and accept His principles for true freedom. He will faithfully supply all of your needs and give you victory over your trials. You will be truly free when all of your joy comes from Him.

Lord, I am so easily drawn to material things and temporal values
that don't last. Keep my mind fixed on You so that I may enjoy Your
eternal riches.

THE STRUGGLE WITH TEMPTATION

SCRIPTURE READING: LUKE 4:1–13
KEY VERSES: LUKE 4:1–2

*Then Jesus, being filled with the Holy Spirit, returned from the Jordan
and was led by the Spirit into the wilderness, being tempted for
forty days by the devil. And in those days He ate nothing,
and afterward, when they had ended, He was hungry.*

Everyone faces temptation. Even the Son of God was tempted by Satan to turn away from God. But Jesus saw through the enemy's schemes and remained firm in His love and devotion to the Father (Luke 4:1–13).

One of the reasons Jesus came was to personally identify with our needs and struggles. He understands how you feel under the weight of temptation. He has faced the tempter and overcome the darkness and adversity associated with Satan's fiery trials.

When you face temptation, know that you do not face it alone. Jesus is with you, and He provides the strength you need to say no to every dark thought or evil imagination. In times of temptation, when the enemy whispers lies to defeat and discourage, take your stand against him by clothing yourself in the mighty armor of God (Ephesians 6). Also know that you can never disappoint God. He knows exactly what you are doing even before you do it, and He loves you still.

Temptation is not a sin. Sin is the result of our acting on the temptation. God provides the strength we need to steer clear of temptation. You can say no to all evil because Jesus lives in you, and He has given you the Holy Spirit to lead you into all truth and knowledge. Therefore, take your stand as a child of God and claim His strength and victory!

*Father, I know temptation is common to all. Give me the strength to
steer clear of temptation and reject evil.*

Dealing with Temptation

SCRIPTURE READING: 1 CORINTHIANS 10:11–13
KEY VERSE: 1 CORINTHIANS 10:13

No temptation has overtaken you except such as is common to man;
but God is faithful, who will not allow you to be tempted beyond
what you are able, but with the temptation will also make
the way of escape, that you may be able to bear it.

Imagine yourself standing in the middle of a blazing forest fire. Flames leap from above, rise from below, and dance back and forth on all sides. You are scared, breathless, and certain that all is lost. Then you notice a clear, fire-free path that leads from where you are standing to a spot out of harm's way. What do you do? Well, you run like crazy down the safe path, of course!

How would you respond to someone who says, "You know, I'd rather just jump headlong into the fire and see what happens"? We would not be able to understand! Why on earth would someone choose to run toward danger and refuse to take advantage of a clear way of escape?

When we face temptation, it is like standing in the middle of a forest fire. Danger beckons from all sides, inviting us to jump into the fray. The problem, though, is that the fire looks inviting in these situations. Not only does the danger seem moot, but it actually appears to be a source of joy.

Joy never results from giving into temptation. Surrendering to the tempter only brings heartache and sin. Fortunately, God has promised that He will never allow us to be tempted beyond what we can bear; He always provides a way of escape. If you would run from fire, then it is only reasonable that you would flee from temptation; the only difference between the two is that temptation is more dangerous.

Lord, Your truth has shown me that yielding to temptation is like
willingly running into a forest fire. Give me the strength to turn my
back on those things that tempt me.

FLEEING TEMPTATION

SCRIPTURE READING: JAMES 4:7–10
KEY VERSE: MATTHEW 6:13

And do not lead us into temptation, but deliver us from the evil one.
For Yours is the kingdom and the power and the glory forever. Amen.

A popular response to temptation has made waves in the Christian community in recent years. This method of resistance makes perfect sense—flee from the temptation. On its face, this is a perfectly understandable response. After all, removing yourself from compromising situations is crucial to maintaining solid Christian character.

However, simple flight is not the ultimate answer. Unfortunately, fleeing temptation is only a temporary solution. One way or another, that old temptation will always seem to find you, wherever you have fled.

The idea of fleeing from Satan's ploys is a slight distortion of biblical counsel. Rather than running away from Satan, Scripture instructs, "Resist the devil and he will flee from you" (James 4:7). Through the power of the Holy Spirit, believers have the ability to send Satan himself running in terror.

Also, it is important for Christians to remember that temptation is not a problem that we can solve ourselves, by fleeing or any other manner. Instead, we need deliverance from temptation. Jesus taught, "And do not lead us into temptation, but deliver us from evil" (Matthew 6:13 NASB).

Evil is a God-sized problem. Thinking that we have within ourselves any means to defeat it negates the need for a Savior. We cannot win this spiritual war; however, we can rest in the assurance that Jesus has already secured the victory. When temptation comes, remove yourself from the situation, but also stand firm in the Lord. Remember, you are part of the victorious army.

Lord, I cannot always flee from temptation. And temptation has legs to follow me. Give me the strength to resist temptation wherever I meet it.

SNARES OF THE WORLD

SCRIPTURE READING: JOHN 10:11–18
KEY VERSES: HEBREWS 13:20–21

*Now may the God of peace who brought up our Lord Jesus from the
dead, that great Shepherd of the sheep, through the blood of the
everlasting covenant, make you complete in every good work to do His
will, working in you what is well pleasing in His sight, through
Jesus Christ, to whom be glory forever and ever. Amen.*

Cattle ranchers know all too well that the barbed-wire fences designed to
protect their livestock can become dangerous traps for curious animals.
In an effort to reach grass that is just outside of the fence, cows often poke their
heads between the twisted wires and become entangled in their razor-sharp
snares.

At this point of entrapment, the cow is generally helpless. Though it may
pull and thrash, the barbs only dig deeper into its flesh. It must now cry out
for help. A seasoned rancher will be able to quiet the animal and carefully
release it from its place of bondage.

Though it may not be quite as obvious, we, too, can become deeply
entangled in the world's snares. Many times traps can exist deep within the
hearts of those around us. Inner struggles can often prove to be more painful
and destructive than external trials.

How wonderful it is to know that we have a "seasoned rancher" in our
lives! Jesus is often referred to as the Good Shepherd, and for good reason.
Throughout the Bible, we are likened to sheep in need of direction and rescue.
Jesus came to earth to physically, spiritually, and emotionally experience our
trials firsthand. He came to answer our cries of help and to release us from the
barbs of the evil one.

When the devil tries to ensnare you, there is no need to fight, struggle,
and thrash. Instead, be still and call out to the attentive Good Shepherd. He
tends to His flock faithfully and will be there for you in your time of need.

*Lord, keep me from the snares of the world. Give me direction so I
will not be entrapped by the barbs of the evil one.*

CAPTIVES OF SIN

SCRIPTURE READING: LUKE 4:14–30
KEY VERSE: LUKE 4:18

The Spirit of the LORD is upon Me, because He has anointed Me to
preach the gospel to the poor; He has sent Me to heal the brokenhearted,
to proclaim liberty to the captives and recovery of sight to the blind,
to set at liberty those who are oppressed.

Imagine what it must be like to accidentally get locked in your own bedroom. At first, you probably would not even realize it. After all, the room would be the same; there would be no reason for you to think there was a problem. Your furniture would be there, neatly arranged. Your bed would still beckon you with the hope of peaceful slumber. Your window would still offer the pleasant view that you see every day. There would really be nothing out of the ordinary.

Then, say you wanted to make a sandwich. You click the television off, climb out of bed, and head for the door. Reaching for the knob, you are immediately struck with the realization that your door lock has broken, and the door will not open. You pull and jerk on the knob, but the door does not move. You yell for help, but no one is home. You are trapped; and the worst part is, you never even realized you were a prisoner.

This scene is a bit of a parody, but it aptly represents a biblical truth: all people, whether they realize it or not, are captives of sin. Everyone is locked in his own private prison. The good news, however, is that Jesus came into the world to release the prisoners. That is, He came to free the entire world from the grip of sin.

Thank Him today for the glorious freedom offered by the Cross of Christ. He paid the fine, He bore the punishment, and He has set you free!

Father, thank You for the glorious freedom offered by the Cross.
Thank You for paying the price, bearing the punishment, and setting
me free!

EXPERIENCING GOD'S LOVE

SCRIPTURE READING: HEBREWS 5:6–10
KEY VERSE: HEBREWS 5:8

Though He was a Son, yet He learned obedience
by the things which He suffered.

What happens when you ignore God? In your mind, do you picture Him just walking away, looking forlorn and rejected? Or do you have a mental image of God getting mad at you and banishing you to forty years of wilderness wandering?

Neither is correct. God loves you perfectly. And His love for you is not based on your obedience. Though He tells us in His Word that obedience is better than sacrifice, the thing that God wants most from you is a love that comes from your heart.

He doesn't stop loving you just because you do something wrong. None of us can earn God's love by being good or trying to be perfect. For one, we do not have the ability to do either of these on our own. We need a Savior. And this is why Jesus came to die for you and me. He does the very thing that you cannot do for yourself. He makes you acceptable in God's eyes. He sets you free from sin.

When we ignore the Lord, we are the ones who suffer and miss a great opportunity for blessing. God is not a strong and mighty taskmaster who waits for us to do something wrong so He can pounce. He is a loving God who listens for our cry. When He draws you to Himself, He uses love, not a rod of thunder. God knows that once you drink of His love, the world's appeal will fade. Give Him your heart, and you will be blessed by what you receive from Him.

Thank You for Your love, Father. It sets me free from sin and makes me acceptable in Your sight. I rejoice in that!

ATTACKING THE ROOTS OF SIN

SCRIPTURE READING: 1 JOHN 1:5–2:2
KEY VERSE: 1 JOHN 1:9

*If we confess our sins, He is faithful and just to forgive us our
sins and to cleanse us from all unrighteousness.*

If you hurt someone as a result of a sin you committed, would you go to him
or her for help in overcoming that sin? If you are like most people, you
probably would not. Why? Because you would likely feel guilty or ashamed.
Our human minds think this way because we have trouble understanding true
forgiveness.

The beauty of this scenario is that God is not limited by human understanding. His thoughts are higher than ours, and His ways are different
(Isaiah 55:8). When we sin against God, He is the very One we need to help
us break free from the cycle of sin. Though this sounds ironic, it is the truth.

First John 1:9 tells us God will forgive us and cleanse us when we confess
to Him. Essentially, no matter what we have done, God is willing to forgive
us and to wash away the damaging residue that disobedience can leave upon
our lives.

If you have an unconfessed sin in your life, do not feel like you have to
hide from God. Instead, bring the matter to Him in prayer and receive the
gift of His forgiveness. Being out of fellowship with God is a terrible place to
be. Do not let fear keep you away from the One who loves you unconditionally. Return to Him today just as you are. There is no need to feel ashamed.

*Lord, I do not know why I try to hide my sin from You, for You will
not condemn a contrite heart. Search my soul and bring forth those
hidden things so that I may confess them.*

SAVED BY GRACE

SCRIPTURE READING: ROMANS 11:1–6
KEY VERSE: ROMANS 11:6

*And if by grace, then it is no longer of works; otherwise grace is
no longer grace. But if it is of works, it is no longer grace;
otherwise work is no longer work.*

Freedom is a word with many political and religious applications. In its purest sense, however, freedom is defined as liberty from bondage or enslavement. When the apostle Paul addressed the church of Galatia, he spoke of a specific type of freedom—the freedom Christ offers from "works." Paul provided this clarification because many Galatians had been mistakenly led to add unnecessary qualifications to obtaining salvation. They were still trying to earn favor with God and forgiveness of their sins by doing good works and offering sacrifices. Paul reminded the church that their efforts were futile because Christ's death on the cross had paid the price for the world's sins. Therefore, there was no need to attempt to achieve perfection by obeying the old law, which had formerly enslaved them.

The liberating news is that we are saved by God's grace alone. If that wasn't true—if we can earn God's favor—then grace isn't really grace at all (Romans 11:6). If a person believes he can earn salvation, he feels no need for God's grace. As believers, we know this to be untrue.

Use your prayer time today to intercede for the citizens of our world who are still in bondage to the law. Ask God to reach their hearts with the news of the free gift of eternal life made available through Jesus' shed blood.

*Dear Lord, thank You for freedom from the works of the law and
salvation by grace alone. I pray for those still in bondage to the law.
Let them learn of Your precious gift of salvation.*

FREE TO REJOICE

SCRIPTURE READING: MATTHEW 28:18–29

KEY VERSE: PSALM 139:13

For You formed my inward parts;
You covered me in my mother's womb.

How often do you stop to thank God for your freedom? Whether or not you live in a free country—even if you are reading this message from inside a jail cell—if you have trusted Jesus Christ as your Savior, you are the recipient of the greatest kind of freedom. It is freedom from eternal suffering and death.

The Bible tells us that no one is worthy of this gift. We have all sinned and fallen short of God's likeness (Romans 3:23). But Jesus' death on the cross removed our collective death penalty once and for all. Therefore, you are now secure in Him.

Why did God give you this great gift? It is because He has something wonderful in mind for your life (Jeremiah 29:11). He wants you to accomplish great things for His kingdom and to share the joy of your faith with others (Matthew 28:18–20). God designed you for a purpose when He formed you in your mother's womb (Psalm 139:13).

If you are struggling with feelings of doubt, regret, or depression surrounding something in your past, receive this message of hope today: God sent His Son to die for you so that you may have freedom from the bonds of sin. You are forgiven because of His great love.

Before you end your quiet time today, read John 15:13–15. In it, Jesus explains that He made so great a sacrifice because He loves us so much. No longer are we slaves to sin, but we are instead free to rejoice in the love of our Savior and Friend, Jesus Christ.

Lord, I have been created by design to walk in the way of freedom. I praise You for forgiving me and setting my feet free to follow You.

REACTING TO TEMPTATION

SCRIPTURE READING: JAMES 1:1–8
KEY VERSE: JAMES 1:2

My brethren, count it all joy when you fall into various trials.

Temptation is an enticement to go beyond the bounds of our God-given desires. While we ourselves have to take responsibility for caving in to such an attraction, it should nonetheless be helpful to recognize the source of all temptation: Satan, the enemy of our souls.

The enemy is crafty and intelligent. He also is savage and relentless. His goal is to alienate you from God, to destroy your fellowship with your Creator and Savior. His purpose is to stunt your growth as a believer and minimize your impact for God's kingdom. He knows your weaknesses; he also knows how to surprise, stage, and camouflage.

This is why it is imperative for every believer to maintain his or her defense by means of a vibrant, abiding fellowship with Jesus Christ. He is our refuge and rear guard, and His Word is our very effective weapon.

It is a mistake to accuse others for your own failures. For instance, some people attribute their current faults to the mistakes of their parents. While parental influence can be great, every person is responsible for his or her own choices and actions. Even more so, it is an error to try and blame God for the temptations that lure you. God is holy; Satan is evil.

React to temptation with the knowledge that its source is an evil enemy who attempts daily to steal your joy and destroy your effectiveness as a child of God. Then turn to the Lord and ask Him to help you overcome. He is the One who is able and eager to free you and give you victory.

Lord, help me to overcome the temptations of the enemy. Give me the victory and set me free!

The Lifeline to Freedom

SCRIPTURE READING: JAMES 1:12–17
KEY VERSE: JAMES 1:12

Blessed is the man who endures temptation; for when he has been approved, he will receive the crown of life which the Lord has promised to those who love Him.

Satan cannot have your soul, so he wants nothing more than to ruin your fellowship with the Lord and to sidetrack your walk and your witness.

James, Jesus' half-brother, describes the destructive progression Satan sets in motion through temptation: "But each one is tempted when he is carried away and enticed by his own lust. Then when lust has conceived, it gives birth to sin; and when sin is accomplished, it brings forth death" (James 1:14–15 NASB).

We can be carried away and lured to go beyond the limits of our God-given desires and interests. Our own lust can conceive and give birth to sin. But this birth is not one involving life. Rather, it brings forth death.

Jesus, however, is a God of hope. While it sometimes seems as if Satan is throwing everything in his formidable arsenal at us, we can trust in God's Word and believe Him when He tells us that He is faithful. He will never allow us to be tempted beyond what we are able, in His power, to withstand. God will always give us the opportunity to escape. He always honors His Word. And He is always trustworthy.

The key to overcoming temptation is simple obedience. At times, that may seem impossible. But keep in mind that what is impossible with man is possible with God (Matthew 19:26). The Bible says that He will make a way of escape. The lifeline to freedom forever will be there. It is simply a matter of whether we are willing to grab hold.

Dear Lord, I thank You that You will not allow me to be tempted beyond what I am able. Thank You that the lifeline to freedom is available to me today as I reject temptation.

AUGUST
Pathway to Peace

Peace I leave with you, My peace I give to you; not as the world gives do I give to you. Let not your heart be troubled, neither let it be afraid.

—John 14:27

Prevailing Peace

Scripture Reading: Psalm 34:1–8
Key Verse: Psalm 34:8

Oh, taste and see that the LORD is good;
Blessed is the man who trusts in Him!

Even before he was king of Israel, David understood feeling overwhelmed with life. While he was being hunted by Saul, David fled to Gath, where he found out his reputation as a warrior preceded him. He pretended to be insane so that King Achish of Gath would not have him killed.

No one should doubt that David experienced stress during this episode. Yet during that time, he wrote about God's goodness in Psalm 34. David found true sanctuary in the Lord.

Today, as in David's time, peace is still a difficult thing to come by. The day is often filled with conflicts and stressful interruptions. Sometimes it can seem impossible to escape the tumult and achieve serenity. Yet Jesus offers you the same tranquility that David found: "Peace I leave with you, My peace I give to you; not as the world gives do I give to you. Let not your heart be troubled, nor let it be afraid" (John 14:27).

The only way to have peace is to trust God wholeheartedly, as David did. Allow His peace to permeate your life, and you will be able to say as Charles Wesley did, "I rest beneath the Almighty's shade, my griefs expire, my troubles cease; Thou, Lord, on whom my soul is stayed, wilt keep me still in perfect peace."

Father, thank You for the peace that passes human understanding.
Thank You for keeping me in perfect peace.

PEACE BARRIERS

SCRIPTURE READING: PSALM 23:1–6
KEY VERSE: 2 PETER 3:14

*Therefore, beloved, looking forward to these things, be diligent
to be found by Him in peace, without spot and blameless.*

Our quest for true peace begins at birth. As babies, we long for our mother's comforting arms; as children we yearn for happy experiences that are void of fear; and as adults we strive to find success and fulfillment through jobs and relationships.

These pursuits are desirable, but temporal. Lasting peace cannot be attained through our own efforts, but rather through Christ in us. The peace that comes from Him is eternal.

If you have accepted Christ as your personal Lord and Savior and are not experiencing peace, it is time to examine your relationship with God. Your bond with Him is the foundation upon which real peace is built. Until you have peace *with* God, you cannot experience the peace *of* God.

What causes disruptions in our peace with God? "Peace barriers" are often composed of habitual sin, unresolved guilt, and unforgiveness toward others. Obstructions can also occur when we blame God for difficult circumstances, or when we decide to live in a state of rebellion against God's truths.

If you are ready to experience true peace, ask God to expose anything that may be preventing you from receiving the peace that only He can give. Listen with an open heart and receive what God reveals to you through teaching, the Scriptures, or His own voice. When the barriers are removed, rejoice in His faithfulness.

Lord, I long for Your peace as surely as I have sought peace on my own throughout my life. Please show me the barriers to everlasting peace in my life.

CONFIDENT PEACE

SCRIPTURE READING: PHILIPPIANS 4:11–13
KEY VERSE: PHILIPPIANS 4:13

I can do all things through Christ who strengthens me.

God wants us to live a confident, peace-filled life, but far too often, feelings of inadequacy and unworthiness prevent us from doing this. There is only one way for God's people to face life, and that is to face it confidently. He is the One who loves us, has saved us from eternal death, and is committed to guiding us through every moment this life has to offer.

The apostle Paul lived through horrendous circumstances. He was rejected by his Jewish peers, stoned, and abandoned for dead. He was ridiculed, ignored, and often beaten for His devotion to Christ and the gospel message. But Paul continued to maintain a confident hope. His life was not set on earthly accomplishments. When he did not think he could face another day, he recalled one simple truth: "I can do all things through Christ who strengthens me" (Philippians 4:13).

Paul could get up each day because he understood that it was not his ability or strength that was needed. It was the strength of God flowing through his life that gave him the confidence he needed to face every task and challenge. If you try to achieve your goals apart from God, you will find that it is impossible. When you give God complete access to your life and place your dependency in Him, He builds a power base of truth, hope, and love in your life that will sustain you through every challenge and give you peace in every circumstance.

Confidence is an emotion that empowers us by energizing and strengthening us to do whatever God has called us to do.

Heavenly Father, take my feelings of unworthiness. Give me confident peace that will empower me to do what You have called me to do.

THE TRUSTWORTHINESS OF GOD

SCRIPTURE READING: PSALM 89:1–9
KEY VERSE: HEBREWS 13:8

Jesus Christ is the same yesterday, today, and forever.

Sometimes we find ourselves in deeply threatening situations where we can't see how God can possibly carry out His promises of being with us always or sustaining us through difficulties. Yet, as we read in Psalm 89 (NCV), David, in spite of the many times he felt his life was threatened and feared he had lost everything, said with conviction, "Your love continues forever; your loyalty goes on and on like the sky" (verse 2).

So, too, God's loyalty to us is everlasting. His promises are trustworthy. God sees beyond the here-and-now to what was and what will be.

In this one truth, we find our reason for hope and for unwavering confidence. God's unchanging nature teaches us that even when we feel unlovely, we are beautiful to Him. There is nothing we can do to change His love for us. It is unconditional, and it flows freely from His throne of grace.

Do you trust Him? Have you experienced a strong assurance that comes from placing your faith in His unfailing ability? Roll the burden of your heart onto Him.

Lord, my confidence is in You. My peace comes from the assurance that You know what is best, do what is best, and provide Your best.

THE POSITIVE POWER OF JOY

SCRIPTURE READING: PHILIPPIANS 2:13–18
KEY VERSE: PHILIPPIANS 2:17

*Yes, and if I am being poured out as a drink offering on the sacrifice
and service of your faith, I am glad and rejoice with you all.*

It was not uncommon for Jesus to instruct those He healed to go to the
temple and offer a sacrifice. In doing this, the people were acknowledging
God's mighty work while giving praise to Him, instead of just focusing on
the healing itself. There was a release of joy and praise as the people went
before God, thanking Him for what He had done. Joy is foundational to the
Christian life. The Bible teaches us to be joyful in all things.

Can this mean that even when we fail to see God's miraculous hand at
work in our lives, there is joy? Yes. Imprisoned and away from those he loved,
the apostle Paul wrote, "Even if I am being poured out as a drink offering . . .
I rejoice and share my joy with you all" (Philippians 2:17 NASB). It is possible
to have peace and be joyful even though our world seems to be coming apart
at the seams.

Because of Christ's love and devotion to you, you can have peace and
joy in times of disappointment, heartache, and personal loss. This is because
joy is not based on your circumstances; it is based on a Person—the Lord
Jesus Christ.

When you feel sorrowful, take your sacrifices of praise to Him. Let His
arms of encouragement engulf you and hold you close. Joy and peace reside
deep within the heart, not in external circumstances.

*Lord, I claim peace and joy to reign in my life today, regardless of
my circumstances. I offer a sacrifice of praise to You.*

Joy in the Lord

Scripture Reading: 1 Thessalonians 2:17–20
Key Verse: Nehemiah 8:10

Then he said to them, "Go your way, eat the fat, drink the sweet, and send portions to those for whom nothing is prepared; for this day is holy to our Lord. Do not sorrow, for the joy of the Lord is your strength."

Author and Bible teacher Warren Wiersbe writes:

Joy takes the burden out of service. "The joy of the Lord is your strength" (Nehemiah 8:10). God loves a cheerful servant as well as a cheerful giver . . . God wants His family to be happy, and this means that each member must contribute to the joy.

Have you ever thought about how your personality affects others? What type of employee or family member are you: positive, encouraging, a team member, and someone who prompts warm comments?

The Thessalonians struggled with being cheerful believers. Their joy had been dampened because they had allowed doubts and fears to creep into their thinking. False teachers had convinced them that the rapture of the church had already taken place.

Paul wrote his letter to encourage them not to give in to negative thinking. Instead, he admonished them to keep their focus on what they had been taught concerning this event: "For who is our hope or joy or crown of exultation? Is it not even you, in the presence of our Lord Jesus at His coming?" (1 Thessalonians 2:19 NASB).

Don't allow fears or doubts to control you and your emotions. Even though you face times when you do not sense God's closeness, He has not left you. Your greatest joy is in knowing that He has an eternal love for you that cannot be destroyed. This knowledge gives peace in the midst of turmoil.

Lord, thank You for the spirit of joy that yields strength, power, and peace to endure difficult circumstances.

EMPOWERING CONFIDENCE

SCRIPTURE READING: PSALM 40:1–5
KEY VERSE: PSALM 40:5

Many, O LORD my God, are Your wonderful works
Which You have done;
And Your thoughts toward us
Cannot be recounted to You in order;
If I would declare and speak of them,
They are more than can be numbered.

What is the basis for your confidence? Is it in an ability or a talent that you feel you have perfected? God allows you to do many things—some of which seem to come naturally. But in reality, it is God working in and through your life that enables you to do what He has called you to do. Never be guilty of taking credit for what only God can do.

David grew to be a mighty warrior and king. However, as is obvious in Psalm 40, he never lost sight of the fact that it was God who trained his hands for battle.

How can you avoid becoming overconfident and insensitive to God's ability in your life?

- Keep your focus on the Lord. Ask Him to point out any pride you may have displayed.
- Set aside time each day to be alone with the Lord. Prayer and meditation teaches us to rely on God and not on ourselves.
- Choose to trust God. An active faith builds our character and confidence. David confidently faced Goliath because he knew the Lord would grant him the victory.

Is your confidence in the eternal source of God's power and strength?

Lord, thank You for a strong confidence that will drive away doubt, fear, and anxiety and give me peace.

GOD IS IN CONTROL

SCRIPTURE READING: PSALM 147:1–7
KEY VERSE: PSALM 147:3

He heals the brokenhearted
And binds up their wounds.

In *A Godward Life*, author and pastor John Piper offers these thoughts: "Human strength can never impress an omnipotent God, and human bigness can never impress a God of infinite greatness. . . ."

Psalm 147 is a thrilling statement of hope for people who enjoy God being God: "He determines the number of the stars, he gives to all of them their names" (verse 4 ESV). Now this is more than we can absorb! "Such knowledge is too wonderful for me; it is high, I cannot attain it" (Psalm 139:6 ESV).

The earth, where we live, is a small planet revolving around a star called the sun which has a volume 1.3 times that of the earth. There are stars a million times brighter than the sun. There are about a hundred billion stars in our galaxy, the Milky Way, which is one hundred thousand light years across. . . . The sun travels about 155 miles per second, and so it would take two hundred million years to make a single revolution on its orbit in the Milky Way. . . .

The good news for those who enjoy God being God is that He enjoys them. He delights in those who hope in His immeasurable power. It is therefore no literary coincidence that the verses on either side of God's greatness in Psalm 147:4–5 show Him caring for the weak (verses 3 and 6). He loves to be God for the weak and childlike, who look to Him for all they need.

Lord, my peace comes from the knowledge that You are in control.
Thank You for that assurance.

GRACE AND PEACE

SCRIPTURE READING: ROMANS 6:11–14
KEY VERSE: ROMANS 6:14

For sin shall not have dominion over you,
for you are not under law but under grace.

Once we enter into a relationship with Christ, confessing Him as our Lord and Savior, we are redeemed. The guilt that shadowed our past vanishes in the light of God's deep forgiveness. While God views us as His sons and daughters, righteous in His sight, we still stumble. Feelings of guilt can rush over us, whispering that we are unworthy in the eyes of our heavenly Father and robbing us of our peace.

When those thoughts enter our minds, we must put them aside and remember what God has proclaimed over us: we are righteous. But we still must confess those sins to the Lord in order to restore our relationship with Him.

Paul writes, "Therefore do not let sin reign in your mortal body, that you should obey it in its lusts. . . . For sin shall not have dominion over you, for you are not under law but under grace" (Romans 6:12, 14). Living under grace does not mean we have a free pass to sin; rather, it means when we do stumble, God graciously extends a hand of mercy to us when we go before Him and repent. We can never do anything to earn God's grace and forgiveness in our lives. No matter what we do, it's only by His grace that we are righteous. It's only by His grace that our guilt is washed away.

I can do nothing to earn Your grace, dear Lord. It is a gift, and I praise You for it. Your forgiveness covers all my failings.

ABIDING IN CHRIST

SCRIPTURE READING: JOHN 15:1–8

KEY VERSE: JOHN 15:1

I am the true vine, and My Father is the vinedresser.

Troubles may seem to overwhelm you. It may seem that at every turn, no matter what you do, heartache awaits. It may seem that life is one trail of confusion and frustration leading to another.

It is at these times that you must remember the Lord's words that He will never leave you nor forsake you (Hebrews 13:5). It is at these times that you must draw close to Him. Is peace possible even in hard times? Absolutely. But the only way it is possible is through an abiding, abounding relationship with Jesus Christ. John 15 describes the beautiful "vine and branches" relationship we have with Christ if we truly are "in Him."

To enjoy true peace, we first must have peace with God. This means that we must be reconciled to God through faith in His Son, Jesus Christ. You may know unbelievers who seem to have it all together and are at perfect peace. But many times, beneath the veneer, they are as empty as any other lost soul. The truth is that peace cannot be purchased by human efforts. There is no such thing as peace, without the Prince of Peace.

A child of God enjoys all the blessings of personally knowing the God of the universe, who promises to be with us until the end of the age and beyond. All He asks of us is devotion, faith, and trust. Then peace becomes the natural by-product resulting from abiding in Him.

Lord, I am so grateful for the blessing of personally knowing You! Thank You also for the natural by-product of abiding in You—Your supernatural peace.

A CHRIST-CENTERED MIND

SCRIPTURE READING: PSALM 37:1–8

KEY VERSE: PSALM 37:1

Do not fret because of evildoers,
Nor be envious of the workers of iniquity.

It sometimes seems so difficult to live in peace in our frenzied world. The business and burdens of everyday life overshadow the joy we should be experiencing. We forget that the Bible repeatedly says that we are Christ's and He is ours. The enemy tries to distract us from this truth, and one of his most effective tactics is to get us to pull tomorrow's burdens into today.

Billy Graham's *Christian Worker's Handbook* states:

The term anxiety covers a wide range of problems resulting from unfounded fears. Someone has said that the anxious person and the worrier are so preoccupied about what may happen in the future that they forget to cope with the present. It is characteristic of such a person to worry about anything. They build "mountains out of mole hills," as insignificant matters assume great importance in their lives. They are anxious about imagined shortcomings, the future, their health, their families, and their work. They are often unable to pinpoint the reasons for their anxieties and fears.

Mankind has always been beset by worry, and the pressures of modern life have aggravated the problem. . . . Many of you are filled with a thousand anxieties. Bring them to Jesus Christ by faith. . . . I am learning in my own life, day by day, to keep my mind centered on Christ; the worries and anxieties and concerns of the world pass, and nothing but 'perfect peace' is left in the human heart.

Keep my mind centered on You, Lord, so that I can continually experience Your perfect peace.

A SENSE OF SELF-WORTH

SCRIPTURE READING: ROMANS 12:1–6

KEY VERSE: COLOSSIANS 3:3

For you died, and your life is hidden with Christ in God.

In Romans 12, Paul indicated that some people tend to think more highly of themselves than they should. It is also true that other people are tempted to think lowlier of themselves than is appropriate.

How are we to think? A godly sense of self-worth offers a valuable solution here. It lies at the heart of a peaceful life and provides the solid middle ground between the ditch of self-disparagement on the one hand and the precipice of self-exaltation on the other. This resting place in Jesus stems from simply seeing yourself the way God sees you.

When you are born again, God sees you as His beloved child and the owner of a new identity. Because your life is hidden with Christ in God (Colossians 3:3), you can say that you are complete in Christ. It is because of His Spirit within that it is possible for you to live a righteous life.

At the same time, you retain a sin nature, which is still capable of expressing itself. It is all right, therefore, to be grieved by some things you do, while rejoicing over others. That is how God feels. You should always keep in mind, however, that God's delight or displeasure with your conduct in no way alters either His love for you or your identity as His child. He always sees you as His own and a person of infinite worth.

Ultimately, you will reach full maturity in Christ, but in the meantime, never forget that you are not what you do. You are who you are.

Dear Lord, I am so glad I am not what I do, but who I am in You. Thank You for a godly sense of self-worth that enables me to be at peace with myself.

PROVERBS OF PEACE

SCRIPTURE READING: PROVERBS 17:13–15
KEY VERSE: PROVERBS 17:22

A merry heart does good, like medicine,
But a broken spirit dries the bones.

The book of Proverbs is rich in wisdom. It amplifies the truth that we can have peace and be content in all circumstances. Let's examine a few of these proverbs of peace:

- Proverbs 1:7: Fear and reverence of the Lord, which leads to surrender and submission, is the first step in enjoying contentedness.
- Proverbs 1:10–19: There are those who seek happiness through ill-gotten gains and wickedness. Never look at the world in envy, especially when you consider that their methods take away the life of the possessors.
- Proverbs 11:5, 30: Righteousness brings true contentment because right thinking and right actions are a joy to the Lord.
- Proverbs 16:32: It is better to have self-control than one's own dynasty.
- Proverbs 17:22: There is no way to put a price tag on good health brought on by joy and peace through a life lived for the Lord.
- Proverbs 18:12; 22:4; 25:6–7; 29:23: Humility is a cornerstone to peace and contentment, because humility never allows you to make yourself more than what God would have you to be.
- Proverbs 21:26; 22:1: Generosity and a good name are the natural results of honoring the Lord with obedience and staying our minds on Him.
- Proverbs 25:27; 27:23–24; 28:19: Delighting yourself in the Lord, His work, and His will for your life produces gains beyond measure.

Father, make me content in every circumstance. Give me peace in every situation. I claim these proverbs of peace to be manifested in my life today.

The Power of Solitude

Scripture Reading: Psalm 4:1–8
Key Verse: Psalm 4:7

You have put gladness in my heart,
More than in the season that their grain and wine increased.

The phrase "quiet time" has become widely used in Christian circles over the past several years. Preachers preach it, teachers teach it, and prayer warriors rely on it. However, when we say "quiet time," what are we really thinking?

Most likely, as you read this very passage, you are in the midst of your own quiet time. Perhaps you have soft Christian music in the background, a Bible on the table, and a soothing cup of coffee at your side. Maybe you have a cat nestled at your feet, and a lovely green yard outside the window. What warm and comfortable images!

All of these things are conducive to a refreshing prayer experience, a lengthy discussion with the Lord, or a moment of individual worship. However, even this peaceful scene is full of distractions.

Right now, you are actively reading; in a moment, you will spend a minute or two in prayer. However, this is not true "quiet time." Your mind is full of thoughts, words, and quiet conversation. Although this time is vital, it is not solitude.

Richard Foster writes, "Without silence, there is no solitude." A true moment of silence does not involve formulating your next thought or action, but instead is a moment of complete silence. Calm your mind, and even stop praying for a moment. Sit back and listen for a while. You may be surprised by what you hear.

Lord, I am unaccustomed to solitude—the deep silence in which You dwell. Teach me how to quiet the noise around me to hear Your voice.

PEACEFUL SOLITUDE

SCRIPTURE READING: PSALM 9:1–5
KEY VERSE: PSALM 9:1

I will praise You, O LORD, with my whole heart;
I will tell of all Your marvelous works.

Clearly, we live in a loud society. This is not simply a problem in some parts of the world; rather, industrialized society and fast-paced living have filled the world's airwaves with what can only be described as "noise." Some of the noise is useful; for example, a late-breaking news report on all channels that warns of an approaching storm. However, many things that fill our ears are practically pointless. Why is the noise there, and why do we need it?

In *Celebration of Discipline*, Richard Foster speculates, "One reason we can hardly bear to remain silent is that it makes us feel so helpless. . . . If we are silent, who will take control?" Very often, words are not only our means of communication, they are our means of control. We use words to manipulate our environment, to indelibly set our fingerprints on any given situation. If we don't speak up, someone else will swoop in and take charge.

Sometimes, this is exactly what needs to happen. Foster continues, "If we are silent, who will take control? God will take control." Our prayer lives are too often marked by an overabundance of talking, petitioning, and posturing. It is of extreme value to spend time daily talking with the Lord. However, it is also necessary to spend time in utter solitude before Him, allowing Him to speak to you uninterrupted. Take a moment to filter out the noise, and listen for God's voice.

Lord, am I guilty of using my voice to control situations? Give me the will to silence my voice so that Yours can be heard and You can have control.

GUILTY FEELINGS

SCRIPTURE READING: PSALM 103:6–12

KEY VERSE: PSALM 103:12

As far as the east is from the west,
So far has He removed our transgressions from us.

Just when we think we are free of some past sin, the enemy discreetly reminds us from where we came. He places sin around our necks like an albatross. Is it possible to shed those feelings of guilt forever and find spiritual peace?

The motive of the devil is to lie to us so that we become confused and wander away from the narrow path that leads to our heavenly Father. That's why we must ask the Lord for discernment from the enemy's lies so that we can put them aside and move forward.

When we ask God to forgive us of any sin we have committed—whether it be in the distant past or just today—He gladly obliges us. Suddenly, the sin that was a barrier in our relationship with God is removed. God never reminds us of our past sins.

David wrote that God removes our sins as far as the east is from the west (Psalm 103:12). We know that, yet we still struggle with past sins. In overcoming those feelings of guilt, we must be in constant remembrance that it is God's grace that brings freedom.

Whenever the enemy brings our past to mind, we can defeat him by recalling our source of forgiveness and reminding ourselves of what God's Word says: our sins are gone as far as the east is from the west.

Lord, when I am reminded of past sins, I know it is not You who is dangling them under my nose. I renounce the works of the enemy in trying to discourage me.

THE WATERS OF PEACE

SCRIPTURE READING: ROMANS 5:1–5
KEY VERSE: ROMANS 5:5

Now hope does not disappoint, because the love of God has been poured out in our hearts by the Holy Spirit who was given to us.

A favorite American gospel hymn contains the powerful but unusual lyric, "I've got peace like a river in my soul." When you think of peace, do you imagine a river?

In the book of Romans, we are told that "the love of God has been poured out in our hearts by the Holy Spirit" (5:5). Again in John 4:14, the analogy of water is used when Jesus told the woman at the well, "Whoever drinks of the water that I shall give him will never thirst. But the water that I shall give him will become in him a fountain of water springing up into everlasting life."

Just as a clear mountain stream refreshes and nourishes the wildlife in its midst, the peace of God fills our hearts with comfort through the Holy Spirit. There is no greater peace than that which is available through Jesus Christ.

Try to imagine His peace washing over you like a cool stream of water—soothing your heartache, washing away doubt, and cleansing the wounds of sin and pain. Is the river of peace becoming clear to you now?

The peace that comes from God is not a static, stagnant emotion. Rather, it is a fluid, energetic wave of confidence in the One who holds the universe in His hands. Open your heart. Receive the satisfying waters of peace into your soul and give praises to God for His mercy and love.

Lord, when I am distraught, help me to immerse myself in the running waters of Your peace, so that I may be refreshed.

EXPERIENCING PEACE

SCRIPTURE READING: JOHN 14:1–27
KEY VERSE: JOHN 14:27

*Peace I leave with you, My peace I give to you; not as the world gives do
I give to you. Let not your heart be troubled, neither let it be afraid.*

When God initially placed Adam and Eve in the Garden of Eden, surrounded by fragrant flowers, beautiful trees, and delicious fruits, do you think they felt peaceful? Of course they did. They were in true communion with each other and with God. They had no knowledge of evil, heartache, pain, or death.

We all know what happened next. Temptation entered the garden, and mankind began its earthly bondage to sin and death. Despite God's foreknowledge of what would occur in Eden, it was never His will for humans to experience pain. God's perfect, peaceful world was tainted by the author of evil, Satan.

Though we live in a world plagued by violence, anger, and hostility, we can still experience the peace that God intended us to know. By sending His Son, Jesus, to die for our sins, the door of peace and forgiveness was opened once and for all to those who believe.

To obtain God's peace, you must make three key decisions: accept Jesus Christ as your personal Lord and Savior, believe that the peace God offers is yours for the asking, and live in obedience to God's will. Remember—it is impossible to live with peace in your heart and rebellion in your actions.

It is God's will for you to be tranquil in your heart and serene in your spirit, despite the chaos around you. Seek His peace today.

I will know, Lord, when I am seeking Your will: I will have an untroubled heart because of Your peace within.

LOSING YOUR PEACE

SCRIPTURE READING: PHILIPPIANS 4:1–8
KEY VERSE: PHILIPPIANS 4:8

Finally, brethren, whatever things are true, whatever things are noble,
whatever things are just, whatever things are pure, whatever things are
lovely, whatever things are of good report, if there is any virtue and
if there is anything praiseworthy—meditate on these things.

Our thoughts play a great role in the level of peace in our lives. When our minds are occupied with negative, nagging, and unproductive thoughts, we push peace away and invite anxiety and worry into our lives. Therefore, we must learn to recognize and replace negative thought patterns before they rob us of peace.

There are seven categories of thoughts that steal peace from us: sinful, negative, erroneous, unrealistic, rebellious, obsessive, and enslaved thoughts. Each category represents a different area in which Satan aims to establish a stronghold in our minds.

Whether you are plagued by one or several of these types of thoughts, it is important to properly extinguish the flames of their fiery path through your mind. Until they are put down, you will be unable to experience God's gift of peace.

When these thoughts surface, first reach out to God in prayer. Confess that you are struggling with troublesome thoughts and ask Him to remove your burden. Then turn your mind's energy to that which is positive, uplifting, and of God.

Philippians 4:8 encourages us to think on things that are true, noble, right, pure, lovely, admirable, excellent, and praiseworthy. Allow God to quench your desire to ponder more negative concepts and ideas with positive thoughts of His plan for peace in your life.

Lord, keep me from bulldozing Your gift of peace into a corner when
my spirit is driven by negative, nagging, and unproductive thoughts.
Help me lift my thoughts to You.

SEEKING PEACE

SCRIPTURE READING: PSALM 46:1–10
KEY VERSE: PSALM 46:10

Be still, and know that I am God;
I will be exalted among the nations,
I will be exalted in the earth!

Do you feel peaceful? If you do not, you are probably seeking peace. Most likely, peace is something you desire. As humans, we are all born with a need for comfort and peace. We seek out pleasing relationships, work environments with low stress levels, and comfortable furnishings for our homes. We volunteer at charitable organizations, spend time with loved ones, and attend church services—all in an effort to find true peace. Why, then, do we still feel unfulfilled?

It is because we are working too hard. As we toil and fret, struggle and strive, God is waiting patiently for us to slow down. You see, peace is not something we can achieve; rather, it is something God gives to us when we are ready to accept it.

The writer of Psalm 46:10 said to stop struggling and recognize God's presence. What a simple and beautiful statement! When you accepted Jesus Christ as your personal Savior, Jesus came to dwell inside of you through the Holy Spirit. The Bible tells us that Jesus is our peace, meaning that when you received Him, you also received the gift of His peace.

Do you need a refresher course on what the peace of Jesus feels like? Slow down for a moment. Stop striving and meditate on the person of Jesus. Accept the gift of peace He can bring to your life.

Lord, let me cease striving and meditate on You and the truth of Your Word. I accept Your gift of peace through Jesus Christ.

UNSHAKABLE PEACE

SCRIPTURE READING: ROMANS 8:18–28
KEY VERSE: ROMANS 8:28

*And we know that all things work together for good to those who love
God, to those who are the called according to His purpose.*

The Lord has only good plans in store for your life. You may go through
difficult times, but God promises to use every trial to build "good"
into your life (Romans 8:28). When Satan tells you to worry, God has the
opposite in mind. He wants you to trust Him and to experience His peace
on a daily basis.

How do you gain and retain the true peace of God?

- Recognize your dependence on God. The heart that finds its identity in Jesus Christ is a heart of peace. The person who rushes here
  and there to solve his own problems quickly can become a person
  of strife and worry. Take responsibility for your actions, but let
  God have the reins to your life.
- Pray. The enemy cannot defeat you when you are on your spiritual
  knees before God in prayer. This is the true pathway to unshakable
  peace.
- Trust God. When thoughts of fear invade your mind, tell the Lord
  what you are feeling and claim His presence as your protection and
  shelter.
- Focus only on God. Don't cling to negative thoughts. Set the focus
  of your heart on God and His possibilities. When God views your
  life, He sees only potential. You can live life to the fullest because
  Christ is alive in you and all things are under His control.

*God, I am totally dependent upon You. I trust You. I focus my mind
on You. I will live this day in unshakable peace.*

PROTECTING YOUR PEACE

SCRIPTURE READING: MATTHEW 6:25–34
KEY VERSE: MATTHEW 6:25

*Therefore I say to you, do not worry about your life, what you will eat
or what you will drink; nor about your body, what you will put on. Is
not life more than food and the body more than clothing?*

Webster's Dictionary defines *peace* as "an agreement or treaty to end
hostilities." If we are to experience peace in our daily lives, what are
the "hostilities" that need to be reckoned with? Most of the time, peace
ceases when concern becomes anxiety.

Concern stems from a caring feeling about someone or something, and
allows God to be involved. Anxiety, however, is a tormenting form of worry
that focuses on the problem instead of on God. To protect our peace, we
must learn to thwart anxiety before it begins.

There are three ways to recognize the onset of anxiety:

- If you find that you are more concerned with what you desire rather
  than the will of God, you are heading for a period of anxiety.
- If you find yourself feeling hurried into making unwise decisions,
  you are inviting anxiety.
- If you are living in a constant state of agitation and uneasiness,
  you are likely suppressing anxious feelings.

Walking in peace does not involve escaping reality or responsibility;
rather, peace enables us to face trials and hardships with genuine confidence
in God. Peace guards our hearts and minds from damaging thoughts.

Use your quiet time today to conduct a "peace check." Examine your
spirit in the presence of the Lord and commit to banish anxious feelings
when they arise.

*Lord, examine my heart to see if I am resisting Your divine peace by
focusing on what I want, making unwise and hurried decisions, or
experiencing agitation.*

The Offer of Peace

*These things I have spoken to you, that in Me you may
have peace. In the world you will have tribulation;
but be of good cheer, I have overcome the world.*

In John 14:27, as Jesus prepared for His imminent death, He spoke these words of comfort to His disciples: "Peace I leave with you; My peace I give to you; not as the world gives do I give to you. Do not let your heart be troubled, nor let it be fearful" (NASB).

This heartfelt revelation established a reason to hope for generations of Christians to come. Jesus' message of peace remains a beacon to us today in a world of conflict and unrest. His peace is different from the world's, different from the fleeting glimpses of happiness and joy we receive from worldly pursuits. The peace of Jesus quiets anxious hearts and soothes troubled minds as nothing else can.

When you accept Jesus' offer of peace, be prepared to experience spiritual wholeness and mental clarity like you have never known. Worry will suddenly become useless, and anxiety will soon evaporate like the morning dew.

Though no life on this earth is exempt from trials and occasional heartaches, when our confidence is in the One who has overcome the world (John 16:33), we can live with hope in our hearts. When our trust is in God, the enemy cannot win. Instead, God will use difficult times to increase our spiritual maturity and to demonstrate that He is the sustaining power in our lives.

*Lord, Your peace is a promissory note that says You are in charge—
You have already overcome the world that is trying to drag me down.*

DEMONSTRATING PEACE

SCRIPTURE READING: 2 CORINTHIANS 13:5–11
KEY VERSE: 2 CORINTHIANS 13:11

Finally, brethren, farewell. Become complete. Be of good comfort, be of one mind, live in peace; and the God of love and peace will be with you.

Here is a scene that you could witness on almost any playground in the world. Two boys are playing together in a sandbox or at the base of a slide. Suddenly, a fight breaks out and the two young children are embroiled in a heated exchange with fists flying. Their peaceful playtime has come to a violent end.

Where did these children learn to act like this? Apparently, human beings are not programmed for peace. Too often, a person's initial response to displeasure or stress is to strike out violently against the source of his frustration. The base nature of sinful man is to protect oneself first and foremost. However, one's disposition toward anarchy is certainly no excuse for failing to strive toward peaceful living.

The New Testament contains no less than eight direct commands for peace among believers. This clearly reveals that God's will is for men and women to live in peace with one another. Knowing that God demands His people to live in peace may seem too much to ask when countered by mankind's sinful, selfish desires. Yet, if peace is God's will—and it is—then He must have made it possible to achieve. Sometimes peace may not be one's natural reaction, but according to God's Word, it is possible.

Pray today for the Holy Spirit to reveal ways in which you can demonstrate the peace of God.

Dear heavenly Father, reveal ways in which I can demonstrate Your peace to those with whom I come in contact today.

PEACE WITH OTHERS

SCRIPTURE READING: ROMANS 12:10–18
KEY VERSE: ROMANS 12:18

If it is possible, as much as depends on you, live peaceably with all men.

Have you ever encountered a person who would not allow you to be kind to them? Despite your loving comments or gestures, perhaps they insulted you or accused you of having some ulterior motive. How should Christians respond to those who will not accept another's attempt at peace?

While the New Testament contains several passages instructing believers to practice peace, Romans 12:18 does so with the understanding that some people will not accept your peace offerings. As such, the apostle Paul added two qualifications to the command to be peaceful.

First was the condition, "If it is possible." This indicated that there are times when peace with another person is not possible. These people may not be interested in a peaceful environment, or they may even enjoy causing other people harm.

Second was the phrase, "as much as depends on you." This should only be taken to mean as far as you can go without sacrificing your God-given principles. When one's conditions for peace countermand God's rules for living, then this peace is unacceptable.

Despite the occasions when peace may be impossible, it is still the Christian's responsibility to seek peace. Do not use the above qualifications as an excuse to give up. You will only be excused when you have made every effort for peace.

Lord, I realize it is my responsibility to seek peace. Help me to make every effort to achieve peace with others.

THE PEACE OF GOD

SCRIPTURE READING: ISAIAH 53:4–6
KEY VERSE: ISAIAH 59:2

But your iniquities have separated you from your God;
And your sins have hidden His face from you,
So that He will not hear.

Peace is not merely that state of calmness and ease which we seek in desperate times. It is ultimately the condition that can exist between God and man because of the redeeming work of Christ.

When Adam and Eve sinned in the garden, a barrier was erected between the Creator and His creation, extinguishing any hope of relationship between the two. That barrier is called sin. It destroyed the harmony that had previously existed between God and man, and only a miracle could restore it (Isaiah 59:2).

The miracle came about two thousand years ago on a hill just outside Jerusalem. Jesus Christ submitted Himself to the most horrific death any man has ever suffered. Jesus didn't merely die; He hung on the cross with the weight of all sin—past, present, and future—on His back. The full penalty for my transgression and yours was levied against Him that day. At the moment of Christ's death, the massive temple veil dividing the Holy Place from the Holy of Holies was torn in two from top to bottom, signifying reconciliation between man and God (2 Corinthians 5:18–19). Peace with God was now possible again.

Though an instrument of death and brutality, the cross stands as an eternal symbol of peace. But it is not until we bow at the pierced feet of Jesus and offer our lives to Him as a living sacrifice that true peace becomes a present reality. What greater peace could there be than to know that you have perfect harmony with God. This is His precious gift to you.

Dear Lord, thank You for Your peace that came to me by the way of the Cross. Thank You for paying the price for this priceless gift.

PEACE WITH YOURSELF

SCRIPTURE READING: COLOSSIANS 1:12–18
KEY VERSES: COLOSSIANS 1:13–14

*He has delivered us from the power of darkness and conveyed us
into the kingdom of the Son of His love, in whom we have
redemption through His blood, the forgiveness of sins.*

Have you ever wondered who your staunchest critic is? Who is always
present for your biggest blunders? Who remembers the intimate details
of your past mistakes with pristine clarity?

The answer, most often, is you. Yours are the hands that toil the fields of
sin and rebellion. Yours are the lips that often bring pain upon others. For
many, this leads to a tormenting sense of unrest and guilt. Christians often
have difficulty accepting God's forgiveness because they are the ones who
know for sure how much they do not deserve it.

Even believers who have accepted Christ's atoning sacrifice fall into
unhealthy behaviors. The primary example of this trend may be someone
asking forgiveness for the same past sin every day for weeks, months, or
even years.

This is a trap that we must avoid. Christ did not provide a partial salvation.
There is no in-between; the event of His death and resurrection either
triumphed over sin or it did not. The answer from Scripture is clear—it did.

Pray today for God's help in setting old burdens to rest and taking up the
peace that Christ has so firmly provided.

*Father, I want to set old burdens to rest and embrace the peace that
You have provided through Jesus Christ. Please help me.*

A Barrier to Peace

Scripture Reading: Psalm 85:1–13
Key Verse: Psalm 85:2

You have forgiven the iniquity of Your people;
You have covered all their sin.

Sin robs you of peace with God because it places a barrier between you. Author and Bible teacher Kay Arthur states, "Sin will take you further than you ever want to go." She is right. The enemy entices us to sin. When we do, we suddenly find we have drifted further from God than we would have thought possible.

A lack of peace often indicates that there is something wrong within a person's life. It could be that he is believing Satan's lie by thinking that God has abandoned him. Nothing could be further from the truth. God's love for us is eternal.

Another reason we lose our sense of peace is because of sin. The way to reclaim the joy and peace that sin has stolen is to humble ourselves before the Lord in prayer and ask Him to forgive our transgressions.

The psalmist wrote, "Have mercy upon me, O God, according to Your lovingkindness; according to the multitude of Your tender mercies, blot out my transgressions. . . . Restore to me the joy of Your salvation, and uphold me by Your generous Spirit" (Psalm 51:1, 12). King David wrote these words to the Lord after his adulterous affair with Bathsheba. Anguish over his sin motivated David to pray for forgiveness and for the restoration of the joy of his salvation.

God heard David's prayer and restored him. The Lord will do the same for you. His peace and joy await those who turn to Him.

Lord, forgive me of my sin. Destroy every barrier that blocks me from Your presence. Restore the joy of my salvation and give me peace.

THE PRINCE OF PEACE

SCRIPTURE READING: EPHESIANS 2:14–18
KEY VERSES: EPHESIANS 2:14–15

For He Himself is our peace, who has made both one, and has broken down the middle wall of separation, having abolished in His flesh the enmity, that is, the law of commandments contained in ordinances, so as to create in Himself one new man from the two, thus making peace.

It is one of modern culture's great tragedies: what many people seek and work so hard to achieve is in fact not a product of all their accomplishments and effort. Millions of people are turning the world upside down looking for peace, while never realizing that the "genuine article" is simply not of this world. Money cannot buy it; success and fame can never guarantee it. Until you have peace with God, you will never experience inner serenity.

Since genuine peace is not dependent upon outward circumstances, it is possible to experience a tranquility beyond our comprehension, even in the midst of life's most tragic moments. But this real peace is not possible unless there exists absolutely no impediment between us and God, and the only way the barrier of sin and self can be removed is through the cross of Calvary. If we would simply bring our struggles and needs to the foot of the cross, we would find an abundant source of peace. A heart at rest is not rooted in some worldly principle or philosophy; it can be realized only through an intimate relationship with the person of Jesus Christ (Ephesians 2:14–15).

The devil will take every opportunity to destroy our calm by drawing attention away from Christ to things that may seem important at the time, but in reality have no other purpose than to distract. Don't waste your life looking for peace in all the wrong places—just remember, the Prince of Peace is its only true source.

Lord, I seek no other source of peace. You are the Prince of Peace. Keep my eyes focused on You and eliminate every distraction.

Bearing Unbearable Burdens

Scripture Reading: Jeremiah 6:16–20
Key Verse: Jeremiah 6:16

Thus says the LORD: "Stand in the ways and see, and ask for the old paths, where the good way is, and walk in it; then you will find rest for your souls. But they said, 'We will not walk in it.'"

When we are overburdened, the world seems a colder place. The sun may be shining, but our heads are bowed low so we don't notice. The birds sing, but our ears are filled with the cries of our hearts—cries of pain, sorrow, and weariness.

We put distance between others and ourselves as our problems absorb our time and attention. Perhaps we are weighed down by unmet expectations, sudden trauma or death, or simply too much responsibility. Another possibility is that sin is causing our heaviness of heart. Whatever the cause, however, the result is the same: a crushing weight. Only the amount of the weight varies.

Into our bleakness comes the voice of God Almighty inviting us to draw near and find rest in Him. The old prophet Jeremiah spoke for God, telling his listeners to find the good way and walk in it. That's how we will find rest.

Won't you look up to your heavenly Father right now? Jesus offers living water. Take time to drink until your soul is strengthened enough for you to ask the way. With the Spirit's help, take one step, then another, down that path of obedience, and He will give you the promised peace.

Jeremiah 6:16 ends with God pointing out the Israelites' response: they wouldn't walk with God. Let us stand and look and ask and walk so that we find the rest the Lord has promised for our souls.

Father, I want to walk in the ancient paths, the good way, Your way. I know that it is there that I will find rest for my soul.

The Pathway to Peace

SCRIPTURE READING: PSALM 116:1–7
KEY VERSE: PSALM 116:7

Return to your rest, O my soul,
For the Lord has dealt bountifully with you.

Let's take a closer look at our passage from yesterday, Jeremiah 6:16:

1. "Stand in the ways and see." In a time of turmoil, our minds race ahead to think of all that could happen in the future. We ask ourselves lots of "what if" questions and frequently fall victim to unfounded worry. To "stand" means to turn our mind from its troubling thoughts of the future and to focus on God. It is similar to being at an intersection with signs pointing many different ways. We wait until we know which direction the trail is heading.

2. "Ask for the old paths, where the good way is." The road of trouble has been well traveled by the saints of the faith, and their footsteps have made it into a path of glory to God. Meditate on the cries of King David in the Psalms or on the prayers of others in the Bible. Ponder their responses as well as the way they reveal their faith and trust in God even while suffering greatly. Accept the Spirit's revelation of the ancient path of faith and the good way of trust. Then pray for courage to walk those paths as Jesus did.

3. "Walk in it; then you will find rest for your souls." With eyes firmly fixed on our Savior, resolve to walk down this road of suffering in a way that is honoring to Him. Draw deeply on the Holy Spirit's strength for the next step, and seek to be obedient in thought, word, and deed. You will discover that as you follow Him, sweet, soul-satisfying rest will be found.

Lord, I choose the pathway of peace. Help me to stand firm in times of turmoil. Enable me to ask where the good way is, and then to walk in it.

SEPTEMBER
Pathway to Assurance

These things I have written to you who believe in the name of the Son of God, that you may know that you have eternal life, and that you may continue to believe in the name of the Son of God.

—1 John 5:13

THE REASON FOR OUR HOPE

SCRIPTURE READING: JUDE 1:20–25
KEY VERSES: 1 TIMOTHY 2:3–4

*For this is good and acceptable in the sight of God our Savior, who
desires all men to be saved and to come to the knowledge of the truth.*

It is difficult for us to recommend a business, service, or product to others
when we haven't tried it ourselves. We can tell them what we have heard
about it, but there is no personal experience from which to draw.

When other people come to us and ask us about salvation, and we doubt
the validity of God's promise that our salvation is eternally secured in Him,
how can we share our faith with confidence?

There are many reasons why people doubt their salvation. They question
how a loving God would allow tragedy. They believe that works, not grace,
save them. They fail to take God at His word. They remain living a life of
sin, unwilling to submit to the authority of the Lord in their lives. But God's
Word gives us all the assurance we need in order to know that our salvation
is secure in Him, giving us the confidence to share our faith with others.

First Timothy 2:4 reminds us that God "desires all men to be saved and
to come to the knowledge of the truth." And John the Baptist told us, "He
who believes in the Son has eternal life; but he who does not obey the Son
will not see life" (John 3:36 NASB).

In understanding that our salvation is secure and that God desires all
men to know the truth, we can go forth with boldness and tell those around
us the reason for our hope.

*Lord, I know with surety that my salvation is firm in You. Show me
how to convey this to others who are full of doubt and confusion
about their salvation.*

A SURE ANCHOR

SCRIPTURE READING: HEBREWS 13:1–6
KEY VERSES: HEBREWS 13:5–6

Let your conduct be without covetousness; be content with such things as you have. For He Himself has said, "I will never leave you nor forsake you." So we may boldly say: "The Lord is my helper; I will not fear. What can man do to me?"

As the storm clouds roll across the horizon of our lives, we must prepare to face adversity with confidence. Once the trials or testing times arrive, it is time to evaluate where we have dropped the anchor of our faith. Does our anchor reach deep enough that our faith is securely fastened to the Lord?

When you place your hope and faith in anything other than Christ, you are going to be disappointed. The things of this world may satisfy temporarily, but eventually the emptiness in your heart will overtake any satisfaction.

No matter how much support and encouragement our friends may give us, the peace that is necessary to weather many storms in our lives can come only from God. No matter how much money we have, it will never solve all our problems or fill all our emptiness.

But our hearts anchored in Christ will hold us tightly as we endure all of these storms. God rejoices over His children, delighting in bringing about the best for our lives. Nothing in our lives surprises Him. He knows it all, and He knows the best way for us to stand strong against these difficulties. "For He Himself has said, 'I will never leave you nor forsake you.' So we may boldly say, 'The LORD is my helper, I will not fear. What can man do to me?'" (Hebrews 13:5–6).

Lord, when material goods start to draw my attention away from You, help me to stay anchored in You so that I can withstand life's storms.

THE ASSURANCE OF THE WORD

SCRIPTURE READING: HEBREWS 13:7–9
KEY VERSE: HEBREWS 13:9

Do not be carried about with various and strange doctrines. For it is
good that the heart be established by grace, not with foods which have
not profited those who have been occupied with them.

In seeking to anchor our lives in Christ for those days when storms strike,
we must start with God's Word. Bible teacher Warren Wiersbe explains:

The purpose of spiritual ministry is to establish God's people in grace, so
they will not be blown around by dangerous doctrines (Ephesians
4:11–14). Some recipients of the letter to the Hebrews were considering
going back to Jewish laws that governed foods. The writer warned them
that these dietary regulations would not profit them spiritually because
they never profited the Jews spiritually! The dietary laws impressed people
as being spiritual, but they were only shadows of the reality that we have in
Christ (Colossians 2:16–23).

When local churches change pastors, there is a tendency also to change
doctrines or doctrinal emphases. We must be careful not to go beyond the
Word of God. We must also be careful not to change the spiritual foundation
of the church. It is unfortunate that there is not more doctrinal preaching
today because Bible doctrine is the source of strength and growth in the
church.

Finding our foundation, our anchor, in God's Word is crucial to
weathering the trials in our lives. Nothing prepares us more for life's tests
than a deep knowledge of God's Word.

Lord, I do not want to trade in my rootedness in You for a false sense
of security offered by popular and erroneous doctrines. Keep me
anchored in Your truths.

A God We Can Trust

SCRIPTURE READING: PSALM 85:1–13
KEY VERSE: PSALM 85:7

Show us Your mercy, LORD,
And grant us Your salvation.

Trust is something we earn with one another. However, from the moment God saves us, He trusts us and believes in us. Does He think we will never make another mistake? God knows we will still make mistakes, but His Spirit lives in us—and this is a point of uncompromising trust.

Many people read God's Word and then allow the enemy to twist God's truth in such a way that they doubt God's goodness. When there are people in our lives who promise us things but fail to deliver, an attitude of cynicism can seep into our thinking. Trusting anyone can be a major challenge for us when we have been disappointed time and time again.

However, God has a reputation of trust for several millenniums. Throughout the Bible, we do not read of God promising to do something and then not following up on His promise. For some people steeped in cynicism, this might take longer to believe than others. But in the end, the truth is revealed: God is faithful—always.

God's faithfulness is great. His promises do not always unfold the way we imagined, but He always keeps them. As God proves His faithfulness to us, we learn that He is ultimately trustworthy with everything, including our lives. We can rest confidently in that assurance.

Dear Lord, cleanse me of any cynicism that has seeped into my thinking. I embrace Your faithfulness and trustworthiness with renewed assurance.

FREEDOM AND ASSURANCE

SCRIPTURE READING: EPHESIANS 5:1–7
KEY VERSE: 1 JOHN 4:16

*And we have known and believed the love that God has for us. God is
love, and he who abides in love abides in God, and God in him.*

Halo effect." "Teacher's pet." Regardless of what we call it, it is that
phenomena where a person can seemingly do no wrong. As long as
the person stays within the parameters of defined protocol, he receives
heaps of praise.

Many people may never have experienced that situation within a class-
room or work-related setting, but we can experience that same dynamic in our
relationship with God. Instead of fearing that we will get zapped or punished
for our next words or actions, freedom pervades our spirits. We come to the
understanding of what the Bible means when it says, "God is love" (1 John
4:16). And as we do this, we realize that it is not God's intention to restrict
our beings, but rather to free us to do His will and fulfill all the desires He has
placed on our hearts.

Paul wrote, "Therefore be imitators of God as dear children. And walk
in love, as Christ also has loved us and given Himself for us, an offering and
a sacrifice to God for a sweet-smelling aroma" (Ephesians 5:1–2). When such
freedom is given to us because of God's incredible love, we realize that we can
trust Him with assurance.

As we walk according to His prescribed ways, we will experience freedom
like we have never known—and we will learn to trust Him with everything.

*Thank You for freedom to do Your will, Lord. Thank You that I can
trust You with complete assurance.*

LEAVING DOUBT IN THE DUST

SCRIPTURE READING: JOSHUA 1:1–9
KEY VERSE: JOSHUA 1:9

Have I not commanded you? Be strong and of good courage;
do not be afraid, nor be dismayed, for the Lord your
God is with you wherever you go.

There are many reasons believers struggle with doubt. Sometimes the very people who say they believe every word written in the inerrant, infallible Word of God are the very ones who still struggle with overcoming doubt, which can paralyze a walk.

Sin and guilt can lead a believer to doubt that God is willing to act on his or her behalf. So can other factors like previous failures, the negative influences of others, and a wrong focus. But perhaps the main reason many believers still doubt is an ignorance of the Word of God. The only way we can know how God would have us react, the only way we can bury eternal truths deep into our hearts and minds, is to take Joshua's advice and meditate on God's Word.

Meditating on Scripture means more than just a casual read. It means to read it, study it, ponder it, and ask God questions. "Father, what are You saying to me personally through this passage? Show me how to apply this truth to my life to prepare me for what You have in store for me."

Performing this spiritual exercise prepares you for long-distance tests of faith and leaves doubt in the dust. It programs your mind to think the way God thinks. There is nothing that energizes your faith as knowing Scripture so well that in any situation you are able to recall appropriate passages at the Holy Spirit's prompting.

Lord, program my mind to think the way You think. Energize my
faith through Your Word. I want to leave doubt in the dust.

GOD'S AMAZING GRACE

SCRIPTURE READING: 1 PETER 5:1–12
KEY VERSE: 1 PETER 5:12

*By Silvanus, our faithful brother as I consider him, I have written
to you briefly, exhorting and testifying that this is the true
grace of God in which you stand.*

Though there will be times when we feel alone, we can be assured that God does not desert His children. Once we accept His unfailing love, we are His forever. To understand God's grace, we must lay aside any human, preconceived ideas about grace. Eternal grace is a gift from God.

When we accept Christ as our Lord and Savior, inviting Him to transform our hearts and lives, we enter into God's amazing grace. We receive His grace for more than just a season—it is for a lifetime.

As we grow in our spiritual walk with the Lord, we quickly discover that God's grace toward us never changes. Peter, a man who understood grace thoroughly, wrote, "I have written to you briefly, exhorting and testifying that this is the true grace of God. Stand firm in it!" (1 Peter 5:12 NASB).

When doubts or fears creep into your thoughts, stand firm in the knowledge of God's grace. Realize that He will not leave you emotionally stranded alongside the busy highway of life. He provides for every need you have—physical and emotional. The provision of His grace is an important part of your Christian belief system. Without it, you would not know, understand, or be assured of salvation's call.

God's grace is sufficient for all you face. Ask Him to teach you how to live each day.

Your grace is sufficient, Lord. Teach me how to live each day. Let me stand firm in Your grace.

This Grace in Which You Stand

SCRIPTURE READING: EPHESIANS 2:1–10
KEY VERSE: EPHESIANS 2:5

*Even when we were dead in trespasses, [He] made us alive
together with Christ (by grace you have been saved).*

There are times when we say words that we wish we could take back. Or perhaps we do something in such a way that we wish we could retrieve our actions and correct them. As these moments mount, we wonder how much longer our favor with God will last. We seek His forgiveness, but we wonder if we are in danger of exhausting God's grace for our lives.

The truth is this: you cannot exhaust the grace of God. He loves you even when you act unlovable. He does hold us accountable for our words and actions. When our words or actions hurt another, we need to admit what we have done and ask God and the person we have hurt to forgive us.

Humility is a sign that God's grace is flowing unhindered through us. Realize also that grace is a gift—something God gives us and something we should give others. When you are hurt by another's actions or words, remember the grace that God has extended to you. Forgive and allow God to restore your relationship with the other person. God desires to transform our lives by the realization that His grace never ends. We are saved by grace (Ephesians 2:5), and we are called to live grace-filled lives.

When is the last time you thanked God for His grace toward you? Take time to do this, and extend grace, love, and acceptance to another today.

Lord, thank You for Your grace extended to me. Help me to extend grace, love, and acceptance to someone today.

BLESSED ASSURANCE

SCRIPTURE READING: ACTS 16:25–34
KEY VERSE: ACTS 16:31

So they said, "Believe on the Lord Jesus Christ, and you will be saved, you and your household."

In terms of salvation, all of us fall into one of four categories:

- We are saved and we know it.
- We think we are saved, but we're not.
- We don't claim to be saved.
- We are not saved but would like to be.

In which category do you find yourself?

Salvation is God's deliverance of the believer, through Jesus Christ, from all the effects of sin. It is God's work in the human heart, and it is accompanied by all the benefits He bestows on us now and forever.

We need to know beyond a shadow of a doubt where we are going to spend eternity. That certainty is available to every one of us. Do you have that kind of assurance? If you are not confident that you have eternal salvation, I urge you to settle this most important decision of your life right now.

First, realize that God desires to save everyone (1 Timothy 2:4). Not only does He want to save everyone, but He also provided the way to salvation through His Son (John 3:16). He has told us we must believe in Jesus Christ (Acts 16:31), and we must confess Him before men (Romans 10:10).

Our heavenly Father is faithful to keep His promises. If you trust in Jesus Christ as your personal Savior, He will save you from your sin and welcome you into His family without regard to merit or worth on your part (John 1:12). Eternal life will be yours. He offers this gift freely to all who believe in His Son. Will you receive it?

Lord, I accept the gift of eternal life. I receive salvation through Your Son, Jesus Christ. Thank You for the assurance of my salvation.

THINGS NOT SHAKEN

SCRIPTURE READING: HEBREWS 12:25–29
KEY VERSE: JOHN 14:8

Philip said to Him, "Lord, show us the Father,
and it is sufficient for us."

The *Titanic* was deemed unsinkable, invincible. Yet today it lies at the bottom of the ocean. Its tragic demise is a reminder that no matter how invincible we perceive things to be, nothing on this earth is beyond destruction. Only God and His Word are indestructible.

Jesus told His disciples that He would not leave them as orphans (John 14:18). However, after His arrest they began to doubt His Word to them. By the time He was crucified, their doubts had turned to fear. When Jesus was alive, it was easy to believe that He was the Messiah. However, two days after His death, with their prayers seemingly unanswered, they began to doubt, and their faith sank.

We do the same thing. We place our faith in Christ and then, through a turn of events or sorrows, we find ourselves crying out to God. We also doubt His promises to us and wonder why He allows adversity to touch our hearts. But be assured—even when we feel shaken, God is not. He is our firm, immovable anchor of hope.

Have you placed your faith in something that is unshakable? Or have you given your hopes and dreams to something that will sink whenever the slightest adversity strikes? Only God is unshakable. When your heart is anchored to His, no storm or adversity can harm you.

Lord, when doubt smolders, do not let me fan it into flames of fear.
I choose to believe in the indestructible nature of Your person and
Your word.

ASSURANCE OF SALVATION

SCRIPTURE READING: JOHN 5:24–29
KEY VERSE: 2 PETER 3:9

*The Lord is not slack concerning His promise, as some count slackness,
but is longsuffering toward us, not willing that any should perish
but that all should come to repentance.*

Freedom floods our hearts the moment we learn that we do not have to be perfect to experience God's love and salvation. Living each day worried about how the next downfall might cast us in God's eyes is not the way to live a life of freedom. While we must honor God with our obedience, our salvation isn't going to slip away every time we slip up.

In order to gain a firm grasp of the assurance of our salvation, we need to understand God's will for the redemption of mankind. Paul wrote, "This is good and acceptable in the sight of God our Savior, who desires all men to be saved and to come to the knowledge of the truth" (1 Timothy 2:3–4). God desires that everyone would come to a point of recognition of sin and repentance.

At times, we may think that God is hiding His salvation from us. But He is not. Salvation is available for all people. Peter wrote, "The Lord is not slow about His promise, as some count slowness, but is patient toward you, not wishing for any to perish but for all to come to repentance" (2 Peter 3:9 NASB).

Many fail to realize it, but God desires to be personally involved in our lives. He wants us to experience His grace, but we must take the initial step toward Him. When we do, He provides for every need we have, beginning with the salvation of our souls.

Lord, whether I—in my weakness—am up, down, or crawling back to my feet, You are constant, standing with hands outstretched to help me. Praise You for Your steadfast love.

THE ETERNAL ADVENTURE

SCRIPTURE READING: 1 JOHN 5:6–13

KEY VERSE: 1 JOHN 5:9

If we receive the witness of men, the witness of God is greater; for this is the witness of God which He has testified of His Son.

When someone testifies about something—a product, an event, another's character—the testimony is only as strong as the character of the person giving it. And when it comes to God, there should be no question about what He says. His words are truth.

But there is an even greater benefit to knowing God. As we draw near to Him, we learn that He not only provides the guidance we need at every turn in life, but He also gives us a clear map on how to accomplish His plan for our lives.

John wrote, "If we receive the witness of men, the witness of God is greater; for this is the witness of God which He has testified of His Son. . . . And this is the testimony: that God has given us eternal life, and this life is in His Son" (1 John 5:9, 11). The assurance of our salvation is based on God's Word. We do not have to be afraid that one day we will fall from His grace. This cannot happen to those who have accepted Christ as their Savior. God's love is eternal. There is never a moment in time when He turns His love in another direction. It is always focused on us.

He provides us the assurance we need through what He has testified about His Son. The moment we accept God's Word as truth and receive Christ as our Savior, we are saved. The eternal adventure begins with great assurance!

Thank You for salvation and assurance. Thank You, Lord, that Your love is forever focused on me.

THE BELIEVER'S SECURITY SYSTEM

SCRIPTURE READING: 2 PETER 2:18–21
KEY VERSE: 2 PETER 2:21

*For it would have been better for them not to have known the way
of righteousness, than having known it, to turn from the holy
commandment delivered to them.*

While every child of God has a built-in "spiritual security system," some Christians are far more vulnerable than others to spiritual predators. False teachers, or "wolves in sheep's clothing," will seek out immature believers and exploit their ignorance. The wolves also hunt down people with unresolved guilt, in an effort to salve their consciences with phony remedies.

People who fail to confess and forsake sin according to Scripture remain highly susceptible to Satan's trickery. Another group of people at risk of seduction are those who have gained a head knowledge of Jesus and religious practices but have not followed through in genuine discipleship. They may be church members, and they may even be baptized, but something is missing. They have no root in true godliness and end up entangled in a worse state than before.

Fortunately, believers are equipped to avoid these potholes. We have a security system designed to protect us if we keep it well tuned. First and foremost, we have to saturate our minds continually with God's truth. In so doing, we will eventually develop a mental grid that reacts in alarm when something false comes our way. In this manner, we become rooted and grounded in the truth.

Christians must also learn to know the Holy Spirit personally and listen to Him. He enables us to have a discerning spirit, and He will educate our conscience to provide timely warnings when we start down the wrong path. We can escape the snares of the devil and rest secure in Jesus.

Thank You for Your security system, Lord. Warn me when I start down the wrong path. Help me escape the snares of the devil and rest securely in You.

GOD KNOWS YOU

SCRIPTURE READING: PSALM 18:1–6
KEY VERSE: PSALM 18:6

In my distress I called upon the LORD,
And cried out to my God;
He heard my voice from His temple,
And my cry came before Him, even to His ears.

The concept of God's ability to save mankind is evident throughout the entire Bible. In Psalm 18:1–2, David wrote: "I will love You, O LORD, my strength. The LORD is my rock and my fortress and my deliverer; my God, my strength, in whom I will trust; my shield and the horn of my salvation, my stronghold."

Saints in the Old Testament understood that God was their only hope of salvation. The prophets of God looked to the future and believed that God would save mankind from sin. This truth was a great source of praise and adoration of the Lord. However, while they loved the Lord, their relationship with Him was quite different than what we experience today. Through the power of the Holy Spirit, we can know God intimately and be sure He knows us.

When the darkness of this world closes in, stop and think of God's infinite, unconditional love. Throughout the ages, the one thing that holds true is that God's salvation is there for all who come to Him with a humble and open heart.

David wrote, "In my distress I called upon the LORD, and cried to my God for help; He heard my voice" (Psalm 18:6). God knows your deepest need, and He will answer your cry for help and salvation.

You are the hope of my salvation, Lord. In my distress, I call to You.
I cry to You for help.

SPIRITUAL SAFETY

SCRIPTURE READING: MATTHEW 17:15–23
KEY VERSE: MATTHEW 17:22

Now while they were staying in Galilee, Jesus said to them,
"The Son of Man is about to be betrayed into the hands of men."

Physical safety is on our minds today, especially after the terrorist attacks on 9/11, which changed our world forever. We are rightly concerned about homeland security, yet when it comes to protection, many people neglect the even more precious arena of soul and spirit. The fact is that there are spiritual terrorists on the loose. Jesus called them "wolves in sheep's clothing" and issued some stern warnings to alert us.

These wolves are false teachers and false prophets who appear to be genuine spiritual guides but are instead full of schemes to advance their own agenda. They look good and they sound good, but they are consumed with lust and greed. None of this is apparent at first. Instead, they preach a fine gospel in a most compelling manner. Gradually, however, they begin to blend inaccuracy with fact. At this point, people seem to forget that truth mixed with error is no longer truth; instead, it has become error.

You can recognize these folks in a number of ways. Jesus said they would bear fruit that would eventually reveal their true character. At first you might detect that they are subtly questioning the Bible's authority and its relevance for the twenty-first century. Then you will notice little is said about living a holy life or being careful to obey the whole counsel of God. Later they will begin to equate obedience to God with living the way they want you to live. False teachers desire a following more than they care for your welfare. Here we must be very discerning, so remember: "You will know them by their fruits" (Matthew 7:16).

Dear Lord, protect me from false teachers and false prophets. Let me recognize them by their fruits. Keep me safe spiritually.

GOD'S UNCONDITIONAL LOVE

SCRIPTURE READING: ROMANS 5:6–11
KEY VERSE: ROMANS 5:8

But God demonstrates His own love toward us, in that
while we were still sinners, Christ died for us.

We have all been disappointed on some occasion by someone we love. Many of us have experienced the pain of abuse, betrayal, or abandonment. The remnants of these events often create "memory scars" upon our hearts, causing us to be wary of trusting or loving someone again.

As difficult as it is for our human minds to understand, God's love is complete and unconditional. He is perfect, and therefore capable of exhibiting perfect love. The sheer magnitude of His all-encompassing adoration can be overwhelming. However, God wants us to know that we are worthy of His love. While we were still sinners, Christ died for us (Romans 5:8).

Can you imagine loving someone enough to allow your only child to die for him? God loves you that much. Before you were born, He allowed His Son, Jesus, to be sacrificed to release you from the debt of sin.

For this great act of sacrifice, God requires no repayment. He only asks that you accept His gift of love. If pain from past hurts has caused you to feel isolated and afraid to love, take hope. There is One who will never disappoint you.

Ask God to heal your heart so that you can begin to comprehend the assurance of His loving hand upon your life from this moment forward.

Dear God, heal my heart so that I can comprehend the assurance of Your loving hand upon my life, knowing that You will never hurt or disappoint me.

GOD'S UNDYING LOVE

SCRIPTURE READING: HEBREWS 12:5–11
KEY VERSE: HEBREWS 12:5

And you have forgotten the exhortation which speaks to you
as to sons: "My son, do not despise the chastening of the Lord,
nor be discouraged when you are rebuked by Him."

Have you ever doubted God's love for you? In times of crisis, we are often tempted to blame God, or to accuse Him of instigating our pain.

Oftentimes, believers feel that God is punishing them for a sin they may have committed. It is important to understand the difference between punishment and discipline. Punishment is God executing His judgment upon the wicked. Discipline is God's correction of His children in order to protect them from further disobedience and harmful consequences.

You may wonder how God can discipline us and love us at the same time. The answer lies in Hebrews 12:5–6. Because God loves you, He wants to bless you with opportunities to grow in faith. As your faith increases, your trust in Him will increase, and your life will show the evidence of maturity.

If you feel that you are experiencing a period of discipline from God, do not resist it. God wants to use you in a mighty way. First, He must file away the rough spots in your life. Trust Him and be assured of His undying love as He shapes you into a beautiful vessel that He can use.

Father, I fear discipline, yet I know I cannot become who You want
me to be without it. I give You my heart. I trust You to govern it as
only a loving parent would.

AVENUES OF HOPE

SCRIPTURE READING: PSALM 103:1–22
KEY VERSE: PSALM 103:6

The LORD executes righteousness
And justice for all who are oppressed.

After Peter Marshall's death, three well-meaning friends approached his wife, Catherine, with the news that she had very little money to live on. She listened to their advice but felt something was missing from their counsel. In *The Best of Catherine Marshall* she recalls the experience:

> Alone in my room later, I stared out the window into the moonlight shining on swaying treetops. . . . Suddenly, standing there at the window, I knew what the missing factor was.
>
> My three friends who saw my many inadequacies, who had meant to be so kind, had reckoned without God. I remember how often Peter had faced this same attitude with his church officers. He would come home from a trustees' meeting sad and grim. "Catherine, no matter what's presented for their approval, their litany is always the same: 'But Dr. Marshall, where is the money coming from?' Where's their faith in God?"
>
> Either God was with me—"I am that I am," a fact more real than any figures or graphs—or He was not. If He was there, then reckoning without Him was certainly not being "realistic." In fact, it could be the most hazardous miscalculation of all.

Catherine Marshall discovered one of the purest truths of the Christian life: God is in control of all things. He holds our futures within His omniscient hand. Impossibilities are grand avenues of hope to Him.

Father, help me realize that my impossibilities are avenues of hope.
I am assured that You hold my future in Your omniscient hand.

THE CAUSES OF UNCERTAINTY

SCRIPTURE READING: PSALM 102:1–2
KEY VERSE: 1 JOHN 5:12

*He who has the Son has life; he who does not have
the Son of God does not have life.*

The Scriptures tell us we can be absolutely certain that we are saved, and yet many Christians are plagued by doubts. What causes this uncertainty? Sin can trigger something inside us that gnaws away at our faith. Satan says, "Don't tell me you're saved. Look at your past. Look at your life."

Another cause of doubt is false teachings. Some people claim there is no way to be certain we are saved. But the Bible promises that we can know we have eternal life.

A third reason for doubt is failure to believe God's Word. The Bible promises that if we have His Son, we have eternal life (1 John 5:12). We can either believe or reject what God promises in His Word.

Another reason is that we focus on emotions, which can quickly change. If salvation were based on feelings, we would never know from one day to the next if we were saved. What's more, believers sometimes doubt their salvation because they compare themselves to other people. Take your eyes off them, and start looking to Jesus!

Sometimes trials and tragedies make us vulnerable to doubt. When Satan sees a child of God discouraged or hurting physically, he will often launch a vicious attack. Our faith must not be based upon our circumstances, but on the truth of God's Word.

When you doubt for any reason, go back to Scripture and let the Lord assure you of His love and His provision.

Take away all my doubts, Lord. I confess that You are real, Your Word is true, and my eternal destiny is secure.

Don't Miss Your Miracle

SCRIPTURE READING: MATTHEW 9:19–22
KEY VERSE: MATTHEW 8:26

But He said to them, "Why are you fearful, O you of little faith?"
Then He arose and rebuked the winds and the sea,
and there was a great calm.

When they set sail on a stormy sea, even Christ's disciples were afraid. Jesus asked them why, and then He calmed the storm (Matthew 8:25–27).

You may be faced with a similar situation. It is easy to give in to fear and doubt when things all around you are in a state of tumult. The important thing to remember is this: if Christ is in you, He will be faithful to you. With Jesus on board, the disciples' ship would not have gone anywhere God did not ordain it to go. So it is with your life. Although you cannot see Him, God is aware of your situation and will navigate it successfully.

Ironically, the faith of a woman who had never previously seen Christ dwarfed that of His own disciples. Because she earnestly believed He could heal her, she dared to touch the hem of His garment. Jesus turned to her and said, "Daughter, take courage; your faith has made you well" (Matthew 9:22 NASB).

Jesus is faithful to all of His followers, regardless of the degree to which they trust Him. But you will miss out on the richness of His blessings when you give in to doubt and fear. When Jesus visited His hometown, the people who had known Him as a child could not believe that He was a prophet. Because of their lack of faith, Jesus did not perform many miracles there (Matthew 13:54–58). How many miracles do you miss out on because of your unbelief?

Lord, I do not want to stand in the way of Your miraculous workings. Help me to set aside my human fears and trust You to do what humans can't.

THE BATTLE OF FAITH

SCRIPTURE READING: 2 CHRONICLES 20:1–18
KEY VERSE: 2 CHRONICLES 20:12

O our God, will You not judge them? For we have no power against
this great multitude that is coming against us; nor do we
know what to do, but our eyes are upon You.

Faith is oftentimes a battle. We wake up in the morning feeling drawn toward the Lord and trusting in Him, but by the end of the day, we find ourselves on the other side of the spectrum, doubting Him entirely. The pendulum of our thinking and emotions swings from doubt to assurance to doubt to assurance.

In 2 Chronicles, we find the story of King Jehoshaphat and the key to stabilizing our faith. What is it that causes us to swing toward doubt? When we focus on our circumstances rather than on God's power to overcome them, our faith becomes finite. When we give our feelings more credence than our knowledge of God, we begin to doubt Him. And when we listen to the complaints of others and the lies of Satan, we forget God's faithfulness.

What will bring us back toward faith? The antidote to forgetting God's faithfulness can be found in the Word, where you can meditate on His promises. When you read His Word daily, try to recall the things He has done in your life. Consider the nature of God and how He manifests Himself in the world around you and in your own experience. Finally, ask the Lord for His perspective when you are faced with a difficult situation. Talking to the Lord directly will diffuse doubt more quickly than any other remedy.

In order to stabilize wavering faith, you must commune with God daily. Pray God-centered prayers that earnestly seek His will above your own, and wait upon the Lord.

Stabilize my wavering faith, Lord. Give me assurance based upon
Your Word and Your divine nature.

COME AS YOU ARE

SCRIPTURE READING: ROMANS 5:12–21
KEY VERSE: ROMANS 5:17

*For if by the one man's offense death reigned through the one,
much more those who receive abundance of grace and of the gift of
righteousness will reign in life through the One, Jesus Christ.*

Imagine being approached with this inquiry: "I don't know anything about God. Would you describe Him to me?" How would you explain to that person what God is like? When the conversation was over, how would the person walk away? Would he or she be discouraged about ever having a relationship with the Lord, or confident and assured about being able to have a permanent, personal relationship with God?

There is a lot of confusion, even among believers, about who God is. Some, thinking He's a God of judgment and vengeance, live in fear of Him. That belief can leave us doubting and afraid, wondering exactly what would cause God to stop loving us.

Scripture reveals the truth: He is the God of grace. Grace is God's goodness and kindness that is lavishly shown toward us, and it has two amazing qualities.

First, it is given to us regardless of whether we deserve it. Our good works or stellar personal qualities cannot bring us God's grace, nor can our failures cause God to withdraw it. We look at grades, scorecards, and performance appraisals in determining who receives what, but God does not look at merit. Amazing, but true.

Second, grace is given freely to us. There is no cost. Our world does not operate this way, but our God does. Not only at the point of salvation but throughout our Christian life, we are invited to come as we are, acknowledge our sinfulness, and receive forgiveness and God's grace.

*Lord, I come just as I am with assurance that You will receive me,
forgive me, and bestow Your grace upon me.*

THE GIFT HE HAS GIVEN

SCRIPTURE READING: 1 PETER 2:21–24
KEY VERSE: 1 PETER 2:24

. . . who Himself bore our sins in His own body on the tree,
that we, having died to sins, might live for righteousness—
by whose stripes you were healed.

Have you ever felt guilty for something you've done? Sure you have. The truth is, there are no perfect people in this world, and—it will come as no surprise—that includes you and me. That means every single one of us has done something of which we are not altogether proud.

The question, then, isn't whether or not you have ever experienced guilt, but rather what God thinks about your feelings of self-condemnation. Does your righteousness in Christ require you to mourn continually over your sin?

The answer is a resounding *no!* Too many believers fall victim to the guilt mind-set. This is the inclination to become almost crippled with remorse over poor decisions and sinful actions. Obviously, God is not pleased with our sin, but He does not want us mastered by guilt!

This certainly does not mean that our wrongdoing is insignificant. In fact, it required the highest price imaginable to secure our freedom from sin, death, and guilt. That price was the very life of the Son of God. The only reason believers are not condemned by their sin is that Jesus already bore the punishment (1 Peter 2:24; 3:18).

Please understand what this means: Jesus died, not merely for the sin "of the world," but for your sin. He paid the penalty; He accepted the guilt. God will not send the punishment for your sin a second time. The debt is paid! No one can repay God for what He's done; we can only praise Him and accept the wonderful gift He has freely given.

Lord, I praise You for the gift You have given—salvation and assurance of my eternal destiny. I thank You for paying my debt.

A Grace-Filled Relationship

SCRIPTURE READING: JOHN 1:14–17
KEY VERSE: LUKE 19:5

And when Jesus came to the place, He looked up and saw him,
and said to him, "Zacchaeus, make haste and come down,
for today I must stay at your house."

We need only to look at Jesus to know our God is a God of grace. Jesus' actions personify grace. We see Him dealing with all kinds of people, not to condemn them, but to lift them up, encourage them, and turn them toward God.

He told the adulterous woman He didn't condemn her; she was just to go and sin no more (John 8:11). Although He knew about Zaccheus's ill-gotten gains as a hated tax collector, Jesus was nevertheless willing to visit the man's house (Luke 19:5). Jesus demonstrated grace even to the hypocritical, legalistic Pharisees: He pointed out their sins so they would repent.

Grace also means forgiveness for the times we sin. Does that mean we can live in any manner we choose and get away with it? No. While God forgives His children, He also disciplines them. Allowing us to get by with something God knows will ultimately destroy our lives wouldn't be an act of grace. It would be an act of careless indifference, and that's simply not who He is. He's a God of grace.

The theme of the Christian life is grace—God's abundant goodness, love, and mercy toward His children. The truth is, before we ever finish enjoying the goodness and kindness that He's given us, He piles on more goodness and kindness, and then more again. John calls it "grace upon grace" (John 1:16 NASB).

Having been saved by grace and now walking in a grace-filled relationship with God, we are to respond in grace toward others. Ask the Holy Spirit to widen your vision of God's grace, and seek ways to live it out.

Widen my vision, Holy Spirit. Assure me of Your grace at work in
me and show me ways to live it out each day.

A MIRACLE OF LIFE

SCRIPTURE READING: PSALM 45:1–15
KEY VERSE: PSALM 45:15

With gladness and rejoicing they shall be brought;
They shall enter the King's palace.

Why is it that so many of us who have trusted Jesus Christ as Savior spend our Christian lives struggling and feeling defeated? One reason may be that we have never grasped exactly what took place at salvation, and we furthermore fail to understand its current meaning in our lives.

God's viewpoint is that, before trusting Christ as Savior, we were spiritually dead (Ephesians 2:5), under His wrath (John 3:36), and condemned to eternal separation from Him (Revelation 20:15). He saw us in these ways:

- Walking dead people, who couldn't make themselves alive
- People deserving judgment, who couldn't remove themselves from divine anger by their own efforts
- Rebellious people who were unable to turn to God apart from the Spirit's drawing power

Clearly, something outside of ourselves was needed. The Lord loved us to the point that He was willing to do whatever was necessary to rescue us from our desperate condition. God's solution was grace:

- He provided a Savior who bore our sins, became sin for us, and endured the wrath of God for those sins.
- He sent His only Son to pay the debt we owed for our sins—a debt we could not pay.

What took place? A miracle of life for us, who were once spiritually dead.

Thank You for the miracle, God. Thank You for sending a Savior who bore my sin and paid my debt. Thank You for the assurance of eternal life!

SAVED BY GRACE

SCRIPTURE READING: 2 CORINTHIANS 5:14–17
KEY VERSE: 2 CORINTHIANS 5:17

*Therefore, if anyone is in Christ, he is a new creation; old things
have passed away; behold, all things have become new.*

Grace is God's goodness and kindness freely extended to the utterly un-
deserving—you and me. Because of His grace, He offers salvation
through Jesus Christ so that we might have a relationship with Him. In that
relationship, His viewpoint of us has changed. God, in His grace, does these
things for us:

- Declares we are righteous. Christ's righteousness is credited as our
  own (2 Corinthians 5:21). The guilt and shame of sin has been
  removed (Romans 8:1). We can live boldly for Jesus no matter
  who we once were.
- Claims us as family. A spiritual adoption has taken place so that
  we might become children of God and call Him "Father." No
  matter how insignificant the world says we are, we are to live our
  days remembering we're children of the King.
- Gives us, who were spiritually dead, a new heart and a new spirit. We
  are born again. We have a fresh start in Christ (2 Corinthians 5:17).
- Raises us out of the life we used to live into a new life with Him.
  The seal of this new life is the presence of the Holy Spirit, whose
  fruit is love, joy, and peace.
- Sets us free from the power of sin, Satan, and self. Obedience and
  victory become a reality as we grow in faith and trust.

Praise God for His unending grace!

*Thank You for Your unending grace, Lord. Thank You for declaring
me righteous and claiming me as family, providing an inheritance,
setting me free from sin, and raising me from the old life to a new life.*

THE RICHES OF GOD'S GRACE

SCRIPTURE READING: EPHESIANS 1:3–14

KEY VERSE: EPHESIANS 1:3

*Blessed be the God and Father of our Lord Jesus Christ, who has
blessed us with every spiritual blessing in the heavenly places in Christ.*

What would it take for you to consider yourself rich? Would it require a healthy bank account? A fancy new car in the garage? The freedom to go online, click a few buttons, and have anything you wanted delivered right to your door?

You may not be so bold as to answer yes to the above questions, but does your life reflect this kind of attitude? Sadly, many believers are completely overtaken by the world's standard of riches. This happens whether the individual is wealthy or not. For the well-off, the temptation is to see money as the defining characteristic of their lives. For the poor, money becomes the be-all-end-all goal of comfort and satisfaction. You see, greed is no respecter of persons. It attacks rich and poor alike.

What many believers fail to realize is that in Christ, we are all rich. Sure, you may have a mortgage, a monthly car payment, and credit card bills; however, if you have placed your faith in Jesus, you can boldly acknowledge that the almighty God has already poured His richest blessings upon you. Hallelujah!

Ephesians 1:3 says that God has blessed us with every spiritual blessing. Did you notice the tense of the verb there? He said "blessed," meaning it has already happened. And He does not give just a little bit here and there; rather, He lavishly pours out His blessings upon us.

*Lord, help me to count my blessings according to Your values and not
the superficial values of the world. You have given me gifts that are
eternal. Thank You.*

GOD'S GOLD MEDAL

SCRIPTURE READING: JOHN 16:31–33
KEY VERSES: JAMES 1:2–3

My brethren, count it all joy when you fall into various trials,
knowing that the testing of your faith produces patience.

When difficult times come into your life, what is your response? While it may seem easier to "quit while you're ahead," this is not the kind of attitude God wants us to demonstrate. Instead, we are to hold our heads high and press on through the pain.

This comes as a shock to many new believers. After placing their faith in Jesus, they are often surprised when some unexpected hardship appears. This reveals a terrible misconception. The Bible does not promise an easy life once we accept Jesus as Lord. In fact, the Word assures us of quite the opposite! Jesus Himself declared that if we are found in Him, the world will give us great trouble (John 16:33).

In James 1:2, we are instructed to consider our struggles as a source of "pure joy" (NIV). This makes sense only when we see our difficulties through God's eyes—as opportunities for growth. An untested faith is weak and ineffective. Just like our muscles, our faith must be exercised against some resistance. When we face these trials with wisdom and endure them with godly determination, we will find blessings we never thought possible.

At the end of the struggle, we will see God standing with our reward: the crown of life (James 1:12). This is an athletic reference—essentially, the "crown of life" is God's gold medal for a job well done.

Do you want God's recognition of your spiritual victory? Then press on through the hardship with assurance and perseverance.

Help me persevere with assurance, Lord. I want to receive a crown
of life!

RESTORED BY GRACE

SCRIPTURE READING: LUKE 15:11–16
KEY VERSE: LUKE 15:14

*But when he had spent all, there arose a severe famine in that land,
and he began to be in want.*

Independence is a highly valued quality. We teach it to our children, and we demand it for ourselves. There is even a statue called the Independent Man on top of the state capitol of Rhode Island. It stands as a tribute to self-sufficiency and freedom.

In the story of the prodigal son, we see a different aspect of independence in someone who takes charge of his own life and shuns his father's care and protection. The account reveals both the downward spiral of sin and the restoring grace of God.

Sin means acting independently of God's will. It begins with a desire that is outside His plan. Next comes a decision to act on the desire. When we act, we find ourselves, like the prodigal, in a distant country, which is anywhere outside the will of God.

To remain there requires deception. We deceive ourselves by thinking that we know better than God, and ignoring any consequences. Defeat follows. For a time, all will seem fine, but, like the reckless son in the story, we will find our way leads to defeat. Finally, we will arrive at despair resulting from famine of spirit, emotions, or relationships. That leads into desperation, where our choices are few, and all distasteful.

The prodigal son ended up there. But desperation is not the end of the prodigal's story, nor is it the end of ours when we sin. Jesus gave this account of an earthly father's forgiving love because He desired to point us to the restoring grace of our heavenly Father. God waits with open arms for us, His wandering children.

Father, thank You for the assurance of Your love—that You wait with open arms to welcome Your wandering children home.

MAGNIFICENT GRACE

SCRIPTURE READING: LUKE 15:17–24
KEY VERSES: ROMANS 6:1–2

What shall we say then? Shall we continue in sin that
grace may abound? Certainly not! How shall we
who died to sin live any longer in it?

Family-oriented movies often end by showing a reunion of loved ones. We see family members with arms around each other in an expression of love and support. Through the parable of the prodigal son, Jesus gave us this same picture of our heavenly Father's attitude toward us (Luke 15:20–24). There, Jesus revealed the magnificence of grace. We see that the one sinned against runs out to eagerly welcome back the one who sinned. The one who was wronged takes the initiative, because of love, to restore the broken relationship; the one mistreated shows compassion to the one at fault.

And there is even more. The prodigal did not know his full rights as a son would be restored. As believers, however, we know in advance what awaits us when we humbly return. Because of grace, we can count on acceptance no matter how long we have been absent from the Father or how far we have wandered. Grace guarantees that the Lord will greet us with compassion and forgiveness and lovingly restore us to full rights as His children.

It is not our performance—not good deeds or even the correct apology—that matters; it is our position in Christ. When God sees that we belong to His Son, He forgives us. The parable of the prodigal points us to the truth that, because of Jesus Christ, we are forgiven even before we return. While this does not give us license to sin (Romans 6:1–2), it does give us reason to celebrate. Our Father waits to welcome us home.

You wait to welcome me home, Father. I am assured of Your magnificent grace. Thank You!

OCTOBER
Pathway to Success

Only be strong and very courageous, that you may observe to do according to all the law which Moses My servant commanded you; do not turn from it to the right hand or to the left, that you may prosper wherever you go. This Book of the Law shall not depart from your mouth, but you shall meditate in it day and night, that you may observe to do according to all that is written in it. For then you will make your way prosperous, and then you will have good success.

—Joshua 1:7–8

THE GODLY WAY TO SUCCESS

SCRIPTURE READING: PSALM 1:1–6
KEY VERSE: PSALM 1:3

He shall be like a tree
Planted by the rivers of water,
That brings forth its fruit in its season,
Whose leaf also shall not wither;
And whatever he does shall prosper.

Every time we turn on the television or radio, we can hear someone claiming to have the formula for quick success. The ads tell us that if we want success, we can have it now, and we can have it for only $49.95.

Such is merely man's success. It's a far cry from godly success, the kind that represents God's heart for us and personifies the great joy and fulfillment that comes with knowing Him.

If we want to stand out from the rest of the world, Psalm 1 shows us the pathway to godly success that will bring us fulfillment like we've never known: be careful about your relationships. In order to be successful, you need to hear God's perspective on things and should seek godly counsel, not the counsel of just anyone who has an opinion. There are some well-meaning Christians who relish the opportunity to give their thoughts on a situation without searching out the Scriptures for what God says.

Commit to the principles of the Scriptures. A warning sign of when you might be drifting is when you begin to compromise God's Word. Ask those around you to hold you accountable to what the Bible says. By making His Word the standard for which you live your life, you will experience a world of success.

God desires success for our lives. He wants us to be a people who bring glory and honor to His name as we receive the best He has to give.

Lord, I want true success, not man's success. Help me seek Your counsel and commit to the principles of Your Word.

THE FULLNESS OF BLESSING

SCRIPTURE READING: PROVERBS 12:1–5
KEY VERSE: PROVERBS 12:2

A good man obtains favor from the LORD,
But a man of wicked intentions He will condemn.

While the phrase "walking with the Lord" may sound like a trite, overly-used phrase within the Christian world, its imagery is perfect in describing what a life with God should be like.

Our relationship with God should not wear us out; rather, it should be refreshing. That does not mean that we will not be challenged from time to time and stretched in our faith. However, God isn't trying to leave us behind. A steady, thriving relationship with God is one in which we grow in our understanding of who He is and what He wants to do with our lives. And in the process of nurturing this relationship, we find His favorable hand resting upon us.

Proverbs 12:2 describes a good man. We become "good" men and women when we walk with God. Our desire for righteousness increases as we walk in the light of His glory. We recognize sin in our lives and long for Him to transform us completely.

In order to stay step-for-step with God, we must maintain our pace with Him, seeking to honor and glorify Him in all that we do. It is there that we find His favor and experience the fullness of His blessing upon our lives.

Lord, I want to walk in Your presence, side by side with You. Take my hand and keep me on pace when I am apt to wander or fall behind.

Good Things in Life

SCRIPTURE READING: PSALM 63:1–11

KEY VERSE: PSALM 63:1

O God, You are my God;
Early will I seek You;
My soul thirsts for You;
My flesh longs for You
In a dry and thirsty land
Where there is no water.

To earnestly seek the Lord, to long in your innermost being to know more about Jesus Christ, you must set your mind to do so. It is not an experiential moment in which you are waiting for a feeling or an emotion to affirm that the Lord has spoken to you.

Rather, it is an intentional, deliberate, daily effort at humbly and sincerely trying to find out more about God. If you're going to seek the Lord, you simply must purpose to do it and trust Him to answer your heart's cry.

The primary ways to learn more about God are to read His Word and communicate with Him in prayer. Perhaps you sometimes feel inundated with admonitions to read the Bible and pray, read the Bible and pray. There is a reason. These vital pursuits must be accomplished in earnest before your understanding of Christ is deepened.

The Holy Bible is a product of the mind and heart of God. It is the principal tool He uses to reveal Himself to us. He communicates to us through His Word and His Holy Spirit, and we communicate to Him through prayer.

Yet you also should consciously determine that in your conversations, Scripture study, church attendance, reading, and service, you will be tenacious in longing to discover His will and His ways. These are all methods in which we learn more about God. These are also the ways in which we are richly rewarded with the truly good things in life.

Lord, just as I set my clocks, tune my instruments, and program my computer, let me also set my mind to seek after You through study, prayer, and contemplation.

Accomplishing the Task

Scripture Reading: Psalm 66:1–16
Key Verse: Psalm 66:16

Come and hear, all you who fear God,
And I will declare what He has done for my soul.

Fear has a way of gripping us so tightly that it can squeeze hope from us. However, when we realize how unfounded our fears are, we can begin to see how inaccurate they are. Many believers experience feelings of inadequacy because of fear. Some fear the responsibility that God has given them. Others fear failure or criticism. And still others fear yielding to God's call on their lives.

Fear undermines the understanding of who we are in Christ, leading us to believe that we cannot fulfill the requests God makes. However, we must realize that without Christ, we are inadequate to accomplish God's call on our lives. But God doesn't call us to do things for His kingdom without equipping us to succeed. We must realize the blessings of our inadequacies.

Instead of fearing to venture into the unknown, we boldly go forth, trusting that if God is the one calling us there, He is going to help us every step of the way. In realizing our inadequacies, we begin to see God's power and completeness. No one is beyond His reach nor is any situation beyond His touch. No longer will we try to do kingdom activity on our own. We will trust solely in the Lord to successfully accomplish the tasks He sets before us.

Father, I do not know why I fear Your call. I give my fear to You, claiming Your promise to be with me and equip me for whatever lies ahead.

ACCEPTING OUR INADEQUACIES

SCRIPTURE READING: 2 CORINTHIANS 3:1–6

KEY VERSE: 2 CORINTHIANS 3:5

Not that we are sufficient of ourselves to think of anything as being from ourselves, but our sufficiency is from God.

As we press past all our fears of being inadequate to fulfill the call God has on our lives, we begin to see the full blessing that comes with accepting our inadequacies. Paul wrote, "Not that we are adequate in ourselves to consider anything as coming from ourselves, but our adequacy is from God" (2 Corinthians 3:5 NASB).

Here are some blessings from recognizing our inadequacies:

- They drive us to God. If we feel we are self-sufficient in all things, we may not seek the Lord's guidance.
- They relieve us of the burden of trying to do the will of God in our own strength. The burden rests upon Him.
- They force us to live our lives and do His work in the power of the Holy Spirit.
- They provide God the opportunity to demonstrate what great things He can do with so little. We know we are incapable and that He is capable of all.
- They free God to use us to the maximum of our potential. We stop trying to interject our own contributions, giving all of who we are for His purposes.
- They allow God to receive the full glory for His work. If we know He is responsible, we will point to Him.
- They enable us to walk in contentment and quietness of spirit. Nothing is more satisfying than seeing God use our willingness to advance His kingdom.

Father, it is a miracle in and of itself that You use my inadequacies to fulfill Your purposes and draw me closer to You in the process. You are an awesome God.

The Power of Confession

SCRIPTURE READING: PSALM 138:1–8
KEY VERSE: PHILIPPIANS 4:13

I can do all things through Christ who strengthens me.

Sticks and stones may break our bones, but negative words can crush our spirits. A harsh tone and a cruel accusation from someone may affirm a dreadful misconception we have about our lives. Paul, however, did not let the defeating words of others sway him. Instead of conceding that maybe their accusations were correct, Paul knew what God had to say about his life. And he began confessing it. "I can do all things through Christ who strengthens me" (Philippians 4:13).

Paul's confession was bold, but truthful. He immediately staked his claim on the source of his strength, Jesus Christ. This was not a mere defiant remark from a person with a huge ego. This was a confession from someone who understood his place in God's kingdom and the power of the One he served.

The spoken word is a powerful tool, and we must be careful to use it in the same way God uses His Word to communicate to us: to continue to shape us into His image. When the confessions of our mouth about who we are align with God's Word, we begin to see the healthy benefits of such statements. Instead of a poor self-image, we begin to see ourselves as God sees us: His beloved children whom He longs to bless with His mercy, goodness, and grace.

Lord, let me never forget that when I accomplish things in You, I could not have done them in my own strength.

YOUR GREATEST LEGACY

SCRIPTURE READING: EPHESIANS 3:10–19
KEY VERSE: EPHESIANS 1:7

*In Him we have redemption through His blood, the forgiveness of sins,
according to the riches of His grace.*

People have endeavored to secure their places in history through varied avenues. At one time, great leaders measured their legacies by the vastness of their families or their gains in battle.

Since then, the famous and infamous alike have attempted to break athletic records, flourish in the arts, and perpetrate perfect crimes to remain memorable. Though Christians are often called to competition and dedicated public service, the goal should not be fame in this world. A Christian's treasure is Christ, so it is the hope of heaven that is the legacy.

Ephesians 3:14–16 instructs, "For this reason I bow my knees to the Father of our Lord Jesus Christ, from whom the whole family in heaven and earth is named, that He would grant you, according to the riches of His glory, to be strengthened with might through His Spirit in the inner man."

Man looks to the past for his legacy, but the Christian's legacy lies in the future. Christ desires that you reflect His holiness and love in this world so that others can understand the reality of His kingdom.

Your legacy might not be acknowledged by historians, but you are certainly celebrated by God for every step in love and holiness that you take here on earth. Let your greatest legacy be to love the Lord your God with all your heart.

Lord, I want my greatest legacy to be loving You with all my heart. That is the measure of true success.

THE POWER WITHIN

SCRIPTURE READING: EPHESIANS 3:20–4:6
KEY VERSES: EPHESIANS 3:20–21

*Now to Him who is able to do exceedingly abundantly above all
that we ask or think, according to the power that works in us,
to Him be glory in the church by Christ Jesus to all generations,
forever and ever. Amen.*

Some days the person staring back at you from the mirror appears to be anything but a powerhouse. How well you know your own faults and weaknesses! As you look at yourself, you wonder if you could hope to aspire to the grand plans and goals that have inspired your heart.

Meister Eckhart has a word of encouragement for you: "If it be not the will that fails you, but only the power, then truly, before God, you have done it all, and no man can take it from you or even hinder you for a moment; for to will to do as soon as I can is the same before God as having done it."

If God has called you to some great undertaking, then you have all the power you need to accomplish it. All you need is the will and determination to go forward. Ephesians 3:20–21 admonishes believers that God is able, in His strength, to do things in us and through us beyond anything we could ever imagine.

God's plans are more wonderful than can be imagined, and they include a place for you. You are His child, and His desire is for you to succeed. So, as you look at yourself in the mirror, remind yourself that the power within you is the power of God, and nothing is impossible for Him.

Lord, if You are calling me to be a powerhouse, then I want to stay plugged into You. I know that You alone have everything I need to succeed.

THE RICHES OF GOD'S GRACE

SCRIPTURE READING: EPHESIANS 1:3–12

KEY VERSE: EPHESIANS 1:7

In Him we have redemption through His blood, the forgiveness of sins, according to the riches of His grace.

When God bought your salvation, He spared no expense. He provided the costly blood of Christ to purchase your eternal life. Why is it, then, that some believers spend their lives trying to earn what God has already paid for?

Abraham Lincoln surmised that it is because believers fail to recall God's great grace. Lincoln wrote, "We have forgotten the gracious hand which has preserved us in peace and multiplied and enriched and strengthened us, and have vainly imagined in the deceitfulness of our hearts that all these blessings were produced by some superior wisdom and virtue of our own."

If believers imagine they have earned salvation through virtue, then when virtue is lacking, they believe they have lost the blessing. However, salvation was never based on human acts of piety. Salvation has its foundation in the sacrificial grace of Christ. His grace covers your sin. It was a great penalty to pay, but Jesus deemed that your salvation was worth the price.

Accept the riches of His grace and invest your life in thankfulness to Him.

Your grace covers my sin. Thank You, Lord! I am so glad You deemed my salvation worth the price.

A Powerful Relationship

SCRIPTURE READING: JOHN 15:14–16
KEY VERSE: JOHN 15:15

No longer do I call you servants, for a servant does not know what his master is doing; but I have called you friends, for all things that I heard from My Father I have made known to you.

The night before his wedding, Joseph Scriven's fiancée drowned. Devastated, Scriven moved away from his home to escape the memory of her. He relocated to Canada where he met another lovely young woman named Eliza. Before they could marry, she got sick and passed away.

Joseph Scriven faced these and many other tragedies; however, Christ was his constant comfort. It was Scriven who penned the beautiful poem, "What a Friend We Have in Jesus." He wrote, "Can we find a friend so faithful who will all our sorrows share? Jesus knows our every weakness; take it to the Lord in prayer."

Jesus understands the depth of your suffering too. In John 15:15, Jesus said, "No longer do I call you slaves . . . but I have called you friends" (NASB). You may perceive Jesus in lofty terms as "Savior," "King of kings," and "Almighty," but He also desires for you to know Him as "Friend."

Jesus calls you His friend because He loves you. No one could see more deeply into your heart or is more faithful and trustworthy to care for your needs. He promises to comfort you.

Turn to Him to be your closest friend. You will find in Him a powerful relationship.

Lord, You are both my king and my friend, my creator and my ever-present companion. I bring to You every thought and care, just as You have called me to do.

THE KEYS TO SUCCESS

SCRIPTURE READING: GALATIANS 6:6–10
KEY VERSE: 1 THESSALONIANS 5:24

He who calls you is faithful, who also will do it.

They say that in any organization 20 percent of the people do 80 percent of the work, so this devotion is dedicated to those faithful saints who carry the overwhelming load of responsibility in their congregations.

Though your faithful service is indispensable to the church, there is danger that you will take on so much responsibility that you begin to burn out or, worse, become prideful about your service.

Anthony Hanson has this reminder for you: "The service the Christian does is not his, but Christ's. . . . This knowledge, far from inhibiting action, actually releases the Christian from that appalling feeling of responsibility that has driven so many . . . to despair. . . . Work done conscientiously by the Christian is his share in Christ's service; but it is Christ's service, and therefore the Christian need neither be proud because it has succeeded or overwhelmed because it has failed."

You may feel like the work won't get done if you don't do it—but remember it is God who accomplishes the work through you. First Thessalonians 5:24 promises that it is God who will ultimately do the work. Service is not something we do for God, but something God does through us.

Just as God empowers you to fulfill your duties, He can equip others. Trust Him. Rest in Him, and He will accomplish His will.

Father, I rest in You. I know You will accomplish Your will in and through me.

The Value of Little Things

SCRIPTURE READING: MATTHEW 10:38–42
KEY VERSE: MATTHEW 10:42

*And whoever gives one of these little ones only a cup of cold
water in the name of a disciple, assuredly, I say to you,
he shall by no means lose his reward.*

For evangelists like Billy Graham, ministry consists of preaching the gospel to millions of people at large, preplanned events. However, a great majority of the work God does through His people is on a much smaller scale. Notice Jesus' words in Matthew 10:42—even a cup of cold water to a little one will be rewarded by God.

Acts of service, such as giving water to a child, speak to humility of heart and willingness that truly honor God. It is the person who is willing to set up folding chairs, take food to the homeless, or simply listen to a hurting friend whom God uses in a profound way.

Perhaps those activities seem insignificant compared to preaching a revival or building a mission church. However, they are the backbone of a healthy ministry where the love of God is displayed in authentic ways.

Lest you think your small offerings are lost, Brother Lawrence admonishes, "We ought not to be weary of doing little things for the love of God, who regards not the greatness of the work, but the love with which it is performed."

So make the most of every opportunity to do the little things that make such a big difference. You will certainly not lose your reward.

Lord, help me make the most of every opportunity. I want to do little things in a big way.

GET UP!

SCRIPTURE READING: LUKE 22:31–34
KEY VERSE: LUKE 22:31

And the Lord said, "Simon, Simon! Indeed, Satan has asked for you, that he may sift you as wheat."

In Peter's mind, it was a brave moment of standing with his Messiah. Sword in hand, Peter would do everything he could to help Jesus carve away the Roman Empire and regain Israel's independence.

Christ's battle was not against Rome, though; it was against sin. He saw the truth of the situation, whereas Peter had a limited view. Jesus understood that in the stressful events leading up to the Crucifixion, the disciples would be filled with sorrow and confusion. Jesus knew that Peter would fail. Jesus told him, "I have prayed for you, that your faith should not fail; and when you have returned to Me, strengthen your brethren" (Luke 22:32).

Jesus knows there will be times when you fail too. Things will arise in your life—distresses, perplexities, great pains—that will be extraordinarily difficult to stand against, and you will flounder. However, Jesus is interceding for you. He does not view you in light of your failures but whether you rise again to serve Him.

Henry Liddon said, "Nothing is really lost by a life of sacrifice; everything is lost by failure to obey God's call." When you fall, do not be afraid of God. He always accepts you with open arms. Focus instead on His forgiveness and get up again!

Lord, just as You knew Peter would fail—but would return, humbled, and serve You—so, too, You know my failings and draw my penitent heart back to You.

RISE AGAIN

SCRIPTURE READING: JOHN 21:1–17
KEY VERSE: JOHN 21:15

So when they had eaten breakfast, Jesus said to Simon Peter, "Simon, son of Jonah, do you love Me more than these?" He said to Him, "Yes, Lord; You know that I love You." He said to him, "Feed My lambs."

Have you failed? Are your insides being gnawed away by the insidious emotions of embarrassment and remorse?

Then be encouraged by the failure of one of the great disciples. During Christ's trial and crucifixion, it was crucial that the disciples stayed together and kept their faith strong. Instead, they fled. Simon Peter went as far as denying his beloved Friend three times.

However, when they met again after the Resurrection, Jesus held no malice for Peter. John 21:15 reports, "When they had finished breakfast, Jesus said to Simon Peter, 'Simon, son of John, do you love Me more than these?' [Peter] said to Him, 'Yes, Lord; You know that I love You.' [Jesus] said to him, 'Tend My lambs'" (NASB).

Jesus did not chastise Peter; rather, He stressed that for Peter to truly show his love, Peter would have to take on the commission: feed My lambs. The same is true for you. God does not desire for you to remain ashamed. His direction is that you renew your commitment and take up the purpose for which He called you.

As Oliver Goldsmith astutely notes, "Our greatest glory is not in never falling, but in rising each time we fall." You have no reason to live in shame. Rise again and take on the godly life to which God called you. You may find your biggest failure was only the beginning of your greatest success.

When I wallow in guilt, Lord, I am not doing it for You, but for me. Help me to rise quickly, ignore the naggings of embarrassment and remorse, and be about Your business.

An Immense Blessing

SCRIPTURE READING: JAMES 2:20–24
KEY VERSE: PROVERBS 18:24

A man who has friends must himself be friendly,
But there is a friend who sticks closer than a brother.

The Bible gives us many examples of friendship. God called Abraham His friend (James 2:23). Aaron and Hur stood by Moses' side and supported his hands to ensure victory in battle (Exodus 17:12). David and Jonathan are a well-known example of friendship (1 Samuel 18).

These friendships were more than casual relationships. In the midst of difficulty or hardship, they offered support and strength for each other. When we take time to establish a deep, mutual relationship, we have someone whom we can depend on and who will stand with us no matter what we might face.

We need to be careful as we choose our friends, because they impact our lives. They bring enjoyment, delight, and pleasure. Friends can help us learn how to get along with other people, how to give and take, and how to relate more intimately. They can drive us, motivate us, disillusion us, distress us, or even destroy us.

We all want to feel accepted and loved. If you build a friendship based on a need that you have, it will not last. When the need is satisfied, you will grow weary of the friendship, or you will become dissatisfied if the need is not being met.

Take the time to build true, genuine, devoted, and loyal friendships, and your life will be immensely blessed by the effort.

Lord, the friends I choose either help anchor my faith or create barriers between You and me. Help me to choose wisely those with whom I spend my time.

Wise Relationships

SCRIPTURE READING: 1 SAMUEL 20:1–42
KEY VERSE: 1 SAMUEL 20:42

*Then Jonathan said to David, "Go in peace, since we have both sworn
in the name of the Lord, saying, 'May the Lord be between you and
me, and between your descendants and my descendants, forever.'"
So he arose and departed, and Jonathan went into the city.*

How do we develop wise friendships? Friendship usually begins because of mutual concerns and interests, and deepens as you take time to build your relationship. Whether our interests may be in a sport, classical music, or raising our children—as believers, we have a mutual interest in our faith in Jesus Christ and our relationship with Him.

Many times our past experiences influence our ability in building trusting relationships. If we have been hurt before, we may be less likely to open our hearts again. Or we may base our friendship on personal ambition or selfishness. When we depend on another person for our security or take advantage of someone for our own personal gain, we are not building wise, lasting relationships.

A friendship that is based on the issue of what someone can do for you is not a true friendship. No person can ever satisfy the longing and need in your life. Only Jesus can meet all your needs—spiritual, physical, and emotional.

Building friendships requires risk of possible pain and rejection. However, it is worth the risk to find a friendship anchored by genuine trust, devotion, and loyalty. Ask God to show you how to be a true friend, and begin to work toward a lasting, rewarding friendship.

Lord, thank You for the good friendships You have provided. Help me to be one of those friends who comes alongside others without selfish motives.

HEARING AND OBEYING

SCRIPTURE READING: PSALM 92:12–14
KEY VERSE: PSALM 92:12

The righteous shall flourish like a palm tree,
He shall grow like a cedar in Lebanon.

When we are given an assignment and it turns out wonderfully, but it isn't what the person assigning us the task communicated for us to do, is that success? In the world around us, there are many people who appear to be successful by man's standards—fame, wealth, riches—but by God's standards are complete failures. They missed the mark. They aren't becoming what He intended for them to become.

If our desire in life is to obtain godly success, we must first get our assignment straight: What is God's will for our lives? God's will for everyone is to know Him and to develop a personal, intimate relationship with Him while becoming what He created each person to become. However, how that looks specifically in each person's life varies.

For David, it meant growing in his relationship with God through the trials and struggles of becoming king of Israel. For Jonathan, it meant growing in his relationship with God through the tremendous sacrifice of yielding the throne to David. Godly success looked different in both these men's lives, yet they both achieved it by following God's will.

We establish ourselves as men and women of God if we are willing to hear and obey His will for our lives. It is the only way we can have true, godly success in our lives. It is the only way to measure success—are we doing what He has asked?

Father, establish me as a person who is willing to hear and obey Your
will. Let me measure my success by doing what You have asked.

THIS IS HIS TIME

SCRIPTURE READING: PSALM 40:13–17
KEY VERSE: PSALM 40:1

I waited patiently for the Lord;
And He inclined to me,
And heard my cry.

No matter how hard we tried not to let it get to us, it did. The pressure began building and building—deadlines, irritable bosses, difficult children, commitments we made, a delicate family situation. Then, suddenly, we snapped. We showed the world around us that we could not handle it on our own.

Admitting our inability to handle the sometimes overwhelming stress of life is exactly what God wants. Instead of trying to navigate through these rough waters on our own, He wants to see us turn to Him more than ever. This is His moment to shine through us by leading and guiding us to a place of peace. This is His time.

Paul encourages us in Philippians 4:6–7 to not be anxious, but through prayer to tell God about our worries. Why can we tell God about our problems so easily?

First, God already knows what we're going through, but He still wants to hear it from us. Our admission of frailty oftentimes paves the way for God to work in our lives.

Second, we should tell God about our problems because He knows how to resolve them. We will never experience true prosperity trying to operate on our own wisdom.

And last, God is not surprised by our challenges in life. He knows what is coming, and He knows how to get us through. Who else would be more perfect to talk about our anxieties during a time like this?

Lord, I admit my shortcomings, my anxieties, and my failures. Help me turn them around so that You can be glorified.

Finding Favor with God

Scripture Reading: Proverbs 3:1–4
Key Verse: Proverbs 3:3

Let not mercy and truth forsake you;
Bind them around your neck,
Write them on the tablet of your heart.

Whenever we find favor with someone, we feel their support. In everything we do, we are encouraged. It's not that we feel we can do no wrong, but we feel that we will always do right. Verses pepper the Bible with ways we can find favor with God. The most basic of ways begins with opening God's Word and instilling it into our hearts and minds.

Solomon wrote, "Let not mercy and truth forsake you; bind them around your neck, write them on the tablet of your heart" (Proverbs 3:3). God's truth is written on our hearts when we begin a daily diet of reading His Word, taking time to understand the principles and concepts that make up His kingdom. In the Bible, we find the sustenance for life, the strength to persevere, the hope to conquer our fears.

Every lesson taught in the Bible is a direct reflection of the nature and character of God, pointing us toward the manner by which He desires for us to live. Through reading God's Word, we begin to understand more about Him and more about the nature of Jesus Christ. As we put these principles to practice in our lives, we find that the favorable hand of the Lord is surrounding us.

Lord, as I search Your Word, take Your truths and carve them into my heart so that they may come to me quickly when I need them.

A Successful Combination

SCRIPTURE READING: 2 CHRONICLES 6:1–10

KEY VERSE: JAMES 1:6

*But let him ask in faith, with no doubting, for he who doubts is
like a wave of the sea driven and tossed by the wind.*

Imagine the billions of prayers that reach the throne of God each day: prayers for healing, help, favor, and honor. When you lift your personal prayers to God, do you have faith that He will respond? Faith combined with prayer is a successful combination.

The Bible tells us that we must pray in faith, without doubting, in order to have our requests answered (James 1:2–8). This concept often confuses new and seasoned believers alike. However, clarification can be gained from today's Key Verse. James advises us to pray wholeheartedly unto the Lord. He does not say that when we pray without doubting we will automatically receive exactly what we asked for, in the exact moment we request it. The key is to pray with undivided trust. God always answers prayers, but His solutions and timelines may be different from ours.

Our responsibility is to rid our minds of doubt. Prayer-related doubt can occur when our problems takes precedence over God. Doubt can also stem from a lack of familiarity with God's Word. God will fulfill His promises, even if it is not in the way we expect or in the time frame we want (2 Chronicles 6:1–4, 6–10).

Examine your level of faith the next time you have a need in your life. As you take your request to God, ask yourself, "Do I genuinely trust God, or am I allowing my mind to be divided by doubt?"

*Lord, when my problems get so big that they block my view, it means
I have forgotten to trust in You. Help me to leave my burdens with You.*

DECREASING DOUBT

SCRIPTURE READING: JOB 42:1–6
KEY VERSE: HEBREWS 13:5

Let your conduct be without covetousness; be content with
such things as you have. For He Himself has said, "I will
never leave you nor forsake you."

How should the successful Christian deal with doubt? This question often surfaces during times of tragedy when, for an instant, it may seem to some that God is not present. The Bible, however, tells us that God is always with us, in every circumstance, throughout every moment of our lives. He promises in His Word that He will never leave or forsake us (Hebrews 13:5).

As humans, the concept of someone who is incapable of disappointing us is hard to grasp. Therefore, our wandering minds often give way to veins of doubt—doubt that God can provide for us, meet our needs, and turn impossibilities into possibilities.

When feelings such as these seek to break your confidence in God, you must take action. Your best defense is His Word. The Bible is our reassurance, our guide to the undeniable truth of God's love for us and His desire to know us intimately.

If you are not receiving encouragement from your Bible reading, consider purchasing a Bible study tool, such as a topical concordance. Or you might try inviting a friend to become a Bible study partner with you. This will increase your knowledge in a spirit of fellowship. Be sure to select a person who knows the Scriptures and is capable of directing you to God's truths in times of doubt. As you study the Bible together, your knowledge will increase and thoughts of doubt will decrease.

Lord, when I was a child, I sang that the B.I.B.L.E. was "the book
for me." I still believe that. Draw me to the ways and means to keep
Your Word fresh in my heart.

WISDOM FOR GOOD HEALTH

SCRIPTURE READING: PSALM 34:8–14
KEY VERSES: 1 CORINTHIANS 6:19–20

*Or do you not know that your body is the temple of the Holy Spirit
who is in you, whom you have from God, and you are not your own?
For you were bought at a price; therefore glorify God in your
body and in your spirit, which are God's.*

In a certain office building, it is not uncommon to hear excited whispers in the halls on Thursday mornings. There, Thursdays have practically become weekly holidays, days to look forward to, a bright spot of expectation in an otherwise ordinary workweek. You see, Thursday is the day on which lunch is catered by the culinary genius known only as "The Taco Guy." Nobody leaves work hungry on Thursdays.

However, there are those who wince at the thought of such a fine spread of food. The problem for these unfortunates is that they do not trust their self-control when presented with such a plentiful buffet. Rather than making wise decisions in preparing their lunch plates, they either pile on as much food as possible or avoid the cafeteria altogether.

Does wisdom offer a better solution? Is there not a "middle ground" by which one can enjoy the feast and yet maintain a healthy diet? Scripture clearly teaches that the body is the temple of God's Holy Spirit; cramming tacos, fajitas, sour cream, and salsa into every nook and cranny of that temple is unwise, because that misuses both the body and the wonderful gift of food that God has provided.

Pray for wisdom in maintaining a healthy lifestyle so you can achieve success mentally, spiritually, and physically. Do not deny yourself the occasional indulgence, but be wary of unhealthy habits. Your body is God's temple; fuel it with that which will keep your temple functioning properly for as long as possible.

Lord, I realize my body is Your temple. Help me maintain a healthy lifestyle so I can successfully fulfill Your purposes for my life.

SOMETHING BEAUTIFUL

SCRIPTURE READING: PSALM 139:1–12
KEY VERSES: PSALM 139:7

Where can I go from Your Spirit?
Or where can I flee from Your presence?

Under what circumstances do you most seem to notice God's presence? When does your prayer life become more intense? When do you seek after God with every ounce of energy you can muster?

For most people, times of intense pressure and trials result in a greater awareness of the power of God. It is during these times—not during life's greatest successes—that one's utter dependence on God is at its zenith.

How odd that the hardships in life produce greater faithfulness. Would you not expect the opposite result? After all, it seems perfectly natural to praise God in times of joy; however, when your shattered life lies in ruins at your feet, what is there to be thankful for then?

During these trials, you quickly realize your own inability to positively impact your situation. The feeling of complete helplessness is a shocking eye-opener; in the face of desperation, the only alternative is to turn the matter over to God, who is more than able to meet the need.

It has been noted that those who cry, "A loving God would not allow that to happen," are the people who have never experienced extreme trials themselves. Those who are familiar with pain through loss, famine, disaster, etc., are the ones who elevate the value of the lessons learned through hardships.

If you are facing insurmountable trials and you feel broken in spirit, bring your pieces to the foot of the cross. There you will find the One who can reshape your life into something beautiful.

Lord, when the rug is pulled out from under me and I am already on my knees, I find it easier to pray. Thank You for shaping my character during those times.

JARS OF CLAY

SCRIPTURE READING: 2 CORINTHIANS 4:7–18
KEY VERSE: 2 CORINTHIANS 4:7

*But we have this treasure in earthen vessels, that the excellence
of the power may be of God and not of us.*

The apostle Paul knew true success in ministry, but he also knew something about pain and turmoil. During his ministry, he was hunted, imprisoned, beaten, shipwrecked, and mocked. His fellow Jews branded him a traitor, and he was often scorned or not trusted by his Christian brothers. Paul faced the worst that life had to offer, yet he retained the joy that comes from a relationship with Jesus.

Unfortunately, many new believers assume that the saving work of Christ in their lives will prevent them from experiencing times of trials and troubles. Paul, however, disagreed. In 2 Corinthians 4:7–18, Paul illuminated the pain often associated with discipleship. Dispelling the illusion that Christians are spared hardships, Paul instead praised God for those times in which His power is revealed in human weakness.

In verse 7, Paul wrote about earthen vessels and the power of God. The NIV translates "earthen vessels" as "jars of clay." The image here is of the unimaginable power of God being poured into fragile, cracked containers: you and me.

God's glory is not revealed *in spite of* our brokenness, but rather *through* our brokenness. Just as a cracked jar will seep water, so will the power of God leak out from our fractured lives.

Do not be ashamed of your "cracks." Rather, examine yourself to discover how God may be more fully revealed to you and others through your hardships.

Dear heavenly Father, let me realize that the "cracks" in my jar of clay provide openings for Your light to shine through. Reveal Yourself through me today.

Keys to Successful Parenting

Scripture Reading: Ephesians 6:1–4
Key Verse: Ephesians 6:2

"Honor your father and mother," which is the
first commandment with promise.

U nfortunately, there are many Scripture passages that are often taken out of context, whereby half the passage is lauded and the rest is hushed or dropped off completely. Ephesians 6:1–4 is such a passage. Certainly, most of us recognize the admonition in verses 1–3 for children to honor and obey their parents. This is obviously an important task, as verse 2 points out, in that this was the first of God's Ten Commandments to include a promise of blessing if the command is followed.

However, the fourth verse is often left out of our recollection. This equally relevant instruction reads, "Fathers, do not provoke your children to anger, but bring them up in the discipline and instruction of the Lord" (NASB).

Basically, while children should always seek to respect their parents, the parents themselves must strive to be mothers and fathers worthy of that respect. This can be accomplished by placing God as an important part of your family and your private life.

Are there parts of your life about which you do not want your children to know? Does your language, demeanor, or morality change in the presence of your kids? Children not only need to hear God's instruction; they need to see it as well. Our kids see this dramatically displayed in how we live our lives. From today forward, strive to live a life worthy of the little one in your care.

Lord, I have often failed as a parent. Help me to be an example to
my children and all other children to whom I serve as an example.

EXPERIENCING GOD'S BEST

SCRIPTURE READING: PSALM 138:1–8
KEY VERSE: PSALM 138:8

The LORD will perfect that which concerns me;
Your mercy, O LORD, endures forever;
Do not forsake the works of Your hands.

As we make decisions every day, our choices determine the quality of our lives. This is why it is very important to seek God's guidance in order to experience His best. How do we discover God's best? The answer is two-fold. We must first realize that God's way is the best way, and then we must learn to listen to His voice.

Realizing that God's way is better than our way is a difficult process for many of us, because we like to think that we can figure things out on our own. We pridefully tell ourselves that we don't need help from anyone else as we struggle and toil with burdens and decisions. Yet we must understand that God longs to help and bless us. There is truly no one who knows our needs better than He does.

When we understand these things, our spirits are fertile ground to receive His guidance and instruction. We begin to welcome the promptings of the Holy Spirit and to find practical insight for our daily lives as we read God's Word.

A true indicator of hearing God's voice will be a new and complete sense of peace. Jesus said that He gives peace "not as the world gives" (John 14:27), but a peace that passes understanding (Philippians 4:7). His peace, therefore, must be the governing force of each decision we make.

Choose to let the peace of God guide you in your next important decision, while keeping in mind that God's best will far exceed any good thing you could create on your own.

All of history tells the story of those who let You guide them, Lord, and those who didn't. Help me open the pages of my life to Your instruction.

OBSTRUCTIONS TO OVERCOME

SCRIPTURE READING: 1 PETER 5:6–10

KEY VERSE: 2 CORINTHIANS 12:9

And He said to me, "My grace is sufficient for you, for My strength is made perfect in weakness." Therefore most gladly I will rather boast in my infirmities, that the power of Christ may rest upon me.

Yesterday we discussed the important concept of seeking God's best in our life decisions, which requires accepting God's way and listening to His voice. Today, let us consider some common, potential obstructions that could stand in the way of receiving His best.

A primary inhibitor to wise decisions is taking our eyes off God. Many times, when unforeseen obstacles or trials enter our lives, we place our focus on the problem instead of the ultimate solution—God's wisdom. It is in these times that we must not look at our shortcomings and inabilities. We must also avoid comparing ourselves to others. Instead, in our state of weakness, we must call upon the strength of the Lord. God has said, "My grace is sufficient for you, for power is perfected in weakness" (2 Corinthians 12:9 NASB).

Another set of roadblocks we are likely to encounter are detours from Satan. The enemy will do everything in his power to lead you away from God and into a foolish decision. Therefore, we must discard ungodly counsel and be keenly aware of his conniving schemes. The Bible says that Satan is "like a roaring lion, seeking whom he may devour" (1 Peter 5:8). We must pray for protection and rely upon the discernment of the Holy Spirit in order to avoid disaster.

It is wonderful to know that we can count on the Lord Jesus Christ to help us overcome these obstacles to wise decision making. When our trust is in Him, He will guide our paths according to His will, and we will experience His best.

Dear Lord, remove every obstruction. Help me keep my focus on You, resist comparing myself to others, and avoid detours from Satan. Give me the discernment of the Holy Spirit.

GOD'S PLAN FOR GOOD

SCRIPTURE READING: NEHEMIAH 1:3–11
KEY VERSE: NEHEMIAH 1:4

*So it was, when I heard these words, that I sat down and wept,
and mourned for many days; I was fasting and praying
before the God of heaven.*

Do you sometimes feel that a dark cloud of discouragement is following you no matter what you do? Have your peace and joy been replaced by feelings of hopelessness and frustration?

Certainly the prophet Nehemiah experienced great discouragement as he learned of the distress and destruction in Jerusalem. Chapter one, verse 4, tells us that in response to this news, he grieved and prayed for days.

The interesting part of this passage is the description of what Nehemiah did next. After his period of mourning, he offered God a four-part prayer.

First, Nehemiah offered praise to God for His faithfulness and lovingkindness (verse 5). Next, he confessed the collective sins of his people (verse 7). Then, he acknowledged the appropriateness of God's judgment (verse 8). And finally, he asked God to show him success and compassion (verse 11).

Nehemiah's heartfelt petition contains valuable insight for the discouraged: no matter what happens in the physical world around us, God is in control. He is able to work all things, including our failures, into His plan for our good.

If you are discouraged today, use Nehemiah's words to create your own prayer to God. Give Him praise, confess any sin in your life, acknowledge the authenticity of His Word, and request His favor as you get up and try again.

The Lord is faithful in all things. Don't let discouragement block your view of His awesome love and power.

Dear Lord, thank You for Your faithfulness and lovingkindness. Renew my focus. Help me get up and try again.

Encouraging Others

Scripture Reading: Nehemiah 2:17–20
Key Verse: Nehemiah 2:18

*And I told them of the hand of my God which had been good upon me,
and also of the king's words that he had spoken to me. So they said, "Let
us rise up and build." Then they set their hands to this good work.*

Yesterday we discovered how the prophet Nehemiah used prayer to overcome discouragement. Today, as we move to the second chapter of Nehemiah, we will see how he used the same situation to encourage others to be successful.

Traveling to Jerusalem to assist with the reconstruction of the destroyed city walls, Nehemiah was immediately confronted with a chance to testify to others concerning God's goodness. He told his people of God's guidance and care. Seeing his confidence in the Lord, the people began to help with his project.

Then, in verse 19, we see that as he worked, Nehemiah was challenged by doubters and mockers. They constantly questioned him, but despite their questions, the prophet remained strong, giving glory to God, in whom his trust lay.

Once again we can learn a valuable lesson from Nehemiah's example. When faced with the daunting task of rebuilding the fallen city walls, he did not fear his enemies, nor did he collapse under pressure from skeptics. The Lord had given him a task, and he was bound to complete it no matter what obstacles stood in his way.

What was the source of this confidence? Nehemiah's foundation of faith was firmly established upon the God of promise. Therefore, not only was he able to move forward with confidence, he was also able to encourage others to trust in the Source of his strength.

*Lord, help me to keep You at my core, so that others can be encouraged
by the faith they see at work in me.*

SUCCESSFUL SANCTIFICATION

SCRIPTURE READING: 1 CORINTHIANS 1:1–7
KEY VERSES: 1 PETER 1:1–2

*Peter, an apostle of Jesus Christ, To the . . . elect according to the
foreknowledge of God the Father, in sanctification of the Spirit,
for obedience and sprinkling of the blood of Jesus Christ:
Grace to you and peace be multiplied.*

In many places throughout the Scriptures, we find the word *sanctification.*
Sanctification means "to make holy" or "to separate from a common use
to a sacred use." When you trusted Jesus Christ as your Savior, He sanctified
you, setting you apart for a very sacred purpose.

The process of sanctification begins at salvation, where those who believe
are deemed saints (1 Corinthians 1:1–2). Every believer is a saint, because God
has made it so (1 Peter 1:2). Positionally, we are saints, even if our conduct is
un-Christlike.

This is because, at the pivotal moment of salvation, we changed positions
(Ephesians 2:1–5). We were born again, our sins were forgiven, we were
adopted into the family of God, and we are now living under the grace of God
instead of under His wrath.

It is important to understand that this first stage of sanctification was
done for us by God. No human is holy in himself. We are sanctified only by
the blood of Jesus Christ, the work completed for us by a loving heavenly
Father. Stop to thank and praise God for His purifying love and grace.

*Praise You, Lord, for setting aside this ordinary human to be used
for Your sacred purposes. Thank You that it is not accomplished by
my work, but by Your grace.*

END OF CONSTRUCTION

SCRIPTURE READING: EPHESIANS 4:1–3

KEY VERSE: EPHESIANS 4:1

I, therefore, the prisoner of the Lord, beseech you to walk worthy of the calling with which you were called.

In her book, *Footprints of a Pilgrim*, Ruth Bell Graham provides a suggested epitaph for herself: "End of construction. Thank you for your patience."

Though humorous, her expression is based in truth. In Philippians 1:6, Paul placed his confidence in the fact that God will continue perfecting the good work He began in us until the day of Christ Jesus. This process of perfection began with sanctification—being set apart—and continues until the end of our lives. It is the period of progression between these two events that requires our full attention.

Once we have been born again, we should begin a life of progressive growth toward Christlikeness. We should seek to be conformed to the likeness of Christ in character, conversation, and conduct (Romans 12:1–2). We should also progress by allowing Christ to live out His life through us (Ephesians 4:1).

Of course, as Christians, we will all stumble and fall at times. However, as we understand more truth and apply it to our lives, we will be better equipped to avert the enemy's fiery darts.

Examine your life in terms of spiritual growth and progress. Have you increased in biblical knowledge since your conversion? Are you experiencing new levels of intimacy with God? If not, begin moving forward today—away from complacency and toward perfection in Christ.

I know, Lord, that I am under construction and that I will only be completed when I go to be with You. Help me to be a willing participant in this process of sanctification.

NOVEMBER
Pathway to Spiritual Maturity

Therefore, leaving the discussion of the elementary principles of
Christ, let us go on to perfection, not laying again the foundation
of repentance from dead works and of faith toward God. . . . And
this we will do if God permits.

—Hebrews 6:1, 3

TESTING OUR SPIRITUAL GROWTH

SCRIPTURE READING: PSALM 143:8–12
KEY VERSE: PSALM 143:8

Cause me to hear Your lovingkindness in the morning,
For in You do I trust;
Cause me to know the way in which I should walk,
For I lift up my soul to You.

What is it you crave first thing in the morning? Does a steamy, fresh-brewed cup of coffee or tea catch your attention? Does your morning seem incomplete without your usual cereal or plate of eggs? Do you feel like you can't make it out the front door without reading the morning paper or watching one of the cheerful morning shows?

In Psalm 143:8, David wrote, "Let me hear Your lovingkindness in the morning; for I trust in You; teach me the way in which I should walk; for to You I lift up my soul" (NASB). David saw the necessity of seeking God to direct his steps. He looked to God for guidance for the needs of each day.

A sign of spiritual growth is longing to be with the Lord in a time of Bible study and prayer each day. Whether it be in the morning or at night, is there a time in your day in which you spend time with the Savior? Is it a time that you guard jealously?

Henry Ward Beecher said, "The first hour of the morning is the rudder of the day."

Nothing, not even coffee, will begin your day like time alone with God. Seek Him so that you may grow closer to Him. Go into His presence so that you may sing for joy and be glad all your days (Psalm 90:14). When you make plans to meet God, He will place an intimate joy within your heart. Then you will learn to hunger for His Word.

Father, give me a hunger for Your Word. Let me hear Your lovingkindness in the morning. I lift up my soul to You.

YEARNING FOR CHRIST

SCRIPTURE READING: MATTHEW 13:45–51
KEY VERSES: MATTHEW 13:45–46

*Again, the kingdom of heaven is like a merchant seeking
beautiful pearls, who, when he had found one pearl of great price,
went and sold all that he had and bought it.*

What is the thing you most desire in life? What are the top ten things you seek after? Is Christ among your preferred pursuits? A sure sign of spiritual growth is that you yearn for Christ more than anything else.

Rhea F. Miller wrote, "I'd rather have Jesus than silver or gold; I'd rather be His than riches untold; I'd rather have Jesus than houses or lands; I'd rather be led by His nail-pierced hands."

It is a radical change to want Jesus above all else, but it is evidence that the Holy Spirit is making strides in your life. The Holy Spirit will always point you toward a maturing relationship with Christ and conformity to His image.

Jesus taught the disciples that finding the kingdom of heaven is like finding a pearl of such ultimate value that you would sell everything just to have it (Matthew 13:45–46). To truly experience the Lord is to realize that nothing is worth so much as knowing Him. What stands between you and the desire to seek Christ first? Are you willing to grow to the point where your one dependency is upon Him? You will find that pursuing Christ is the most wonderful investment of your life. In His presence, you will discover the peace your soul longs to enjoy.

Lord, I desire You more than anything in life. I want to know You better and have total dependency upon You.

INTIMACY WITH GOD

SCRIPTURE READING: MATTHEW 17:1–9
KEY VERSE: PROVERBS 3:32

For the perverse person is an abomination to the Lord,
But His secret counsel is with the upright.

Do we understand the magnitude of this statement: "God wants to have a relationship with you"? For all our thoughts toward God and our understanding of what He has done for us, it's difficult to grasp why He desires to have an intimate relationship with us.

God created us in His image, meaning that the innate desires of our hearts—to love and to be loved, to be all we are created to be—were placed there by Him. In all His splendor and majesty, God also desires our fellowship. He wants intimacy with His creations. He wants to love us, and He wants to be loved by us.

In building intimacy with us, God does four things: He chooses us; He reveals Himself to us through His love; He responds to our invitation for Him to come into our hearts; and He reveals Himself to us through experience. Static relationships produce static results. God desires dynamic relationships with us that transform the way we think, act, and live. And it is through intimacy that we learn life-changing principles.

As we seek intimacy with God, we must aim to live a righteous life. And it's through living a righteous life that we discover intimacy.

Lord, thank You for choosing me and revealing Yourself to me. I want to remain close to You.

THE BELIEVER'S CONDUCT

SCRIPTURE READING: 1 PETER 1:17–21
KEY VERSE: 1 PETER 1:21

*. . . who through Him believe in God, who raised Him from the dead
and gave Him glory, so that your faith and hope are in God.*

We must guard against falling into the trap of turning our walk with the Lord into a grocery list of dos and don'ts. Should this ever happen, the passion, the zeal, the fervor that we once had for the Lord will vanish.

It is easy to get away from relationship and enter into a rigid pattern of relating to God. We can come to a point where we don't feel or express anything, acting almost like robots for God. To fear God isn't to be frightened into doing what He wants us to do. To fear God is to worship, respect, and love Him so much that we desire to do what is right. We desire to serve Him in a way that pleases Him and brings glory to His name.

Peter knew that we have to meld discipline with passion. With God's love and forgiveness serving as Peter's motivation, he fulfilled the law. This is the beginning of understanding how a believer needs to conduct himself. At the end of this portion of Scripture, Peter reminds us where our hope is: "Your faith and hope are in God" (1 Peter 1:21).

If you are living a life that supports your words, why would you do anything but serve Him? Our conduct reflects what we truly believe about our God and His Word. What message does your conduct convey?

*Lord, when I asked You into my life, it was so I could be Your disciple,
not Your robot. Keep me from turning our relationship into a list of
rules and duties.*

TRUSTING FOR THE IMPOSSIBLE

SCRIPTURE READING: MATTHEW 19:23–26
KEY VERSE: MATTHEW 19:26

*But Jesus looked at them and said to them, "With men this is
impossible, but with God all things are possible."*

In 1911, when Evelyn Forrest, along with her husband, Richard, established Toccoa Falls College, she never dreamed there would be such
heartache and disappointment in her life. Training young people for
Christian service was her one desire. Soon she realized those whom God uses,
He tests with difficulty to see if their devotion will remain firm.

In March 1913, a horrendous fire swept through the three-story hotel
that housed Evelyn's school. The building and all of its contents were
destroyed. Later, Evelyn reflected on that moment:

With men this is impossible; but with God all things are possible (Matthew
19:26). God loves to have His children pray for the impossible. That is
God's invitation to ask Him to do that which no man can do. . . .

We have lost the eternal youthfulness of Christianity and have aged
into calculating manhood. We seldom pray in earnest for the extraordinary,
the limitless, the glorious. We seldom pray with real confidence for any
good to the realization of which we cannot imagine a way. And yet we suppose ourselves to believe in an infinite Father.

When confronted with a closed door, do you trust God for the impossible?
Evelyn did, and her school remains today as a testimony of what God can do,
if only we will trust Him.

*Lord, if I have become calculated in my faith, if I have failed to ask
for the impossible from You who can make it possible, please change
my heart.*

GOD'S WAY IS BEST

SCRIPTURE READING: 1 SAMUEL 13:5–15
KEY VERSES: 1 SAMUEL 13:13–14

*And Samuel said to Saul, "You have done foolishly. You have not
kept the commandment of the Lord your God, which He commanded
you. For now the Lord would have established your kingdom over
Israel forever. But now your kingdom shall not continue. The Lord
has sought for Himself a man after His own heart, and the Lord
has commanded him to be commander over His people, because
you have not kept what the Lord commanded you."*

Saul grew impatient. He wanted to start the offering ceremony so he could
fight the Philistines, but Samuel had not yet arrived. It was imperative
that they sacrifice to the Lord before a battle!

The army began scattering, so Saul took action. He made the sacrifice
even though he knew it was not what the Lord had commanded. He assumed
that details of the offering were not as important as getting it done.

When Samuel returned, he was furious. He rebuked Saul's foolish
actions (1 Samuel 13:13–14).

Saul had only violated a few details of the command, yet he sinned by
considering his way better than God's and choosing his timing above God's.
Matthew Henry comments, "He covered his disobedience to God's command
with a pretense of concern for God's favor. Hypocrites lay a great stress upon
the external performances of religion, thinking thereby to excuse their neglect
of the weightier matters of the law."

Serve God out of love, respect, and obedience. Allow God to lead you in
His way, and He will show you greater victories than you could have contrived
on your own.

*Lord, You desire above all else a loving, obedient heart. Let me not
hide hypocritically behind the practice of religion but, rather, serve
You sincerely.*

Do Not Fear

SCRIPTURE READING: 1 SAMUEL 15:17–24
KEY VERSE: 1 SAMUEL 15:24

Then Saul said to Samuel, "I have sinned, for I have transgressed the commandment of the LORD and your words, because I feared the people and obeyed their voice."

Fear is never a reason to disobey God's commands. In fact, fear that leads to disobedience is fear that has been wrongly invested.

Saul was misplacing fear when he went against God's commands out of fear of his men. This is a temptation in the life of every believer. Many times situations or people will be threatening enough for a Christian to question God's instructions and commands. When God's will takes the obedient servant into danger, or a situation results in rejection, it is easy to allow fear to paralyze the believer into inaction.

In Matthew 10:28, Jesus said, "And do not fear those who kill the body but cannot kill the soul. But rather fear Him who is able to destroy both soul and body in hell." Christ contrasted the concerns of this world to eternal matters. He pointed out that the pains and difficulties experienced in the working out of God's plan are nothing compared to the glorious victory of helping another be saved from the eternal ramifications of sin.

When you find yourself doing God's will and come upon a frightening situation, do not fear—the God of all creation is your protector.

Lord, the opinion of the crowd is a powerful constraint on doing what is right before You. Be my courage, when I must stand alone.

VISION WITHOUT BOUNDARIES

SCRIPTURE READING: MATTHEW 28:16–20
KEY VERSE: MATTHEW 28:19

*Go therefore and make disciples of all the nations, baptizing them in
the name of the Father and of the Son and of the Holy Spirit.*

The idea that nothing is impossible for God is very comforting. Just think about the parting of the Red Sea, the tearing down of the walls of Jericho, and the Resurrection—great overtures that God has accomplished.

However, when it comes to God doing something miraculous through you, you may have doubts. You wonder if God is interested in using you for a great work. Yet when God formed you, He did so with a very special design in mind. And Jesus spoke about His plans in Matthew 28:19 when He told His disciples to make disciples of the whole world. To Jesus, no nation or tribe is excluded from the gospel. God's desire is for everyone to enter the kingdom of heaven through the blood of His precious Son.

Henry Ford said, "I'm looking for a lot of men with an infinite capacity for not knowing what can't be done." That's what God is looking for too. He seeks believers who know that nothing is impossible with God. He wants disciples who willingly follow with full trust in the Savior. There are no boundaries for what God wants us to do and what He wants us to accomplish.

*Lord, give me vision without boundaries. Work in and through me
to accomplish Your will.*

An Absolute Essential

SCRIPTURE READING: LUKE 24:36–43

KEY VERSE: LUKE 24:36

*Now as they said these things, Jesus Himself stood in the midst of them,
and said to them, "Peace to you."*

The disciples were startled by the figure before them. Though they had
received reports that Jesus had risen from the dead, seeing Him in the
room was almost too much for them to process. Jesus calmed them from the
shock—"Peace to you"—understanding that there are some things too difficult for earthbound minds to grasp right away.

Have you ever experienced the Lord working in an amazing, supernatural
manner and become frightened? Perhaps God's provision startled you and you
realized your dependence upon Him. That is why God sent the Holy Spirit—
to calm you and give you peace.

E. Paul Hovey writes, "The word 'Comforter' as applied to the Holy
Spirit needs to be translated by some vigorous term. Literally, it means 'with
strength.' Jesus promised his followers that 'The Strengthener' would be with
them forever. This promise is no lullaby for the faint-hearted. It is a blood
transfusion for courageous living."

In the midst of God's will, you may find yourself astonished, startled,
and overwhelmed at what the Lord is doing around you. However, allow
Him to speak peace to you through the Holy Spirit, and you will be able to
face any situation with strength and maturity.

*Holy Spirit, as the transfusion that injects courage into my Christian
life, keep me from lacking faith in Your leadings.*

TRANSPARENT INTIMACY

SCRIPTURE READING: MATTHEW 26:36–39
KEY VERSE: MATTHEW 26:38

*Then He said to them, "My soul is exceedingly sorrowful,
even to death. Stay here and watch with Me."*

Transparency is an oft-overlooked element in our path to growing closer to Jesus Christ. Intimacy with the Lord requires our full, humble, and honest openness before Him.

Jesus Himself was a wonderful model of openness as He dealt with His disciples. For instance, we read in today's Bible verse that, in the Garden of Gethsemane, Jesus shared with the disciples His anguish over His upcoming crucifixion and brief separation from God the Father.

Knowing that the sins of the entire world were about to be cast upon Him, Jesus grieved, even to the point of near death. Here was God, clothed in human flesh, being completely honest, open, and forthright about His emotions.

This is how Christ would have us react to Him. A proud, arrogant, ego-tistical, self-sufficient Christianity bristles at the thought of such transparency. "Why should I burden God with this when I can handle it myself? I'm just not going to deal with God about this." Such thinking and behavior go against everything for which God created us. However, God cherishes and honors a humble, contrite spirit from someone trying to be him- or herself before the Lord.

Confess sin, worry, doubt, and fear. He already knows all, but your willingness to intimately share with Him all the details speaks volumes about the bent of your heart.

Father, I confess my worry, doubt, and fears. I want to share all the intimate details of my life with You.

HOW TO WALK WITH GOD

SCRIPTURE READING: PSALM 12:1–8
KEY VERSE: PSALM 12:6

The words of the LORD are pure words,
Like silver tried in a furnace of earth,
Purified seven times.

To find a cause that we will stand behind, fight for, live for, and die for takes us being in complete agreement with the principles and the leadership. How willing would we be to defend something that does not stir us with passion? How eager would we be to risk anything for a cause that merely piqued our interest?

Living in agreement with God and His Word is something we must learn if we truly desire to walk with Him. Keeping in step with God proves more than challenging if our hearts are not unified with His. After we have reconciled our relationship with God by accepting His Son, Jesus Christ, as our Lord and Savior, we must learn to trust Him by living a life in agreement with His principles and precepts.

What God says about His Son, His church, His Word, and sin are all of utmost importance for us. If we think that some of these are flawed or untrue, how can we walk in step with what God desires for our lives?

Disunity results in any organization when there is a disagreement between leadership and the body of people. How can the cause be advanced by someone when he does not believe in the cause he is advancing? As we submit more of our lives to Him, our wills are broken to the point that our wills become what God wills for us.

Heavenly Father, I submit my life anew. Break my will so I can easily submit to Your will for me.

Transformed Through Prayer

Scripture Reading: Psalm 18:1–15
Key Verse: Psalm 18:3

I will call upon the LORD, who is worthy to be praised;
So shall I be saved from my enemies.

In the movie version of *Shadowlands*, which portrays the endearing relationship between Christian apologist C. S. Lewis and Joy Gresham, a friend commented to Lewis that God finally answered his prayers. As part of his response, Lewis said, "Prayer doesn't change God—it changes me."

How profound and true that is! Your communication with God is your intimate connection with Him, and He allows you to participate in the work that He is doing and even to see His actions in relationship to your prayers. God hears and answers every prayer, but His purposes in prayer go far beyond just giving you a measurable response.

God wants to transform your life through the process of prayer. Your personal relationship with Christ is deepened and enlarged when you spend time talking to Him. As you come into His presence with reverence and a quiet heart, ready to listen, He begins to purify your heart and sift your priorities. You develop a passion for obedience to God, and you begin to see Him as the Provider for all your needs.

Most importantly, you experience the peace that comes from knowing God is in control (Philippians 4:6–7). Your anxiety melts away as you learn to trust Him. These are just some of the ways God uses prayer to change your heart. The more you pray, the more transformations you'll discover.

Lord, I am so thankful that, through prayer, You allow me to participate in the work You are doing around the world. Transform my life. Deepen and enlarge my relationship with You.

Forging Ahead

Scripture Reading: John 12:23–26
Key Verse: John 12:26

*If anyone serves Me, let him follow Me; and where I am, there My
servant will be also. If anyone serves Me, him My Father will honor.*

The world is constantly vying for our attention. On the left, on the right—its relentless assault can cause us to lose our way quickly if we are not careful. But clinging to God no matter how good or bad our circumstances are keeps us walking closely with Him.

God is the guiding light in our lives, leading us by the voice of His Holy Spirit to a place of life. However, what we forget in our relationship with Him is that we are followers—*He* is the one leading *us.*

Whenever the distractions disorient us, we forget that God is our leader. Instead, we try to coerce Him to follow us, getting out of step with what He wants for our lives. Jesus told His disciples that following Him meant staying *with* Him (John 12:26). Serving the Lord does not happen if we are not walking with Him. And we cannot walk with Him if we are racing ahead of the pace He sets for us. Sometimes getting ahead of God and forging ahead on our own conveys the message that we do not need His help.

As His beloved children, we know that to serve and honor Him as He deserves, we must listen closely to His guidance for our lives through His Word, His Holy Spirit, and other wise believers around us.

*Remove all the distractions, Lord. Help me to keep my eyes focused
on You so I can keep in step with You.*

CALLED WITH CONFIDENCE

SCRIPTURE READING: MARK 16:14–18

KEY VERSE: MARK 16:15

*And He said to them, "Go into all the world and preach
the gospel to every creature."*

After the Resurrection, Christ appeared to two of the disciples. However, the news of Jesus' resurrection seemed too good to be true, so the other disciples, in their disheartenment, did not believe the reports. When Jesus appeared to them, He rebuked them for their unbelief. He knew they would need great faith to take on the commission God had for them, and that faith had to begin with an understanding of God's power.

Eleven men had the responsibility of spreading the gospel to the whole world. They were eleven simple men with an overwhelming goal, fueled by the power that raised Jesus from the dead. Surely our task is not as daunting as that which the disciples faced, yet Christians often consider evangelism impossible.

Clarence Hall wrote, "The problem is not that we have exhausted our frontiers. The problem is that we fail to recognize them! And as our vision shortens, our pessimism deepens."

Lord, I have been guilty of failing to recognize the frontiers for the gospel. Forgive my shortsightedness and infuse me with a powerful drive to witness for You.

POWER FOR THE TASK

SCRIPTURE READING: LUKE 24:44–49
KEY VERSE: LUKE 24:49

*Behold, I send the Promise of My Father upon you; but tarry in the
city of Jerusalem until you are endued with power from on high.*

You might think that Jesus would have expected the disciples to get
started on the daunting task of global evangelization right away.
However, in Luke 24:49, Jesus instructs them to stay in the city until an
empowering happened.

How could the disciples impact the world if they were confined to the
city? How could they wait to get started on such an important assignment as
spreading the gospel? Jesus instructed the disciples to wait for the Holy Spirit,
because He wanted them to have God's power for their great task.

A. C. Dixon reminds us, "When we rely upon education, we get what
education can do. When we rely on eloquence, we get what eloquence can
do. But when we rely on the Holy Spirit, we get what God can do."

Perhaps you have wondered the same things. God has directed you in
certain areas, but He has also called you to wait. You may work well for God,
but when God's power works through you, astounding things happen. In one
day, the disciples led three thousand people to the Lord. God can do great
things through you too.

Wait for Him to empower you through His Holy Spirit.

*Holy Spirit, I want to rely on You to lead in the sharing of the gospel.
I don't want to be merely a Christian educator or orator.*

PRUNING THE BRANCHES

SCRIPTURE READING: JOHN 15:5–8
KEY VERSE: JOHN 15:2

Every branch in Me that does not bear fruit He takes away; and every branch that bears fruit He prunes, that it may bear more fruit.

Have you ever felt like God was removing things from your life? As if the trials and circumstances you were experiencing have made it necessary for you to reduce your priorities to a manageable minimum?

In the classic devotional by L. B. Cowman, *Streams in the Desert,* there is recorded a simple but poignant poem that asks the question, "Why must this lot of life be mine?" The answer: "Because God knows what plans for me shall blossom in eternity."

God knows what opportunities await you. And He is preparing you so that His glory can truly shine through you. First, however, He must remove what is unnecessary. In John 15:2, He promised, "Every branch that bears fruit He prunes, that it may bear more fruit." Understand that trials are never evidence that God has abandoned you. On the contrary, they suggest that God is molding you for great things ahead.

He has a place of service that is suited perfectly for you. However, He must first develop your trust in Him. Then you will see a great harvest and experience the joy of having the Lord work through you.

Thank You, Lord, that You have a place of service suited perfectly for me. Develop my trust in You. Prune the branches of my life, and then work through me.

PRUNING PASSIONS

SCRIPTURE READING: MARK 12:1–9
KEY VERSE: MARK 12:1

Then He began to speak to them in parables: "A man planted a vineyard and set a hedge around it, dug a place for the wine vat and built a tower. And he leased it to vinedressers and went into a far country."

The spiritual pruning process of our lives includes cutting away all that reflects our earthly passions that are in opposition to God's holiness. A. B. Simpson has this to say:

Before the Holy of Holies can be fully opened to our hearts and we can enter into . . . communion of God, the veil upon our hearts must be rent asunder, and this comes as it came on Calvary—by the death of our flesh.

It is when we yield our own natural self to God to die and He slays us by the power of His Spirit that the obstruction to our communion with God is removed and we enter into its deeper fullness. The greatest hindrance to our peace and victory is the flesh. Whenever the consciousness of self rises vividly before you, and you become absorbed in your own troubles, cares, rights or wrongs, you at once lose communion with God, and a cloud of darkness falls over your spirit.

There is really nothing else that hurts or hinders us but this heavy weight of evil, this seed of Satan. . . . We can never rend it asunder, but the Holy Spirit can. It dies only on the cross of Jesus . . . under the fire of His descending Spirit. Bring it to Him, give Him the right to slay it, and then the veil will be rent asunder. The Holy of Holies will open wide, the light of the Shekinah will shine through all the house of God, and the glory of heaven will be revealed in your life.

I yield myself to You, Lord. Remove every obstruction that hinders my communion with You.

Our Christian Growth

SCRIPTURE READING: EPHESIANS 2:1–10
KEY VERSE: EPHESIANS 2:1

And you He made alive, who were dead in trespasses and sins.

After planting watermelon seeds, you water and eagerly watch for them to sprout. As they grow, you continue to water, fertilize, and anticipate their fruit. From the moment you accept Christ, you begin growing in your likeness to Him (Ephesians 4:24).

The Christian life is a growing process with several stages essential to spiritual growth:

- Unbelief. Without Christ we are dead in our trespasses and sins (Ephesians 2:1).
- Salvation. God's gift of salvation is available to all who believe (Titus 2:11).
- Service. A natural response after receiving new life in Christ is the desire to share the joy and peace that comes from a personal relationship with God and encourage other believers in their faith (Ephesians 4:11–12).
- Frustrated inadequacy. God does not want us to become self-centered or satisfied in our relationship with Him or to feel that we can accomplish His work in our own strength.
- Total dependence on God. Without Christ we are nothing and can do nothing (Galatians 2:20).

By seeking God, you will continue to learn, develop, and grow in Christ— producing spiritual fruit far beyond anything you can imagine (Galatians 5:22–23).

Father, I reject unbelief. Use me in Your service and help me depend totally on You.

WORDS OF ENCOURAGEMENT

SCRIPTURE READING: PSALM 8:1–9
KEY VERSE: PROVERBS 12:25

Anxiety in the heart of man causes depression,
But a good word makes it glad.

Have you ever hesitated to speak words of encouragement because you weren't sure how they would be received? Being an encourager means reaching out even when you're not sure.

You never know the impact you might have. In his book *The Power of Encouragement*, Dr. David Jeremiah explains:

I can be encouraged by what I hear. If I sense someone genuinely cares about me, that person's words can be powerful. As the adage goes, "Nobody cares how much you know until they know how much you care."

The Book of Proverbs speaks often about encouragement. Here's one example: "Anxious hearts are very heavy but a word of encouragement does wonders!" (Proverbs 12:25, TLB). Have you ever been weighed down by anxiety when someone came along and spoke a good word which lifted your spirit?

During one of the deepest, darkest times in my life, a fellow pastor called me just to say, "David, I want you to know I love you, and I know you are going through some hurt. I want you to know I'm here if you need me. I want to pray with you." And he prayed with me on the phone. He called me every week for several weeks with a word of encouragement. He poured courage into my heart. . . . Believe it or not, two or three sentences can turn a person's life around.

Lord, give me the spiritual maturity to help others. I want to be an encouragement and blessing to those with whom I come in contact today.

UNCONDITIONAL SURRENDER

SCRIPTURE READING: PSALM 86:1–17
KEY VERSE: PSALM 86:11

Teach me Your way, O LORD;
I will walk in Your truth;
Unite my heart to fear Your name.

Have you ever shopped at an open-air market or a flea market? Oftentimes, the shopkeepers of these establishments purposely display items without price labels. This clever sales strategy revolves around the premise that customers will bargain with them to arrive at an agreeable price.

When we try to bargain with God, however, the result is not desirable. Have you ever prayed, "God, if You stay out of this area of my life, I will serve You more diligently in all others"?

As we learn more about the character of our heavenly Father, we realize that God wants us to surrender our lives completely to Him. As a loving and compassionate Father, God never forces us to relinquish control. Instead, He calls gently to us, asking us to trust Him with our hopes, dreams, and disappointments. He does not want to control you for the sake of power. He desires to use you in a way that is greater than you can imagine.

Take a moment to think through the areas of your life: your occupation, your hobbies, your health, your relationships. Are you currently allowing God to direct your decisions?

Bring your doubts, fears, and worries to the Lord today in prayer. He loves you and is concerned with even the smallest details of your life. When you are ready to stop bargaining, He will lead you to a place of peace and blessing.

I surrender to You unconditionally, Lord. Lead me to a place of peace and blessing.

SURRENDERING TO GOD

SCRIPTURE READING: ROMANS 12:1–5

KEY VERSE: ROMANS 12:1

I beseech you therefore, brethren, by the mercies of God, that you present your bodies a living sacrifice, holy, acceptable to God, which is your reasonable service.

When many people hear the word *surrender*, images of conflict and overpowering forces come to mind. In contrast, the act of surrendering one's life to God is a beautiful and peaceful experience.

Why then are we so afraid to hand over the reigns of our lives to God's omnipotent leadership? The answer lies in our self-oriented nature. We live in a world that encourages us to take pride in what we have accomplished and accumulated. The concept of surrendering these things to God is unthinkable for most people.

As a believer, however, God has called you to a higher standard of living. He wants to help you reach the goals that He has set for your life. Yet, in order to fulfill His plan, we must choose to lay our selfish desires before Him.

Until you make this important step toward God, you will find yourself in a state of unrest and uncertainty. However, once you surrender your life to God, He will unleash the storehouse of blessings waiting for you.

In Romans 12, God specifically asks you to present yourself as a living sacrifice to Him (verses 1–2). God wants to guide, direct, and bless you. Do not let disobedience stand in the way of His plan for your life.

Lord, I present myself as a living sacrifice. Help me understand Your good and acceptable will.

Spiritual Blindness

Scripture Reading: 2 Corinthians 4:1–6
Key Verse: 2 Corinthians 4:4

. . . whose minds the god of this age has blinded, who do not believe,
lest the light of the gospel of the glory of Christ, who is the
image of God, should shine on them.

A key piece of equipment used in horse racing is a set of blinders attached to the bridle on either side of the horse's eyes. Blinders prevent the horse from becoming distracted—allowing him to focus on the path before him. Focus is admirable, unless your focus is on a path that leads to destruction. The world is filled with people who are guided by good intentions, but blinded by deception.

What causes blindness of the spirit? The Bible tells us that Satan has blinded the minds of the unbelieving (2 Corinthians 4:4). By deceiving unbelievers, Satan creates pockets of doubt and skepticism within racial, social, and political groups. Untruths delivered by false teachers then spread like wildfire. Soon, what started as doubt becomes total rejection of all that is of God.

How can you protect yourself from Satan's schemes? Ground yourself in the Word of God by studying the truth of the Scriptures. Then separate yourself from any organization that is misinterpreting what you know to be true.

When Jesus returns, Satan's lies will be exposed before all. Until then, guard your heart and your mind with the truth. When you seek God, He will grant you wisdom to separate the truth from lies.

Father, guard my heart and mind with the truth. Give me the wisdom
to separate truth from lies.

BLIND SPOTS

SCRIPTURE READING: 1 JOHN 2:7–11
KEY VERSE: 1 JOHN 2:9

He who says he is in the light, and hates his brother,
is in darkness until now.

Of the five senses, sight may be the most appreciated. Our eyes enable us to see the beauty of God's creation and allow us to navigate through it. Imagine for a moment that your sight is suddenly limited. As disturbing as physical blindness would be, the Bible warns us of a more formidable disease called spiritual blindness—an ailment that limits our ability to distinguish dark (evil) from light (that which is of God).

Even those of us who have a personal relationship with Christ are not immune to this condition. If we are not living each day with Christ as the central focus of our lives, we can become desensitized to the lures of the world. Satan enjoys nothing more than to distract a believer away from the truth.

In the second chapter of 1 John, we are provided with an example of how we could unknowingly experience spiritual blindness—hating our brother even though we claim to be in the light (verse 9). Essentially, if we call ourselves Christians and then treat others badly, speak out in anger, or harbor resentment toward others, we are actually living in darkness. Our actions are not only displeasing to God, they are damaging to those around us.

D. L. Moody once said, "Where one man reads the Bible, a hundred read you and me." Pray today that God will show you any "blind spots" in your walk.

Heavenly Father, show me any blind spots in my relationship with
You. Don't let me be distracted from the truth of Your Word.

SPIRITUAL INVENTORY

SCRIPTURE READING: PHILIPPIANS 3:7–10
KEY VERSE: PHILIPPIANS 3:7

But what things were gain to me, these I have counted loss for Christ.

Is there a room or closet in your home that you avoid because it's filled with stuff that needs to be cleaned out? One day, you will probably decide to tackle the task. As you move through the boxes, you will have to make some decisions—some things stay, and some things must go. Some items are garbage, and some are keepsakes.

Sorting through your belongings, in a small way, is a kind of prioritizing. You are forced to assign a value to the things you own and then treat them accordingly. In this passage in Philippians, Paul was conducting a kind of spiritual sorting. He put a "trash" label on anything in his life that didn't count toward his relationship with the Lord. Along the way, he had lost much—from material possessions to public esteem. But Paul wasn't concerned. He knew that his "valuables," the blessings of knowing Christ as His Savior, were always with him.

Is there anything in your life that you value more than Christ? Today is the time for a spiritual inventory.

Father, I want to clean out my spiritual closet and eliminate anything I value more than You. Help me recognize the things that are gain to me but are actually a spiritual loss.

A PASSION TO SERVE HIM

SCRIPTURE READING: PHILIPPIANS 3:12–15
KEY VERSE: PHILIPPIANS 3:14

*I press toward the goal for the prize of the upward call of God in
Christ Jesus.*

Have you ever noticed the passion of football players and coaches? It
is often difficult to determine who has more adrenaline going, the
260-pound linebacker or the fifty-five-year-old man wearing a headset on
the sidelines.

But this passion is quick-burning and explosive. The average tenure of a
professional football player is about four years, and there have been several
high-profile cases of coaches suffering heart trouble or leaving the game
because of "burnout." Often these men relied on their own limited strength.

One of the common mistakes believers make in serving God is attempting
to labor in their own strength and not in the power of His Spirit. It becomes a
trap the enemy uses to discourage those laborers who may have started out in
complete sincerity but who somewhere lost sight of the true objective.
Sometimes believers focus mostly on the work they perform and gradually lose
focus on the God whom they originally were honoring.

The key to fruitful service is remembering to place God first. It is difficult for many of us to intentionally dodge the spotlight, but God's Word and
creation costars no one. We should press on "for the prize of the upward call
of God in Christ Jesus" and allow Christ to work through us. That is reward
in itself. Like the old football coach's T-shirt says: There is no "I" in "TEAM."

*Lord Jesus, let me not seek to be a costar in Your service, but rather
a servant seeking only the prize of the upward call of God in You.*

YOUR POINT OF FOCUS

SCRIPTURE READING: PSALM 84:1–7
KEY VERSE: PSALM 84:5

Blessed is the man whose strength is in You,
Whose heart is set on pilgrimage.

On an early morning walk around their college campus, two students came to a snow-covered football field. One friend said to the other, "I bet you can't walk across the field and leave a perfectly straight line of footprints in the snow."

Not being one to refuse a challenge, the student accepted. He began at one end zone, carefully plodding down the field. His eyes remained focused on his feet, only occasionally glancing up to judge how much farther he had to walk. When he finished, the two young men ran up the stadium stairs to get a clear view of the field. From there, they noticed how crooked and off center the line of footprints were in the snow.

The disappointed student issued the same dare to his friend. "No problem," the challenger replied. Starting at one goal post, he walked rather quickly from one end of the field to the other. When finished, the two ascended the steps to evaluate the tracks. The footprints were in a perfectly straight line!

"How did you do it?" the first boy asked.

The other responded, "Simple. I just forgot about my feet and focused all of my attention on the opposite goalpost."

In your Christian walk, where is your attention—on your own accomplishments or on the goal? If your life has gotten a little off center, ask Christ to help realign your steps by keeping the Cross in constant focus.

Lord, sometimes my feet get out of step because I'm too busy contemplating the path to righteousness, rather than the goal. Help me keep my eyes on the Cross that leads me there.

CHRISTLIKE MATURITY

SCRIPTURE READING: LUKE 2:41–52
KEY VERSE: EPHESIANS 4:13

*. . . till we all come to the unity of the faith and of the knowledge
of the Son of God, to a perfect man, to the measure of the
stature of the fullness of Christ.*

People's perspectives on Jesus seem to shift with the seasons. During
Christmas, Jesus is seen as a tiny infant, nestled in blankets and housed
in a barn. At Easter, Jesus is seen as beaten and broken, or as the shimmering
victor over death. The perspective that is traditionally excluded, however, is
one very important segment of His life: His youth.

Luke 2:41–52, the only biblical account of the adolescent Jesus, reveals
something surprising, in that He was increasing in wisdom. This shows that
Jesus—who was fully God—was experiencing growth! Prayer, Scripture
study, and the use of His gifts were bringing about maturation in the Son of
Man. Jesus was sinless and perfect, yet He still experienced maturity. How
much greater is the need for that growth in sinful man!

Ephesians 4:13 calls all believers toward Christlike maturity, unified as
one body through faith in Jesus. Are you experiencing that growth? Are you
utilizing your spiritual gifts in such a way as to strengthen the body of Christ
and to increase your personal development? Pray for God's help as He directs
you into the fullness of the Christian life.

*Lord, let me use my spiritual gifts to strengthen others around me.
Draw me into a deeper relationship with You so I can increase in
wisdom and knowledge.*

A WORK IN PROGRESS

SCRIPTURE READING: EPHESIANS 4:11–16
KEY VERSE: EPHESIANS 4:7

*But to each one of us grace was given according
to the measure of Christ's gift.*

Have you ever assembled a piece of furniture, a large toy for a child, or some other colossal prefabricated building project? Usually, each of these tasks comes with the proper tools and supplies for the job, as well as detailed instructions on how to complete the task.

Some of these jobs are easy, taking only an hour or so. Others, however, may drag on for days, and even then may require a professional's assistance. Regardless of how difficult the task may be, you can usually depend on one unforeseen realization when you are finished: there are parts left over! Where did these parts come from, and what should you do with them? The world may never know.

Ephesians 4:11–16 portrays the body of believers as a work in progress. Just like your desk, chair, or automobile, the church is comprised of many individual pieces—Christians just like you—who have been joined together into a single, purposeful machine called the body of Christ. In this body, however, there are no leftover parts. Every single piece has a job to do, and each one affects the others. If one piece is not working properly, the entire body knows it and works to correct the problem. This is the joy and safety of being united to other believers.

Thank you, Lord, that I am an integral part of the full body of Christ and that in being part of the body, I find my completion.

The Abiding Life

SCRIPTURE READING: JOHN 14:7–14
KEY VERSE: JOHN 14:14

If you ask anything in My name, I will do it.

How does the believer experience the Spirit-filled life by allowing the Holy Spirit to live the life of Christ through him or her? He must consciously submit to becoming a branch that maintains a vibrant connection to its Vine, its source of strength. Branches cannot produce fruit in their own strength, because branches alone have nothing to support and sustain them.

Bible teacher Merrill C. Tenney explains how this works:

> The connection is maintained by obedience and prayer. To remain in Christ and to allow His words to remain in oneself means a conscious acceptance of the authority of His Word and a constant contact with Him by prayer. The prayer request must be related to a definite need and must be for an object Jesus Himself would desire. He was evidently referring back to the counsel in the preceding part of the discourse: "You may ask me for anything in my name, and I will do it" (John 14:14 [NIV]). He was not promising to gratify every chance whim. But so long as the believer was seeking the Lord's will in his life, Jesus would grant every request that would help accomplish this end. . . .
>
> Love is the relationship that unites the disciples to Christ as branches are united to a vine. Two results stem from this relationship: obedience and joy. Obedience marks the cause of their fruitfulness; joy is the result. Jesus intended that the disciples' lives should be both spontaneous and happy rather than burdensome and boring.

Father, make me obedient to Your will. Let me be fruitful so that I can live a spontaneous and happy life rather than a burdensome and boring existence.

Testing Our Spiritual Growth

Scripture Reading: Psalm 84:10–12
Key Verse: Psalm 84:10

For a day in Your courts is better than a thousand.
I would rather be a doorkeeper in the house of my God
Than dwell in the tents of wickedness.

You know you are maturing in your relationship with Christ when:

- You are becoming increasingly aware of your sinfulness and weaknesses.
- Your response to sin is quick and followed by genuine repentance.
- Your spiritual battles are becoming more fierce, and yet you still rejoice.
- You begin to see trials and temptations as opportunities for growth: "Lord, what are You trying to teach me?"
- You view service to Him as an honor and not a burden.
- You view everything as coming from God. He is sovereign, so He either brought it or allowed it.
- You sense your faith growing stronger. It takes more to ruffle you.
- You desire to spend more time in praise and worship. You are in love with the Lord and want to show it.
- Your desire to obey Him becomes more intense, and sin becomes less attractive.
- You are eager to share with others what Christ is doing in your life.
- You experience more awareness of His presence at all times, not just in places like at church on Sundays.
- You jealously guard your quiet times of prayer and Bible study.
- You prefer to spend time with Him above all others. The more time you spend with Him, the more you become like Him.

Lord, I seek Your face and Your presence in all that I do. Search my heart and show me any impediments to my relationship with You.

DECEMBER
Pathway to the Future

For I know the thoughts that I think toward you, says the LORD,
thoughts of peace and not of evil, to give you a future and a hope.
—Jeremiah 29:11

HOPE FOR THE FUTURE

SCRIPTURE READING: TITUS 2:11–15
KEY VERSE: TITUS 2:13

*. . . looking for the blessed hope and glorious appearing of our great
God and Savior Jesus Christ.*

No matter how shaky things in this world are, we find assurance in the fact that God remains the same as He changes us and those around us. God doesn't expect us to change into perfect human beings overnight, but He does desire to begin a process that changes our lives forever.

Once we enter into a relationship with God by receiving His forgiveness and grace and then inviting Him to be Lord over our lives, He begins to transform us in ways we never imagined possible.

When we accept Christ as our Lord and Savior, God calls us His own, His sons and daughters, joint heirs with Jesus. No longer does He view us as sinners—He sees us as saints. However, there is still much work to be done in our hearts.

We can rest in the assurance that there is no time limit to the process of renewing our hearts and minds. God touches our hearts in calling us His children, but the work of transforming us into His image is a long-term plan.

When looking at our own hearts, we could despair when we realize just how much we need to be transformed. But we don't have to despair, because we receive hope in Him, hope that His Holy Spirit will indeed complete the work that He has begun in the lives of each man and woman who would be willing to live for Him.

*Lord, thank You for the work of transformation that You are doing
in my life, and that You have a master plan for me.*

A Reason for Living

SCRIPTURE READING: 2 PETER 3:8–12
KEY VERSE: 2 PETER 3:9

The Lord is not slack concerning His promise, as some count slackness,
but is longsuffering toward us, not willing that any should perish
but that all should come to repentance.

There are times when the world around us seems mired in despair. Looking at their faces, hope is nowhere to be found. They have no hope because they do not know the source of all hope and strength.

Regardless of how entrenched in their sinful ways the world around us appears, they desperately want hope. They want a reason for living. And after much searching, those who never find Christ fail to discover that reason.

But as believers, we are called to show the world the reason for which we live, the One for whom we live. God desires for everyone to come to repentance and enter into relationship with Him. And as those who already have found Him, we are called to share with others the way to Him.

Because of someone's love for Christ and love for us, we heard the truth and accepted Christ. For some of us, it was a simple message that we heard in church. For others of us, it was watching someone live as a representative of Christ day in and day out. For others still, it was understanding the reality of God through a miracle.

God introduces Himself to us through many different avenues. As His children, we, too, are called to be faithful in introducing the hope of salvation to others, whether it be through our words, actions, or lifestyle. Through followers of Christ, the world sees hope for their lives.

Lord, the ways in which You work in the heart are customized to each person's need. Please help me be obedient to the call to be an instrument of the gospel.

TRUSTING GOD'S PLAN

SCRIPTURE READING: GENESIS 12:10–20
KEY VERSE: HEBREWS 11:8

*By faith Abraham obeyed when he was called to go out to the place
which he would receive as an inheritance. And he went out,
not knowing where he was going.*

The Lord's plan for our life often involves different timing than we would choose. I picture the pathway of faith as a highway with two signs on it. The first one says, "Slow down"; the other one says, "Wait here."

We don't like either of those signs, do we? We want to keep moving so we can quickly arrive at our destination. But God is all-knowing; He sees when rushing would land us on our face.

He is also a God of purpose. He knows what He wants to accomplish in our lives, so He erects a sign that says, "Wait." If we are wise, we will keep pace with Him, not lagging behind, but not taking five steps in place of the three He has sanctioned.

Abram provided an illustration of this, demonstrating what not to do. When famine threatened the land, he took matters into his own hands and journeyed to Egypt without consulting God. Though he rightly assumed that Pharaoh would want his beautiful wife in the royal harem, Abram willingly took the risk of never seeing her again. Then, to save his own life, he had Sarai say she was his sister, not his wife.

Even a person of faith (Hebrews 11:8) can resort to the "flesh" and respond from old thought patterns. It is absolutely essential that we wait for the Lord. Even if we don't understand His purpose, that is still no excuse for coming up with our own course of action. What situation in your life is tempting you to run ahead of your heavenly Father? Have patience. God is never late.

Lord, give me patience, for I know You are never late. Keep me from acting in the flesh. Deliver me from old thought patterns.

THE GREATEST GOAL

SCRIPTURE READING: ROMANS 4:13–22
KEY VERSES: ROMANS 4:20–21

He did not waver at the promise of God through unbelief, but was strengthened in faith, giving glory to God, and being fully convinced that what He had promised He was also able to perform.

When Abraham was about to die, his descendants did not number the stars in the sky or the grains of sand on the seashore. However, that did not stop him from believing that God would do just as He had promised.

Abraham saw his reward from afar and didn't waver, and ultimately his relationship with God was strengthened. The true gift for Abraham was that he was able to know God intimately. The promise of many descendants was an additional benefit of that relationship.

In your own life, God has given you promises that He is faithful to fulfill. Yet it is not just the promises that you pursue; it is the Promise Giver. In Colossians 4:12, we learn that Epaphras's prayer was for believers to stand assured of God's will.

It is God's will that you know Him and help others receive Him. Even if you are only able to see His promises fulfilled from afar, you are still gaining the far greater gift of knowing God more. Jesus is the greatest goal of all your pursuits. Do not waver in your faith, but grow strong. Life with Christ is a blessing above and beyond all you could ask or imagine.

Lord, in trusting You to see beyond what I am able, I come to know You and rely on You more completely. I give You my future so You can shape my today.

CONFIDENCE TO FACE THE UNKNOWN

SCRIPTURE READING: EXODUS 2:1–10
KEY VERSES: HEBREWS 11:23–25

*By faith Moses, when he was born, was hidden three months
by his parents, because they saw he was a beautiful child; and they
were not afraid of the king's command. By faith Moses, when he
became of age, refused to be called the son of Pharaoh's daughter,
choosing rather to suffer affliction with the people of God than
to enjoy the passing pleasures of sin.*

As Jochebed looked into her baby's eyes, could she have known the way God would use him? As she sent him floating down the Nile, could she guess the impact that Moses would have on the nation of Israel? Jochebed probably did not even know if Moses would survive his journey, yet she had faith. She was confident that he would be safe, because she trusted God.

You, also, will face the challenge of releasing loved ones and possessions for the promise of a better future. You are called to have faith, even though the future is unknown. Augustine said, "Faith is to believe what you do not yet see; the reward for this faith is to see what you believe."

Will God reveal to you every turn of your journey or explain each step? No, but take heart. Even though Jochebed could not see the way the papyrus basket traveled, she believed her son would survive, because her faith in God was strong. The miracle of the story is this: not only did Moses survive, but he became the deliverer of God's people (Exodus 2:1–10).

You may not be able to see your future, but you can be confident that God will help you when you trust in Him every step of the way. Believe in Him who is unseen, and He will lead you to see what you have believed.

*Lord, help me to believe as Jochebed did, that my acts of faith will
be met by Your acts of loving intent. Even if I do not always see the
results, I trust You.*

INHERITING GOD'S PROMISES

SCRIPTURE READING: GENESIS 15:1–6
KEY VERSES: HEBREWS 6:11–12

And we desire that each one of you show the same diligence to the full assurance of hope until the end, that you do not become sluggish, but imitate those who through faith and patience inherit the promises.

God wouldn't have made all the promises in the Bible if He didn't want to give His children great blessings. Yet we cannot simply assume such benefits belong to us. So how can we claim God's promises with the expectation He will take pleasure in answering our petition?

There are several questions we must ask in order to test the needs we bring before our heavenly Father:

- Does this promise meet my personal need or desire?
- When I request that God keep this promise, do I ask with the spirit of being submissive to His will?
- Does the Holy Spirit bear witness to my spirit that God is pleased with my petition?
- Will God be honored by fulfilling this promise?
- Does my request to claim this promise contradict God's Word?
- If God fulfills this promise, will it further my spiritual growth?

Once we have satisfactorily answered these questions, inheriting God's promises depends upon just three requirements. First, we need to have faith. Our Father wants us to trust Him, and He rewards those who do (Genesis 15:6; Hebrews 11:6). Second, we must be obedient to God's will for us. We will never attain His best if we knowingly disobey. And third, we must be willing to wait for the Lord's perfect timing. It is well worth our while, considering the blessings He longs to give us.

Father, give me faith to inherit Your promises. Give me strength to walk obediently in Your ways. Give me patience to wait for Your timing.

THE SEASONS OF LIFE

SCRIPTURE READING: PSALM 16:1–11
KEY VERSE: PSALM 16:8

I have set the LORD always before me;
Because He is at my right hand I shall not be moved.

In this wintry season, you may look outside and see brown, barren trees. Where the colorful leaves of fall used to beautify the countryside, there are now no splashes of red, green, and yellow. The bare branches afford only a reminiscence of the inspiring autumn foliage.

The same is true for seasons of life when joy and prosperity seem to be a memory. In the difficult times of emptiness and despondency, it is always important to remember that your winters will not last forever.

You can cling to the words of Lamentations 3:22–23, which show the amazing hope that lies beyond the desolation: "Through the LORD's mercies we are not consumed, because His compassions fail not. They are new every morning; great is Your faithfulness." C. H. Spurgeon echoes this sentiment: "Fear not, Christian, for Jesus is with you. In all your fiery trials His presence is both your comfort and safety. He will never leave one whom He has chosen for His own."

Springtime is near to you. Just as new blooms and fragrant petals are sure to ornament the sad limbs, this time of sorrow for you will surely be followed by a time of joy in the Lord. Keep focused on His compassion and mercy, and you shall see the flowers of your faith bud into a beautiful new season.

Lord, in the chill of my spiritual winter, let me realize that spring is just ahead. Keep me focused on Your compassion and mercy. Let the flowers of my faith bud into a new season.

FUTURE SECURITY

SCRIPTURE READING: PSALM 123:1–4
KEY VERSE: LAMENTATIONS 3:22

Through the LORD's mercies we are not consumed,
because His compassions fail not.

The book of Lamentations was written by Jeremiah soon after the fall of Jerusalem. It reflects the great mourning of those whose homes had been destroyed. It was an awful time for the people of Judah. Their loved ones were deported to Babylon, and enemy armies occupied the holy temple of Solomon.

All that had represented security to Judah was gone. The country was dispersed, the center of worship desecrated, the armies defeated, and families disbanded. If you have ever experienced this deep a loss, or have had your security stripped from you, you know the awful despair that can overcome the soul.

Yet Jeremiah was not completely given over to desolation. He believed God's compassions would never fail (Lamentations 3:22). Jeremiah held on to a security which was deeper than anything the nation could offer. William Gurnall writes, "The Christian, like a chalice without a base, cannot stand on his own nor hold what he has received any longer than God holds him in His strong hands."

You have protection that goes beyond armies and buildings, because you have God's strong hands holding you. When you go through difficulties, you have security that can never be taken away. You can know your future is secure.

Oh Father, I have put my focus on physical security. Yet there are always new threats. Help me to realize that Your compassions are with me no matter what the circumstances.

THE RETURN OF CHRIST

SCRIPTURE READING: MATTHEW 24:36–42
KEY VERSE: MATTHEW 24:36

But of that day and hour no one knows, not even the angels of heaven,
but My Father only.

As believers we know that Christ will return to conquer His enemies and establish His kingdom. While there are many details about Christ's second coming that we do not know, we do know He will come as reigning Judge, King, and Lord. No one can know the exact day or time of Christ's return. However, we should be watchful for His coming and careful not to neglect what He has called us to do (Matthew 24:36, 42–51).

As His children, our purpose is not only to glorify God but also to share the good news of the gospel with those around us. Don't allow time to become suspended because you are waiting for Christ to return. At some point, every believer will stand before God in order to give an account for his or her life. Are you doing what God has called you to do? Are you doing it with all your heart?

Regardless of the fears you may have or your ability to accomplish the goals God has established, when you allow God to work in your life, His purpose is accomplished, and you will experience His joy and peace.

Is your life a reflection of God's unconditional love? Your challenge is to live as if you expect Christ to return at any moment, and to make a difference in someone else's eternal destination. Pray that God will use you to bring eternal hope to someone today.

Lord, help me to live my life as if You will return any minute, not because of fear but because of a passion to reach others for Christ.

YOUR ETERNAL FUTURE

SCRIPTURE READING: REVELATION 22:1–5

KEY VERSE: REVELATION 21:27

But there shall by no means enter it anything that defiles,
or causes an abomination or a lie, but only those who
are written in the Lamb's Book of Life.

Do you ever wonder what heaven will be like? John Newton said, "If I ever reach heaven I expect to find three wonders there: first, to meet some I had not thought to see there; second, to miss some I had expected to see there; and third, the greatest wonder of all, to find myself there."

The Bible tells us that heaven is a very definite place. Jesus said, "In My Father's house are many mansions; if it were not so, I would have told you. I go to prepare a place for you" (John 14:2).

Do you know if you will be in heaven? Do you know how to get there? It is not something you can work to make happen. You cannot earn your way. There is only one way to receive eternal life—accept what Jesus Christ did at the cross.

The Crucifixion is God's way of making it possible for every single person who believes in Jesus Christ to spend eternity in heaven. The Bible tells us that when you are saved by the grace of God, you become a citizen of heaven. Your name is in the Lamb's Book of Life (Revelation 21:27).

As His child, God wants you to have a personal relationship with Him now and for eternity. As you anticipate with great joy your eternal future, hunger and thirst to know God more each day.

Lord Jesus, I am speechless at the thought of You preparing a place in heaven for me. I am unworthy. Thank You for dying for me so I could spend eternity with You.

How to Live Your Life

SCRIPTURE READING: 2 CORINTHIANS 5:14–17
KEY VERSE: 2 CORINTHIANS 5:17

Therefore, if anyone is in Christ, he is a new creation; old things have passed away; behold, all things have become new.

The woman explained how she had witnessed her love for Christ to another friend over a period of several years: "I tried not to preach to my friend. Instead, I sought to 'live out' God's love by loving this person unconditionally. I wondered if what I had said and lived made a difference. Then one day, my friend came to me and thanked me for loving her and telling her that Jesus loves her too."

The unconditional love of God changes hearts and people, though we may not see the immediate results. Jesus was serious about sin, but His first concern always was the sinner. He wanted those who came to Him to understand one thing: God loves them.

If we live for ourselves, the fruit of our labor will be obvious: a need to be noticed first, receive credit for what we do, and a continual striving for a material reward. We could summarize the self-centered life with four words: convenience, comfort, covetousness, and compromise.

Servanthood, personal sacrifice, and a genuine love for others mark the Christ-centered life. Instead of asking what you can get out of this situation, job, or friendship, ask, "Lord, how can You use me to bring glory to You in this particular situation? Whom can You love through me?" Pray that you will live your life in such a way that men and women will see your good deeds and glorify your Father in heaven.

Lord, I know that the Christ-centered life is the only effective life. Use me. Love through me. Let my life bring You glory today and in the days to come.

Stopping Short of God's Plan

Scripture Reading: Ephesians 2:1–10

Key Verse: Ephesians 2:10

For we are His workmanship, created in Christ Jesus for good works,
which God prepared beforehand that we should walk in them.

What would you think of a marathon runner who, only fifty feet from the finish line, decided to stop running without completing the course? How much esteem would you attribute to a football player who stopped five yards from the end zone? In the world of sports, fans rarely applaud half-hearted efforts. Instead, crowds cheer for those who defy all obstacles in their pursuit of victory.

The Christian life is like a sporting event in many ways. For this reason, the apostle Paul referred to one's spiritual life as a "race" five times throughout his epistles. This race takes preparation, determination, and diligence, and it requires completion.

Ephesians 2:1–10 lays out God's plan for His children. First, God demonstrates amazing patience toward sinful people. Second, He extends His saving grace to those who seek Him. For many people, these two steps are all that matter.

However, the third part of God's plan is just as vital. The third step is to accept the responsibility that comes with salvation. While salvation cannot be attained through good works, a godly change in character is essential to the Christian life.

Have you allowed the grace of God to change your outward behavior, or have you stopped short of God's plan for your life? Pray for God's strength as you strive to finish the race.

Lord, I don't want to stop short of Your plan. Give me divine strength to finish my race in victory.

GODLY DEPENDENCE

SCRIPTURE READING: 2 CORINTHIANS 5:1–8
KEY VERSE: 2 CORINTHIANS 5:7

For we walk by faith, not by sight.

So much is written about faith these days. We think and talk about trust-ing God, and try, even though we stumble at times, to walk by faith. Many times, it is our trying that trips us up.

God wants us to learn to live by faith and not by sight (2 Corinthians 5:7). This means living with the idea that He is able to do what we cannot do for ourselves. What a victorious thought! It is also a marvelous invitation to experience freedom from doubt, worry, and disbelief.

Before we can trust God fully, we must come to a point of helpless dependence. It is here that we realize we simply cannot do it all, be all that is needed, and have all the answers. If we could, there would be no need for God. We would be in total control and very proud of it.

While God gives us the ability to solve many of the problems we face, His greater desire is for us to live our lives dependent on Him. Godly dependence is not a sign of weakness but one of immeasurable strength and confidence. There are problems in life that only God can solve, tasks only He can perform, and solutions that can only be discovered through the wisdom He gives.

The basic foundation to faith is this: trust God more than you trust yourself. When you do this, you gain wisdom and hope for the future.

Father, I want to depend on You even more in the days ahead. I know there are problems only You can solve, tasks only You can perform, and solutions that can only be discovered through Your wisdom.

PART OF HIS FLOCK

SCRIPTURE READING: 1 PETER 2:21–25
KEY VERSE: 1 PETER 2:25

*For you were like sheep going astray, but have now returned
to the Shepherd and Overseer of your souls.*

Oftentimes in Scripture, God is portrayed in ways that are easy for us to understand. Perhaps the most touching and poignant representation of God is found in Psalm 23, in which David described Him as a shepherd.

In ancient times, shepherds entered into a special relationship with their flocks. They spent each day with the animals, guiding their paths, protecting them from danger, and corralling those who went astray. To the sheep, the shepherd was a constant companion, to the extent that the sheep actually grew to recognize the shepherd's voice and, therefore, to respond only to his call.

In Psalm 23, David acknowledged his position as a wandering sheep under the direction of the Great Shepherd. As such, he rejoiced that he was part of the Lord's flock, with such a gracious, loving Guide.

Because of his assurance of God's protection and guidance, David was able to boldly exclaim, "Even though I walk through the valley of the shadow of death, I will fear no evil, for You are with me" (Psalm 23:4 NIV). This is truly a remarkable statement, because it reveals that David was aware he would face hard times, and yet he was able to rest in the confidence that God would safely see him through the ordeal. Just as a shepherd knows his flock, so does God know you. You are part of His flock.

Oh Lord, I am so thankful that You allow me to graze in the pasture of Your blessings. Even in the hard times that may lie ahead, I know You will safely guide me through each difficulty.

PATIENCE TO WAIT

SCRIPTURE READING: JOB 19:23–26
KEY VERSE: JOB 2:10

"Shall we indeed accept good from God, and shall we not accept adversity?" In all this Job did not sin with his lips.

Job was someone who knew pain. We read in the first two chapters of the book of Job that everything in his life—his family, wealth, and health—was taken away from him. It is clear that at this point, Job had nothing . . . except faith. Job did not know why his life had taken such a dramatic, insufferable turn. However, he remained steadfast in his conviction that God was able to restore his life.

Twice in the opening chapters of the book, the text says Job did not sin or abandon God during his time of loss (Job 1:22; 2:10). Moreover, Job underscores the total sovereignty of God by proclaiming, "Shall we indeed accept good from God, and shall we not accept adversity?" (Job 2:10).

It is important to see, though, that Job did not mask his pain with a false smile, and he did not belittle his own problems in order to "protect" God from blame. Job was honest about his despair.

Despite his brokenness, however, Job praised God's faithfulness. Chapter 19, which contains Job's heartbreaking recount of all that he has lost, concludes with the assurance that God, his Redeemer, not only lives but will also come to restore that which has been lost. Even in the darkest pain, Job knew that God was in control.

If you are in the midst of trial, praise God for His faithfulness. Ask God for the patience to wait for the coming day when He will make His power known to you.

Lord, it is easy to give in to despondency in the face of adversity. Thank You that no matter how deep the hole we are in, Your arms can reach us there.

THE ONE IN CONTROL

SCRIPTURE READING: MARK 9:17–27
KEY VERSE: MARK 9:23

*Jesus said to him, "If you can believe, all things
are possible to him who believes."*

In today's Scripture passage, a father brought his demon-possessed son to Jesus. Nothing was more important to this father than to see his son restored, and he knew Jesus had the power to do it.

When he finally reached Jesus, the father experienced a slight falter in his faith. He requested, "If You can do anything, have compassion on us and help us" (Mark 9:22). Jesus, sensing the man's subtle doubts, replied, "If you can believe, all things are possible to him who believes" (verse 23). Without hesitation, the father realized the disparity between his words and his actions, and he pleaded, "Lord, I believe; help my unbelief!" (verse 24).

What an odd statement! What are we to think? Does this man have faith or not? Yet, when we look closer, we realize that this father was crying out in complete, unashamed honesty. He knew that there was no point in attempting to "puff up" his faith before Jesus. Instead, he humbly admitted that, while he did in fact believe in Jesus' saving power, there were still some things—such as concern for his son—that could interfere with his faith in God.

Do you believe that God has the power to change your life? Do you allow outside influences to affect your faith in Jesus? If so, be honest with God about your fluctuating faith, but always remember that His power does not ebb and flow along with our confidence in Him. Regardless of how we feel, God is always in control—today, tomorrow, and forever.

*Lord, thank You that when my faith falters, You do not; that when
I am most powerless, Your power remains constant. I believe; help
my unbelief!*

LEARNING TO WAIT

SCRIPTURE READING: LAMENTATIONS 3:24–26
KEY VERSE: LAMENTATIONS 3:26

It is good that one should hope and wait quietly
for the salvation of the LORD.

We live in a time when we do not have to wait very long for the things we want, and we like it that way. To paraphrase a recent ad campaign for a restaurant chain, we want the events of our lives to happen "our way, right away."

Perhaps this is why we get so frustrated when our time frame is delayed by someone else's inability to make a decision. Think about the last time you were in a lunch line and someone in front of you simply could not decide what he wanted. There you were, ready to get your sandwich, get out the door, and get on with your life, but someone stood in the way. We usually do not respond well to someone else misusing our time.

This haste carries over into our prayer lives as well. We rejoice when God answers with yes, and we try to understand when He says no. However, there is a third answer to prayer, and it may well be the most frustrating one of all: "Wait."

As we grow in spiritual maturity, we will begin to realize that we are not made to wait because God needs more time to make a wise decision. He knows the best answer to our prayers before we even ask. Instead, we are often made to wait upon the Lord because we are simply not ready for a yes or no answer.

Our human view is dreadfully limited to our own time frame and circumstances; God is not so encumbered. Take time to thank Him today for His wisdom in making us wait sometimes, even when we don't want to.

Lord, I am prone to wanting things my way and right away! Thank You that in Your unencumbered wisdom, You ask me to wait, sometimes, because You know it is best.

Your Eternal Destiny

SCRIPTURE READING: ROMANS 3:10–12
KEY VERSE: MATTHEW 11:28

*Come to Me, all you who labor and are heavy laden,
and I will give you rest.*

When Jesus lived on the earth, He issued a general call of salvation to mankind, saying, "Come to Me, all you who labor and are heavy laden, and I will give you rest" (Matthew 11:28). This passage gives each of us the assurance that, if we respond, God will rescue us from the guilt, penalty, and punishment of sin and restore us through a relationship with Himself.

Salvation is not something we acquire or earn, but something God gives to us freely. When a person thinks he is morally good enough to be saved, he has allowed his own pride to deceive him. The essence of pride tells a person that he does not need God, but rather he can earn the rewards of heaven through self-righteousness.

Romans 3:10–12 reveals to us God's view of the human heart: "There is none righteous, no, not one." No one can take credit for his own salvation. None of us comes into this world saved. We are born as lost souls because of the condition of our hearts, not due to our actions or behavior.

The only thing we can do about our salvation is to get on our knees before the almighty God in absolute, total humility and thank Him and praise Him for reaching down and saving us out of our sinfulness. For in His mercy, grace, goodness, and love, He makes us His true children, writing our names in the Lamb's Book of Life and assuring our eternal destiny.

Lord, I can do nothing to earn the gift of salvation that You have given me. Thank You that I can rest in Your grace knowing that You have already accomplished that which I cannot.

An Eternal Lifestyle

SCRIPTURE READING: LUKE 11:1–14
KEY VERSE: LUKE 11:1

*Now it came to pass, as He was praying in a certain place, when
He ceased, that one of His disciples said to Him, "Lord, teach
us to pray, as John also taught his disciples."*

Just as God has a purpose and plan for our lives, He has the same thing in
mind for our prayer lives. In Luke, we read how Jesus taught His disciples
to pray. This is exactly what He wants to do for each one of us. However, it
is not just a matter of teaching us how to pray. Instead, it is a matter of our
learning how to be sensitive to God's Spirit in prayer.

When it comes to prayer within our devotional times, far too often we
quickly read a passage of Scripture, hurry through a printed devotional,
and recite what sounds like a "canned" prayer. Then we hurry off to start
the day. God wants to spend quality time with us. He longs for us to know
Him intimately.

While Jesus provided a pattern for prayer in Luke, He by no means meant
for us to stop at that point. The Lord lived fully to please the heavenly Father
by seeking to be in tune with His Spirit at all times. Prayer should permeate
our lives so that we seek God's mind and heart at every turn in life.

However, before we can enjoy the benefits of prayer, there must be a
deep, abiding hunger to know God. This means that within our hearts we
long to hear God's voice. Prayer ushers us into the throne room of God where
we find a personal, loving, and holy God eager to share Himself with us.
Prayer is a lifestyle worth living for all eternity.

*Lord, I want to know You better. Give me a deep, abiding hunger to
spend more time with You in Your throne room. I know You are
eager to share Yourself with me.*

THE PERFECT SAVIOR

SCRIPTURE READING: LUKE 2:25–32
KEY VERSES: LUKE 2:30–31

*For my eyes have seen Your salvation which You have
prepared before the face of all peoples.*

To the other people in Bethlehem, there was nothing magical about the day. There was nothing extraordinary about the child who was receiving the ritual circumcision. Yet Luke 2:30–31 reports that Simeon exclaimed, "My eyes have seen Your salvation, which You have prepared in the presence of all peoples" (NASB).

The Lord sent Jesus to be the perfect sacrifice for humanity. When Jesus comes again, He will come as a great warrior and king, not a baby. So why was Jesus born the first time? Why did Christ leave His throne in heaven to work as a carpenter? Why didn't He come as a thirty-year-old man? Wouldn't three years of sinlessness have been sufficient?

In order for Christ to be the Son of Man, He had to endure everything from birth to death. In order for Him to share in our humanity, He had to encounter every part of it. There was nothing extraordinary to the people in Bethlehem, because Christ was experiencing what they encountered every day. Yet consider the miracle that the God with perfect power, understanding, and love has participated in every aspect of human life and sits on the throne of grace as He intercedes for you.

Jesus did not miss one moment of knowing what your life is like. In God's wisdom, He truly became the perfect sacrifice and Savior.

*Lord Jesus, You humbled Yourself to a life of lowly humanity in order
to raise me to the life of a child of the King, through Your death and
resurrection. No words can express my gratitude.*

THE MESSAGE OF CHRISTMAS

SCRIPTURE READING: LUKE 2:1–13
KEY VERSE: LUKE 2:10

Then the angel said to them, "Do not be afraid, for behold, I bring you good tidings of great joy which will be to all people."

For the shepherds watching their sheep outside Bethlehem one evening, the sudden sight in front of them was terrifying. A glorious angel shining brightly in the sky was enough to make anyone rub his eyes and take a second look . . . and run.

But the first words from the angel's mouth were words to calm their frightened hearts: "Do not be afraid" (Luke 2:10). One of the messages that we learn from the Christmas story is that of peace. While God might appear overwhelming at times, He always wants to give us the assurance that with Him, peace reigns, even in the announcement of His Son's birth.

The peace we receive from the Christmas message calms our hearts, letting us know everything will be all right as long as we trust God. However, it also includes a message of peace that assures us that Jesus and His methods of teaching were all designed to draw us to the heavenly Father.

Jesus' birth was no different. Salvation would soon be realized for all mankind. Some people have never heard the message of Christmas. They don't understand its purpose. When we tell them, they might get frightened. However, like God desired to assure the shepherds that there was no need to fear, He gives us the peace we need to submit to Him.

Dear Father, You laid Your mighty plan of salvation before a humble band of shepherds. Thank you that those who humble themselves before You receive those same good tidings today!

GOD'S AWESOME LOVE

SCRIPTURE READING: LUKE 2:15–20

KEY VERSE: LUKE 2:20

Then the shepherds returned, glorifying and praising God for all the things that they had heard and seen, as it was told them.

With great awe and in complete reverence, the shepherds looked upon the baby Jesus. It was true. Everything. All the words spoken to them by the angel in the sky were truth! The Savior had arrived!

And almost instantly, the shepherds realized that this kind of news didn't need to be hidden. Others needed to know that the Savior had arrived—even more prophecy was about to be fulfilled. Were these the first missionaries? No, these were the first witnesses, understanding that along with the knowledge of this great information came the responsibility to tell others.

As we grow in our relationship with Christ and deepen our knowledge of Him through intimacy, there is no need for us to keep this information to ourselves. In light of what Christ has done for us—through not only His birth, but also His death and resurrection—we should desire to share this with others.

Our method of sharing the good news with others might vary. But regardless of the method in which we proclaim Christ, the message of Christmas—God's awesome love for mankind—is a story that warrants being told again and again.

Lord, we are Your witnesses on earth as surely as were the shepherds of Bethlehem. Help us to announce the Christmas message with the same enthusiasm and urgency.

NO ONE BUT JESUS

SCRIPTURE READING: MATTHEW 1:18–25
KEY VERSES: ACTS 4:11–12

This is the "stone which was rejected by you builders,
which has become the chief cornerstone." Nor is there salvation
in any other, for there is no other name under heaven given
among men by which we must be saved.

The humble entrance into the world by Jesus does not instantly conjure up images of power and authority. Yet it was the beginning of God's plan to save the world from its sin. That is power and authority. No one but Jesus could bring about such a radical change in people's lives. It is through the life, death, and resurrection of Christ that we can enter into a relationship with God.

Sleeping in a manger, Jesus may not have looked like He had the beginnings of a man who would transform the world forever, but He did. He wasn't just another baby. In a challenging sermon given by Peter to the religious rulers and leaders following Jesus' death and resurrection, he explained why this man named Jesus was so different: "This is the 'stone which was rejected by you builders, which has become the chief cornerstone.' Nor is there salvation in any other, for there is no other name under heaven given among men by which we must be saved" (Acts 4:11–12).

Jesus' birth began fulfilling the prophecies of His coming from years past. And His impending life would do the same, helping the world realize its need for a Savior and recognizing that it was through Him that they could obtain eternal life. No other but Jesus would become a man who would reshape history.

Father, the cornerstone of Your kingdom was once a baby in a lowly manger. Thank You that Your sacrifice and the human faithfulness over the millennia that have brought the gospel from Bethlehem to me were known to You from the beginning of creation.

A PERSONAL PROMISE

SCRIPTURE READING: JOHN 14:1–4
KEY VERSE: JOHN 14:2

In My Father's house are many mansions; if it were not so,
I would have told you. I go to prepare a place for you.

Jesus came to earth with the view of offering you salvation. He wanted you to have a restored relationship with the Father, a relationship that was so close, so intimate, that you would have your special place in the Father's house (John 14:1–4). In John 14:2, Jesus said, "In My Father's house are many mansions; if it were not so, I would have told you. I go to prepare a place for you."

Christmas is the holiday that we celebrate God coming to make His home with us for a season, so that He could make our eternal home with Him in heaven. Charles Wesley describes the relationship Jesus came to establish:

Hail the heaven-born Prince of Peace! Hail the Sun of righteousness!
Light and life to all He brings, Risen with healing in His wings.
Mild He lays His glory by, born that man no more may die,
Born to raise the sons of earth, born to give them second birth.
Hark! the herald angels sing, "Glory to the newborn King."

Christ's birth was God's reaching out to you. Celebrate the season. Rejoice in the knowledge that God loves you so much that He left all the glories of heaven in order to build a loving relationship with you. Christmas means you have a home in heaven waiting for you. That should make more than the angels sing!

Lord, I am so grateful that through the death of Your Son, Jesus,
my relationship is restored with You and I have a home in heaven
waiting for me.

THE CELEBRATION OF CHRISTMAS

SCRIPTURE READING: MATTHEW 2:1–12

KEY VERSE: JOHN 1:9

*That was the true Light which gives light to
every man coming into the world.*

Has anyone ever given you a birthday party? Most likely, at some point in your life, you discovered the joy of having your friends and family gather together to celebrate your birth. How did that make you feel? By celebrating your birthday, they testified to the fact that your very existence has made their own lives somewhat better.

Now, a second question: Have you ever been to a birthday party to which the birthday boy or girl was not even invited? Of course not! What sense would it make to throw a party to celebrate someone and then fail to invite the guest of honor?

Today is Christmas. Chances are, you have already attended one or two Christmas parties, or maybe you have one scheduled for later today. Do you realize what a Christmas party is? Is it a simple gathering of friends? A chance to exchange presents? An hour of free time in the middle of a workday? If any of these describe the gathering that you attended, then you have not been to a real Christmas party.

A Christmas party is the ultimate birthday extravaganza! We celebrate Christmas because we want to testify that Jesus' existence has made our own lives infinitely better. Was Jesus at your Christmas party this week? Take a moment right now to escape the hustle of the holiday and rejoice in your Savior's birthday.

Lord, You came wrapped in rags so that I could have eternal life. If my wrappings and glitter are not about You, then help me to readjust my focus. Thank You for this great gift.

THE GREAT COMMISSION

SCRIPTURE READING: MATTHEW 28:19–20
KEY VERSE: ACTS 1:8

But you shall receive power when the Holy Spirit has come upon you;
and you shall be witnesses to Me in Jerusalem, and in all Judea
and Samaria, and to the end of the earth.

If God is in absolute control of our salvation, and it is He who brings us to repentance, then why should a Christian pursue missions or ministry? The answer involves a simple, but devoted, act of obedience. Jesus said, "Go into all the world and preach the gospel to all creation" (Mark 16:15 NASB). He further proclaimed, "As the Father has sent Me, I also send you" (John 20:21 NASB).

If and when a Christian answers the call to "go and preach," he is not left to pursue the task in his own strength. When any follower of Christ is called to the harvest, he receives the power of the Holy Spirit, equipping him to be an effective witness for Christ (Acts 1:8).

Not only did Christ exhort all Christians to witness to the unsaved; He also instructed us to disciple new believers in the ways of God. "Go therefore and make disciples of all the nations, baptizing them . . . teaching them to observe all that I commanded you" (Matthew 28:19–20 NASB).

Although Christians are called to share the gospel message, we must remember that salvation itself is left to God. No man comes to the Father but through Christ (John 14:6). Who will be saved and who won't is not our ultimate responsibility.

When we obey the Great Commission—proclaiming the good news of Jesus Christ as far and wide as God allows us—our only remaining task is to watch the Lord perform miracles in the lives of the lost.

Lord, I do not always have the courage to witness, nor the patience
to trust the seed sown to grow. Help me to "go and preach," and leave
the results to You.

FAITH FOR THE FUTURE

SCRIPTURE READING: ISAIAH 40:27–31
KEY VERSE: ISAIAH 40:29

He gives power to the weak,
And to those who have no might
He increases strength.

You are emotionally exhausted with no place to turn. Your troubles are so great that you believe no one would understand them. "Doesn't God see that I'm being mistreated?" you ask yourself. "Doesn't He see how I am feeling?"

All of us, at one time or another, will experience times such as these. But the words of Isaiah 40:27–31 provide great encouragement. The Lord never grows tired. Instead, "He gives power to the weak, and to those who have no might He increases strength" (verse 29).

In addition, verse 28 explains that God's understanding is far beyond our grasp. Therefore, we can have confidence in the fact that God will always comprehend our predicament regardless of its complexity.

As if the Lord's strength and understanding were not enough, verse 31 tells us He offers even more: when we are willing to wait upon God, He will provide us with new strength so that we can soar like eagles. What a wonderful image for our times of complete despair.

As you consider the difficulties in your life, envision yourself receiving from God the ability to surge up and over them with the grace and power of an eagle in flight. This amazing strength is available to you today if you are willing to exchange your weariness for God's divine assistance.

There is nothing you have to do to earn this favor and aid. Simply trust Him and hand over that which seems hopeless, allowing Him to restore your faith for the future.

Lord, just as the eagle harnesses the air currents to glide above the earth, let me also allow Your strength to carry me up above the predicaments and complexities of my life.

WHEN THE GOING GETS ROUGH

SCRIPTURE READING: ISAIAH 40:9–12
KEY VERSE: ISAIAH 40:12

Who has measured the waters in the hollow of His hand,
Measured heaven with a span,
And calculated the dust of the earth in a measure?
Weighed the mountains in scales
And the hills in a balance?

Do you know how to receive God's strength in your life when the going gets rough? Do you know how to rest in Him when all your hope for the future seems in ashes? If you do not know, find comfort in today's Scripture passage. It provides a wonderful reminder of what we should do, and Whom we can count on in the worst of times.

Isaiah 40:9 contains a simple but powerful statement: "Here is your God!" (NASB). From this, we can deduce an important first step: when troubles arise, we should immediately focus on God. Verse 10 describes His great power. We are aware that God is all-knowing and all-powerful. So we know that everything needed to overcome our circumstances is available in Him.

Verse 11 continues with a reminder of God's gentle and compassionate nature. He is the Good Shepherd, who is intimately involved in the lives of His sheep. And because He loves them, He gathers them close and carries them when they are too weary to walk.

Finally, in verse 12, we are provided with the "big picture." God is the Supreme Ruler of the universe, the Creator of all things. And His great plans include each one of us. When your problems seem insurmountable, submit your concerns to the one God, who is available, powerful, compassionate, and supreme. There is no one like Him, and no one better in whom to trust.

Lord, You are my God! You are the one who has measured the heavens, weighed the mountains, and designed each person. I give You control of my life and trust Your plan for me.

TAKING RISKS

SCRIPTURE READING: ACTS 9:1–20
KEY VERSE: ACTS 9:17

*And Ananias went his way and entered the house; and laying
his hands on him he said, "Brother Saul, the Lord Jesus, who appeared
to you on the road as you came, has sent me that you may receive
your sight and be filled with the Holy Spirit."*

Many Christians like playing it safe by gathering as many facts as possible, analyzing the options, and making choices in order to be reasonably certain of the outcome. We have declared uncertainty and risk undesirable because they could end up causing loss. The loss might involve suffering caused by an unwanted result or missing a desired outcome. It might have to do with appearing foolish or incompetent, incurring financial loss, or encountering physical danger.

From a human viewpoint, eliminating uncertainty makes sense. But how does God view uncertainty? Are there times when we're to take risks? The answer is a resounding yes, when He is the one asking us to take risks. From God's viewpoint, there's no uncertainty, because He has control over all things and He will never fail to accomplish His good purposes.

The Bible is full of real people who took risks to obey the living God. One was Ananias, a disciple sent by God to minister to the newly converted Saul. Ananias risked his reputation and his life. Another was Saul himself, who was commanded to preach to the Jews the very gospel he and they had so violently opposed. By focusing upon God, His character, and His promises, both of these men obeyed, despite uncertainty, doubt, and fear.

We're not going to grow in Christian maturity without learning to live with uncertainty and being willing to take risks. What risk is God asking you to take? Won't you step out in obedience and face the future in faith?

Lord, make me willing to take risks. Help me focus on You, Your character, and Your promises despite my uncertainties, doubts, or fears.

OUR ALL-SUFFICIENT GOD

SCRIPTURE READING: 2 CORINTHIANS 3:1–6

KEY VERSE: 2 CORINTHIANS 3:5

*Not that we are sufficient of ourselves to think of anything as being
from ourselves, but our sufficiency is from God.*

Many people would scoff at the idea of inadequacy as any kind of blessing. Too many of us have been tormented by such feelings rather than blessed by them. At the same time, Christians can use them as stepping-stones to blessing:

1. Our inadequacy forces us to do our work in the power of the
   Holy Spirit. Anything that drives us to God has to be good.
2. An awareness of our limitation can relieve us of the burden of
   trying to do God's will in our own strength. Without the Holy
   Spirit, we will be crushed by weights we cannot carry.
3. Another blessing is that such awareness "frees" the Lord to use
   us to the maximum of our potential. When we are lowly enough
   to feel our need, then God will raise us to great heights.
4. Acknowledging our shortcomings allows God to get all the glory
   for His work. Spiritually minded people can tell when something is of God and when it's not. If you are in the Spirit, the
   glory will rightfully go to the Lord.
5. Inadequacy can enable us to live in contentment and quietness of
   spirit. Either we will give God our burdens and cease striving, or
   we will proceed in our own strength and become overwhelmed.

Like the apostle Paul, we should not claim competence in ourselves but rather acknowledge that our adequacy is from God (2 Corinthians 3:5). What area in your life are you trying to manage in your own power? Relinquish control and watch for God's blessing in the days ahead.

*Lord, I relinquish total control of my life. I acknowledge my in-
adequacies and rest upon Your divine sufficiency for the days ahead.*

The Challenge to End Well

SCRIPTURE READING: PHILIPPIANS 1:3–6

KEY VERSE: PHILIPPIANS 1:6

. . . being confident of this very thing, that He who has begun a good work in you will complete it until the day of Jesus Christ.

A writer once penned a story about Hudson Taylor, the great missionary to China. He reported that the government of China commissioned a biography to be written portraying the missionary negatively. Yet the purpose of the assignment backfired: "As the author was doing his research, he was increasingly impressed by Taylor's saintly character and godly life, and he found it extremely difficult to carry out his assigned task with a clear conscience. Eventually, at the risk of losing his life, he laid aside his pen, renounced his atheism, and received Jesus as his personal Savior."

Taylor's life spoke of God's goodness beyond the grave. He followed Christ faithfully, and was rewarded for carrying out the mission given to him. This principle encourages Christians to continue living faithful, godly lives that will impact future generations.

The apostle Paul knew that the only real difference that could be made in a person's life was to introduce him or her to Christ. He performed his duty faithfully until his death, and his testimony endures.

You are challenged to end well so that God's grace will show itself in you. Just like Paul and Hudson Taylor, people will hear of your faithfulness and they will believe in God. Live in courageous godliness to the end.

Dear heavenly Father, thank You for Your loving care throughout this past year. Give me courageous godliness so that I can end not only this year properly but my time on earth as well.

ABOUT THE AUTHOR

Dr. Charles Stanley is pastor of the 15,000-member First Baptist Church in Atlanta, Georgia, and is head of the international In Touch® Ministries. He has twice been elected president of the Southern Baptist Convention and is known internationally from his radio and television program *In Touch*. His many best-selling books include *When the Enemy Strikes, Finding Peace, Seeking His Face, Success God's Way, Enter His Gates, The Source of My Strength*, and *How to Listen to God*.

OTHER BOOKS BY CHARLES STANLEY
PUBLISHED BY NELSON BOOKS

THE IN TOUCH STUDY SERIES

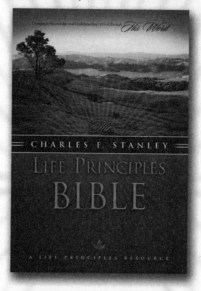

Don't Miss These Bestselling Devotionals by Charles Stanley

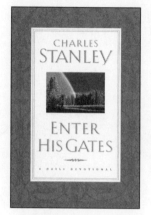

Enter His Gates

Spiritual gates are much like the gates of a city. They are vital to your well-being as a Christian and, if not maintained, leave you open to attack by the enemy. *Enter His Gates* is a daily devotional that encourages you to build or strengthen a different spiritual gate each month.

ISBN: 0-7852-7546-0

On Holy Ground

This daily devotional contains a year's worth of spiritual adventures. Dr. Stanley uses the journeys of Paul, Ezra, Elijah, Abraham, and other heroes of the Bible and his own valuable insights to encourage you to step out in faith and allow God to lead you to new places.

ISBN: 0-7852-7662-9

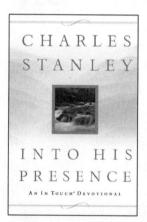

Into His Presence

Readers challenged to enter *Into His Presence* will be encouraged, uplifted, and spiritually renewed with this new devotional. In Scripture we find the Lord's people having dramatic encounters with God in mountaintop situations. There they are given revelation and transformation. To receive what He had for them they had to come away from the spiritual status quo of life and go to a higher level. That is the purpose of this devotional guide—to lift the reader to a new level of intimate, mountaintop encounters with God. Each section will have an introduction explaining the focus for that month's devotional reading and a listing of relevant Scripture along with daily devotional commentary.

ISBN: 0-7852-6854-5

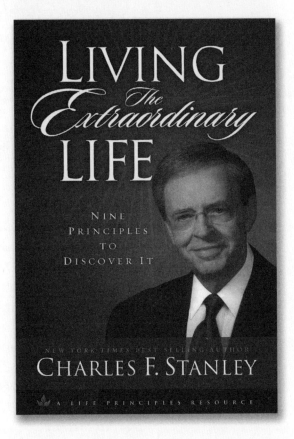